ARCHER & ARMSTRONG

IN THE
BAG

RAFER ROBERTS | DAVID LAFUENTE | RYAN WINN | BRIAN REBER

CONTENTS

Collection Cover Art: David Lafuente with Brian Reber

Writer: Rafer Roberts
Penciler: David Lafuente
Inker: Ryan Winn
Colorists: Brian Reber with SotoColor
Letterer: Dave Lanphear
Cover Artists: David Lafuente with Brian Reber

David Baron
Monica Gallagher
Trevor Hairsine
Phil Jimenez
Kano
David Lafuente
Ben Oliver
Rafer Roberts
Thony Silas
Michael Spicer
Ryan Winn

Assistant Editor: Danny Khazem
Associate Editor: Kyle Andrukiewicz
Editor: Warren Simons

A&A: The Adventures of Archer & Armstrong®: In the Bag.
Published by Valiant Entertainment LLC. Office of Publication:
350 Seventh Avenue, New York, NY 10001. Compilation copyright
©2016 Valiant Entertainment LLC. All rights reserved. Contains
materials originally published in single magazine form as A&A:
The Adventures of Archer & Armstrong #1-4. Copyright ©2016
Valiant Entertainment LLC. All rights reserved. All characters, their
distinctive likeness and related indicia featured in this publication
are trademarks of Valiant Entertainment LLC. The stories,
characters, and incidents featured in this publication are entirely
fictional. Valiant Entertainment does not read or accept unsolicited
submissions of ideas, stories, or artwork. Printed in the U.S.A. First
Printing. ISBN: 9781682151495.

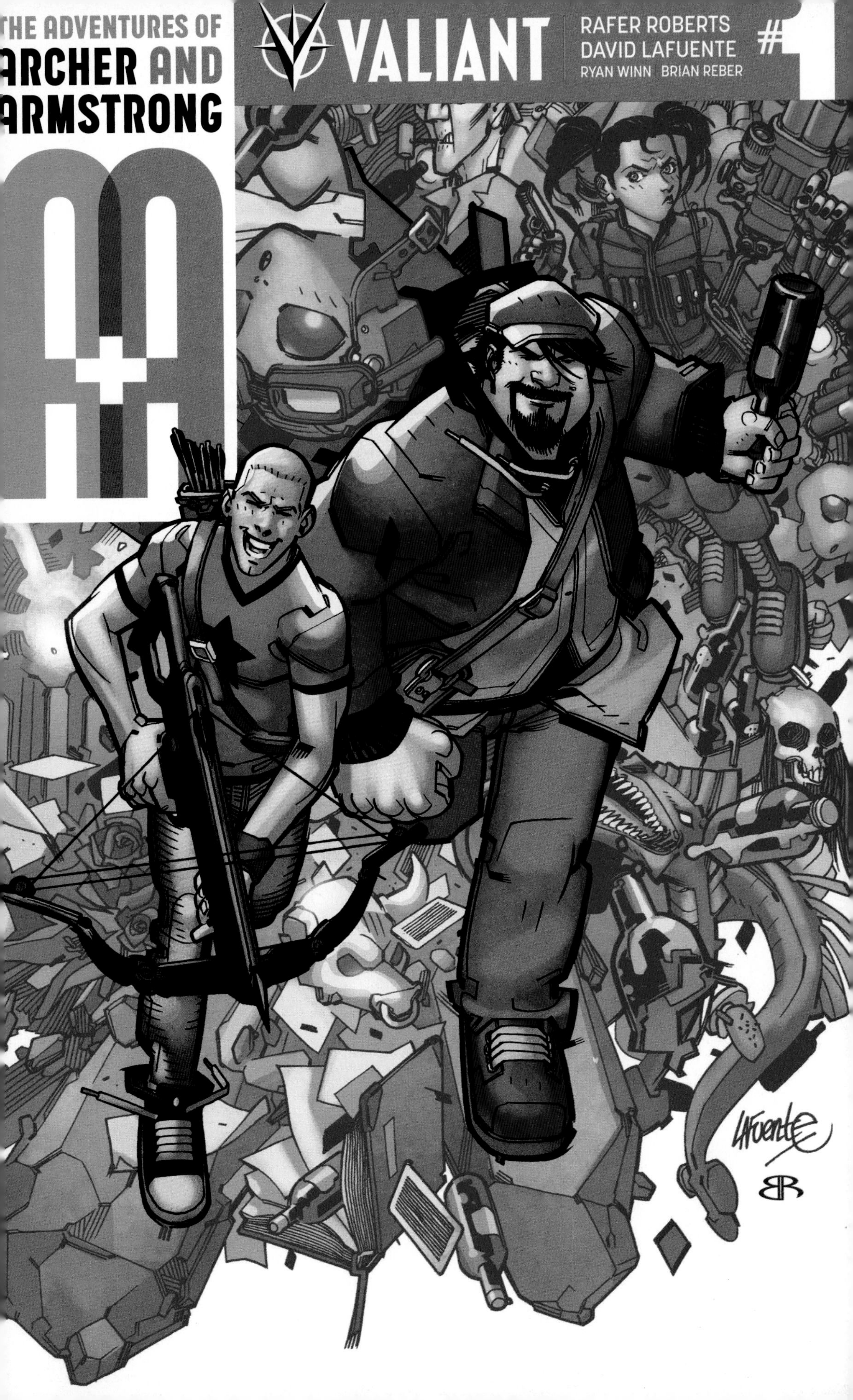
THE ADVENTURES OF
ARCHER AND
ARMSTRONG
A+A
VALIANT
RAFER ROBERTS
DAVID LAFUENTE
RYAN WINN BRIAN REBER
#1
LAFUENTE
BR

WELCOME TO *THE ADVENTURES OF* ARCHER & ARMSTRONG...

MEET ARMSTRONG. Since the ancient city of Ur, this immortal adventurer has spent the last 6,000 years drinking and carousing his way through history alongside some of the greatest merrymakers the world has ever known.

MEET ARCHER. A sheltered teenage martial arts master and expert marksman that was raised for a single purpose: to kill the devil incarnate. Little did he know that this undying evil was actually Armstrong (he's actually a pretty good guy...once you get to know him). Since hitting the road together, the two have become great friends and even better partners.

THIS IS A&A.

ARMSTRONG. 6,000-YEAR-OLD HEDONISTIC IMMORTAL.

ARCHER. TEENAGER. EXPERT MARTIAL ARTIST AND MARKSMAN.

MARY-MARIA. ARCHER'S SISTER. HEAD OF THE NINJA-NUN ASSASSINS, A.K.A. THE SISTERS OF PERPETUAL DARKNESS.

DAVEY THE MACKEREL. LIVES IN ARMSTRONG'S SATCHEL.

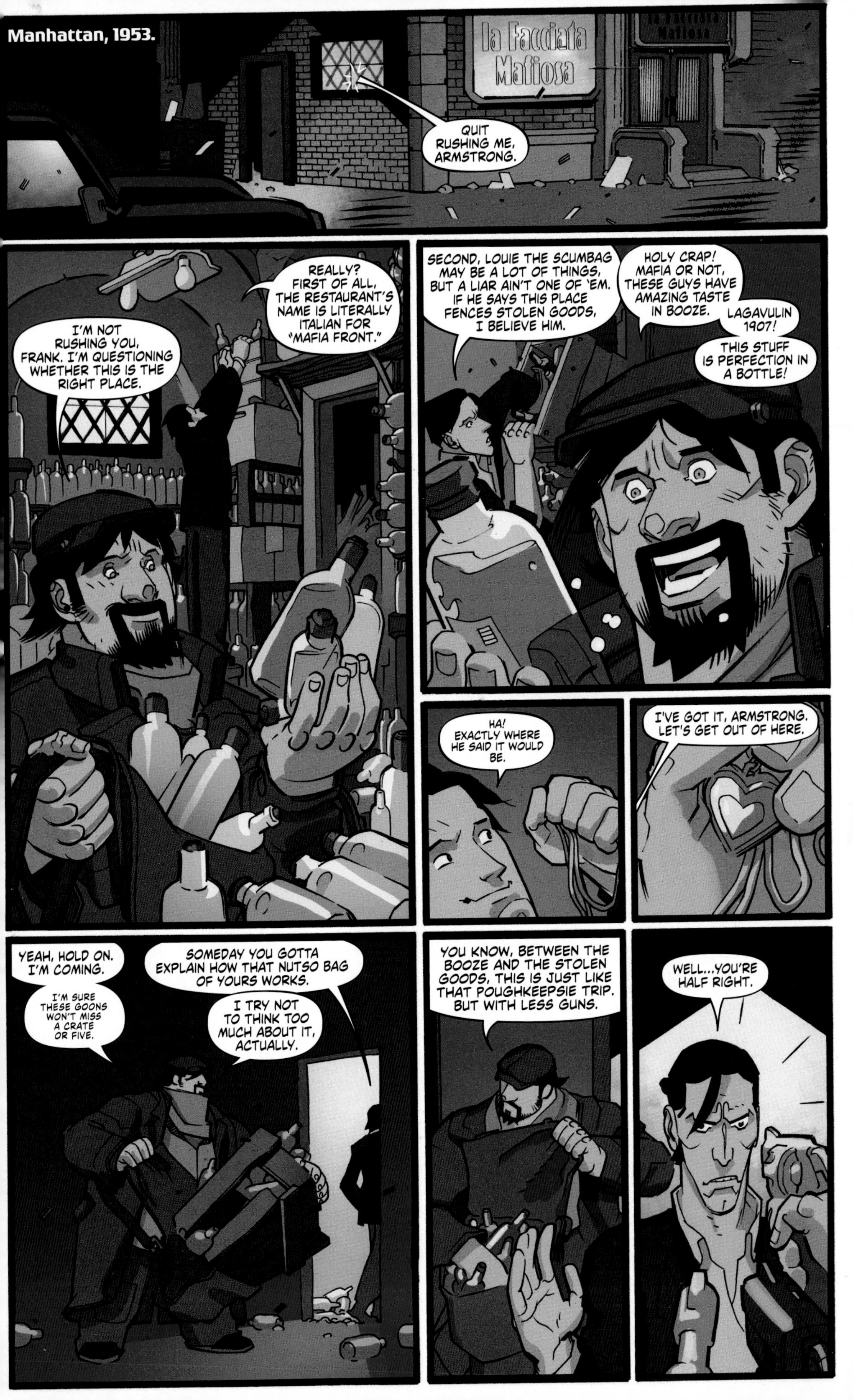
Manhattan, 1953.
La Facciata Mafiosa
QUIT RUSHING ME, ARMSTRONG.
I'M NOT RUSHING YOU, FRANK. I'M QUESTIONING WHETHER THIS IS THE RIGHT PLACE.
REALLY? FIRST OF ALL, THE RESTAURANT'S NAME IS LITERALLY ITALIAN FOR "MAFIA FRONT."
SECOND, LOUIE THE SCUMBAG MAY BE A LOT OF THINGS, BUT A LIAR AIN'T ONE OF 'EM. IF HE SAYS THIS PLACE FENCES STOLEN GOODS, I BELIEVE HIM.
HOLY CRAP! MAFIA OR NOT, THESE GUYS HAVE AMAZING TASTE IN BOOZE.
LAGAVULIN 1907!
THIS STUFF IS PERFECTION IN A BOTTLE!
HA! EXACTLY WHERE HE SAID IT WOULD BE.
I'VE GOT IT, ARMSTRONG. LET'S GET OUT OF HERE.
YEAH, HOLD ON. I'M COMING.
I'M SURE THESE GOONS WON'T MISS A CRATE OR FIVE.
SOMEDAY YOU GOTTA EXPLAIN HOW THAT NUTSO BAG OF YOURS WORKS.
I TRY NOT TO THINK TOO MUCH ABOUT IT, ACTUALLY.
YOU KNOW, BETWEEN THE BOOZE AND THE STOLEN GOODS, THIS IS JUST LIKE THAT POUGHKEEPSIE TRIP. BUT WITH LESS GUNS.
WELL...YOU'RE HALF RIGHT.

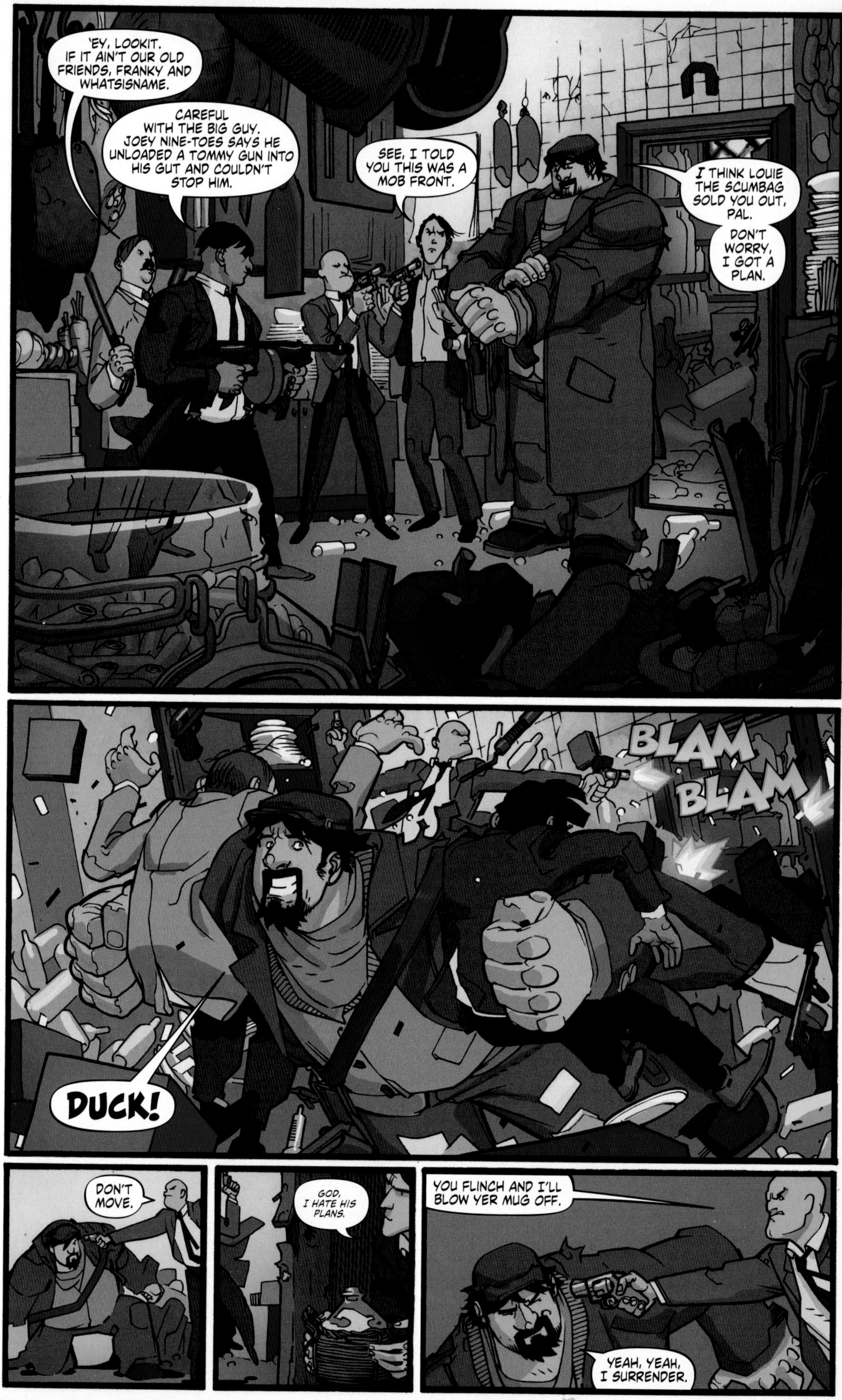
'EY, LOOKIT. IF IT AIN'T OUR OLD FRIENDS, FRANKY AND WHATSISNAME.
CAREFUL WITH THE BIG GUY. JOEY NINE-TOES SAYS HE UNLOADED A TOMMY GUN INTO HIS GUT AND COULDN'T STOP HIM.
SEE, I TOLD YOU THIS WAS A MOB FRONT.
I THINK LOUIE THE SCUMBAG SOLD YOU OUT, PAL.
DON'T WORRY, I GOT A PLAN.
BLAM
BLAM
DUCK!
DON'T MOVE.
GOD, I HATE HIS PLANS.
YOU FLINCH AND I'LL BLOW YER MUG OFF.
YEAH, YEAH, I SURRENDER.

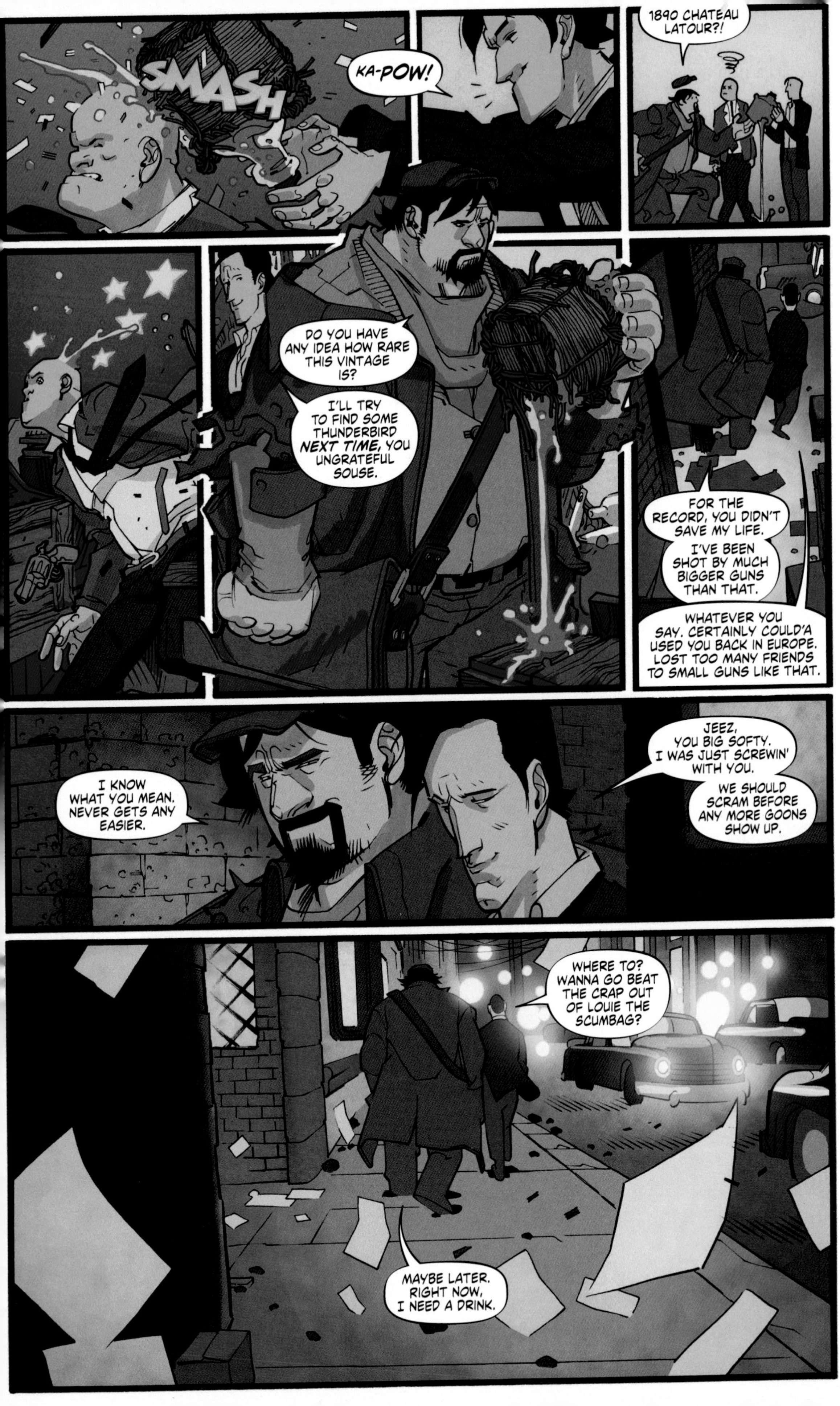
SMASH
KA-POW!
1890 CHATEAU LATOUR?!
DO YOU HAVE ANY IDEA HOW RARE THIS VINTAGE IS?
I'LL TRY TO FIND SOME THUNDERBIRD NEXT TIME, YOU UNGRATEFUL SOUSE.
FOR THE RECORD, YOU DIDN'T SAVE MY LIFE.
I'VE BEEN SHOT BY MUCH BIGGER GUNS THAN THAT.
WHATEVER YOU SAY. CERTAINLY COULD'A USED YOU BACK IN EUROPE. LOST TOO MANY FRIENDS TO SMALL GUNS LIKE THAT.
I KNOW WHAT YOU MEAN. NEVER GETS ANY EASIER.
JEEZ, YOU BIG SOFTY. I WAS JUST SCREWIN' WITH YOU.
WE SHOULD SCRAM BEFORE ANY MORE GOONS SHOW UP.
WHERE TO? WANNA GO BEAT THE CRAP OUT OF LOUIE THE SCUMBAG?
MAYBE LATER. RIGHT NOW, I NEED A DRINK.

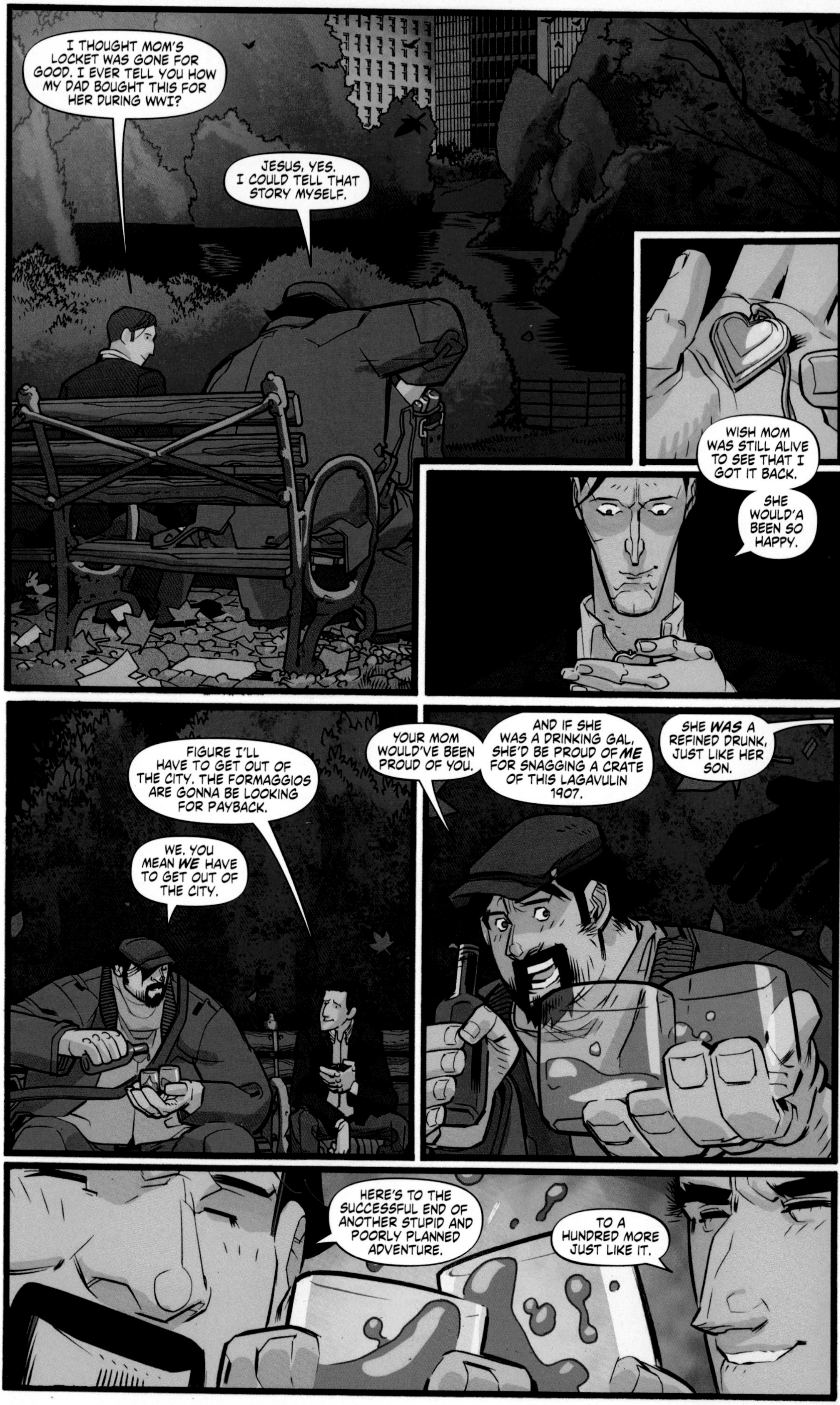
I THOUGHT MOM'S LOCKET WAS GONE FOR GOOD. I EVER TELL YOU HOW MY DAD BOUGHT THIS FOR HER DURING WWI?
JESUS, YES. I COULD TELL THAT STORY MYSELF.
WISH MOM WAS STILL ALIVE TO SEE THAT I GOT IT BACK.
SHE WOULD'A BEEN SO HAPPY.
FIGURE I'LL HAVE TO GET OUT OF THE CITY. THE FORMAGGIOS ARE GONNA BE LOOKING FOR PAYBACK.
WE. YOU MEAN WE HAVE TO GET OUT OF THE CITY.
YOUR MOM WOULD'VE BEEN PROUD OF YOU.
AND IF SHE WAS A DRINKING GAL, SHE'D BE PROUD OF ME FOR SNAGGING A CRATE OF THIS LAGAVULIN 1907.
SHE WAS A REFINED DRUNK, JUST LIKE HER SON.
HERE'S TO THE SUCCESSFUL END OF ANOTHER STUPID AND POORLY PLANNED ADVENTURE.
TO A HUNDRED MORE JUST LIKE IT.

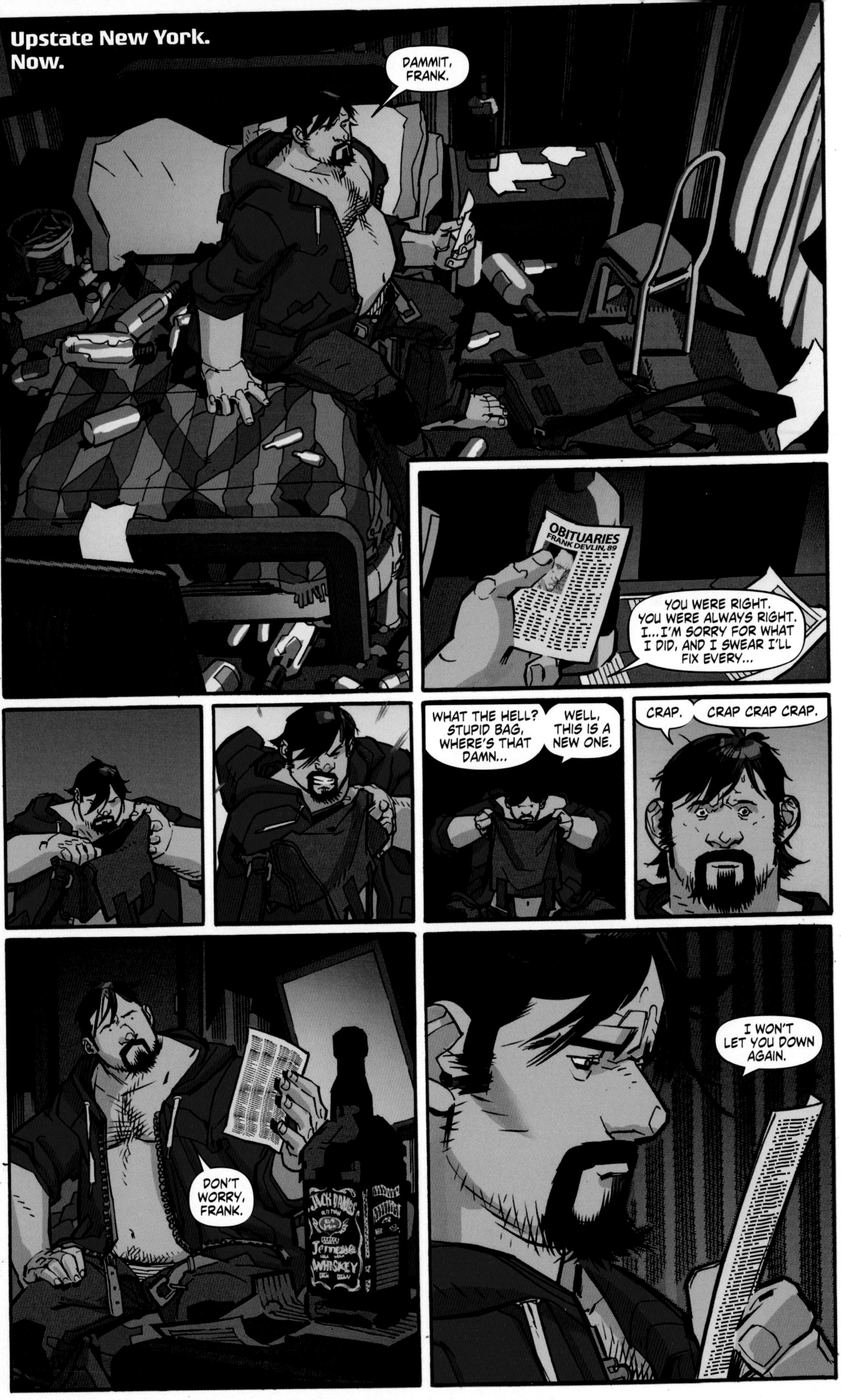
Upstate New York.
Now.
DAMMIT, FRANK.
OBITUARIES
FRANK DEVLIN, 89
YOU WERE RIGHT. YOU WERE ALWAYS RIGHT. I...I'M SORRY FOR WHAT I DID, AND I SWEAR I'LL FIX EVERY...
WHAT THE HELL? STUPID BAG, WHERE'S THAT DAMN...
WELL, THIS IS A NEW ONE.
CRAP.
CRAP CRAP CRAP.
DON'T WORRY, FRANK.
WHISKEY
I WON'T LET YOU DOWN AGAIN.

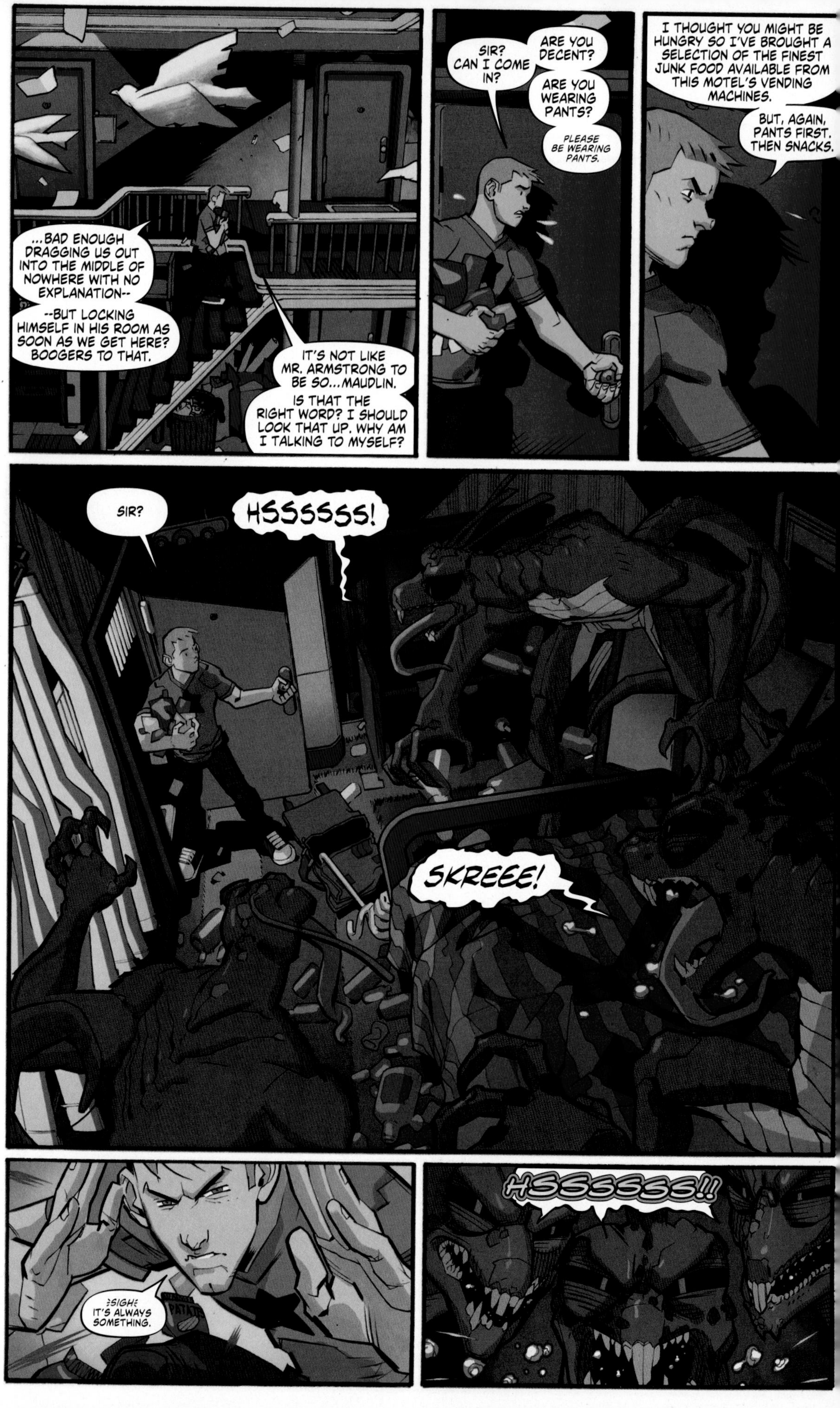
...BAD ENOUGH DRAGGING US OUT INTO THE MIDDLE OF NOWHERE WITH NO EXPLANATION--
--BUT LOCKING HIMSELF IN HIS ROOM AS SOON AS WE GET HERE? BOOGERS TO THAT.
IT'S NOT LIKE MR. ARMSTRONG TO BE SO...MAUDLIN.
IS THAT THE RIGHT WORD? I SHOULD LOOK THAT UP. WHY AM I TALKING TO MYSELF?
SIR? CAN I COME IN?
ARE YOU DECENT?
ARE YOU WEARING PANTS?
PLEASE BE WEARING PANTS.
I THOUGHT YOU MIGHT BE HUNGRY SO I'VE BROUGHT A SELECTION OF THE FINEST JUNK FOOD AVAILABLE FROM THIS MOTEL'S VENDING MACHINES.
BUT, AGAIN, PANTS FIRST. THEN SNACKS.
SIR?
HSSSSSS!
SKREEE!
SIGH
IT'S ALWAYS SOMETHING.
PATATE
HSSSSSS!!

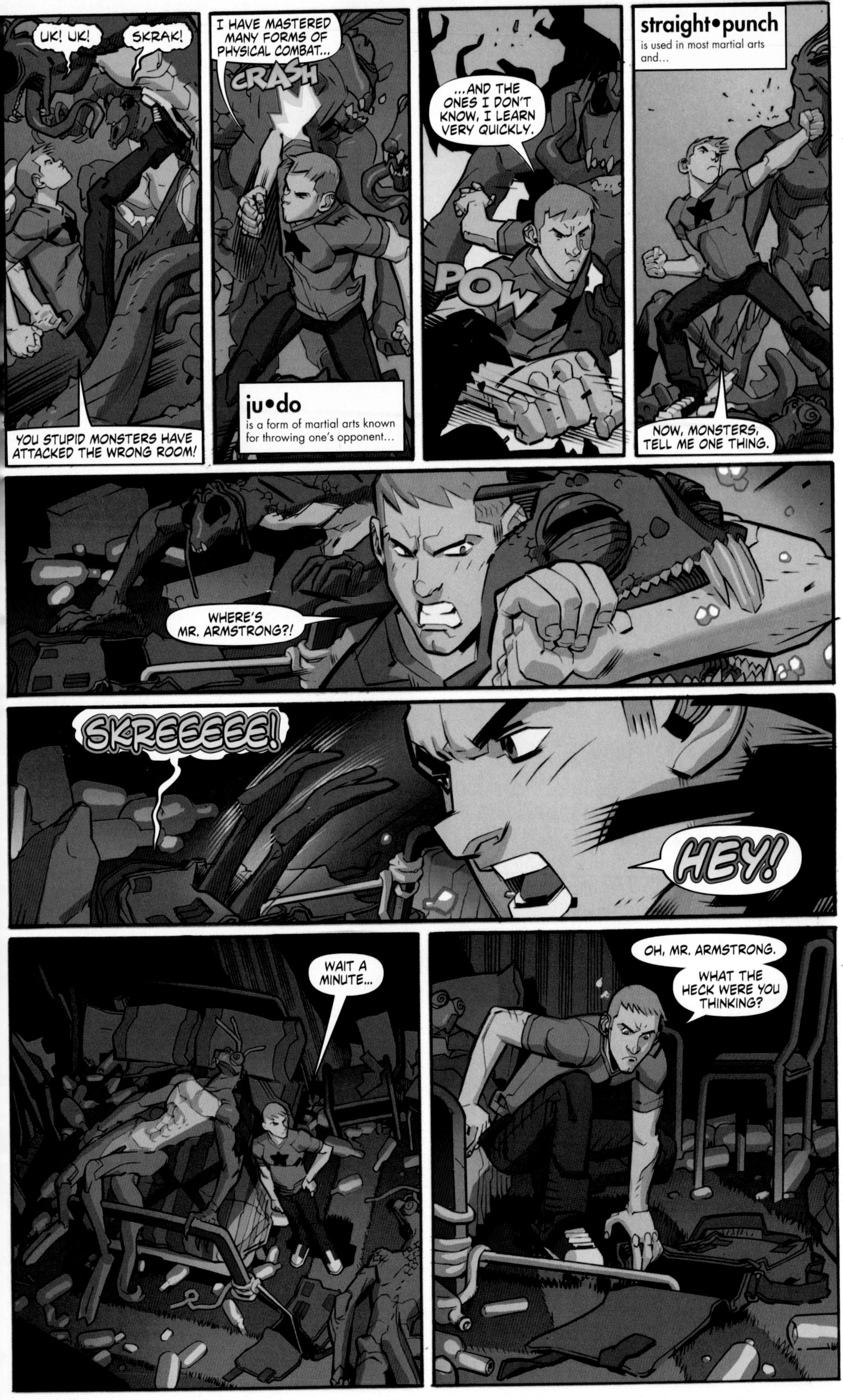
UK! UK!
SKRAK!
YOU STUPID MONSTERS HAVE ATTACKED THE WRONG ROOM!
I HAVE MASTERED MANY FORMS OF PHYSICAL COMBAT...
CRASH
ju•do
is a form of martial arts known for throwing one's opponent...
...AND THE ONES I DON'T KNOW, I LEARN VERY QUICKLY.
POW
straight•punch
is used in most martial arts and...
NOW, MONSTERS, TELL ME ONE THING.
WHERE'S MR. ARMSTRONG?!
SKREEEEEE!
HEY!
WAIT A MINUTE...
OH, MR. ARMSTRONG.
WHAT THE HECK WERE YOU THINKING?

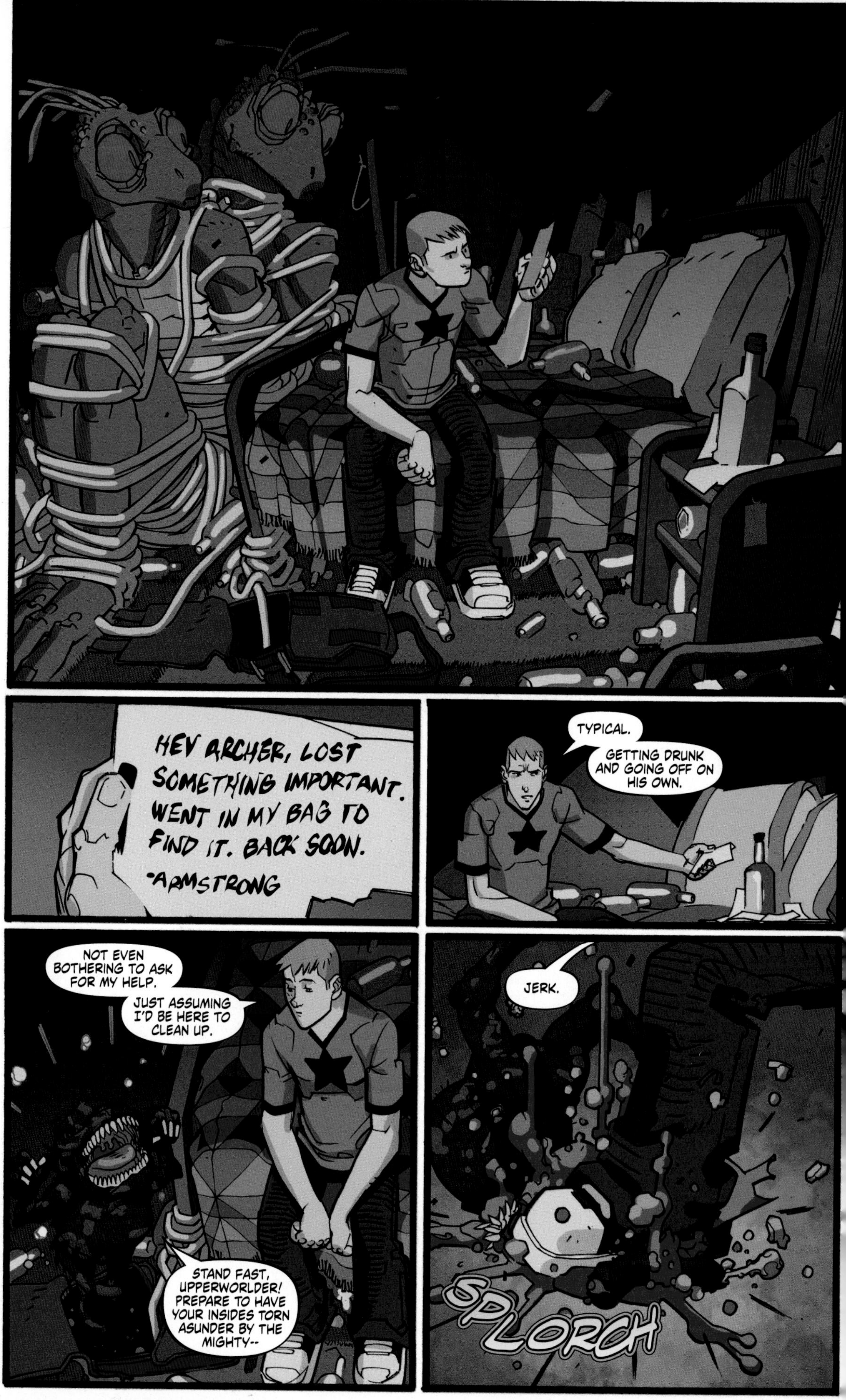
HEY ARCHER, LOST SOMETHING IMPORTANT. WENT IN MY BAG TO FIND IT. BACK SOON.
-ARMSTRONG
TYPICAL.
GETTING DRUNK AND GOING OFF ON HIS OWN.
NOT EVEN BOTHERING TO ASK FOR MY HELP.
JUST ASSUMING I'D BE HERE TO CLEAN UP.
STAND FAST, UPPERWORLDER! PREPARE TO HAVE YOUR INSIDES TORN ASUNDER BY THE MIGHTY--
JERK.
SPLORCH

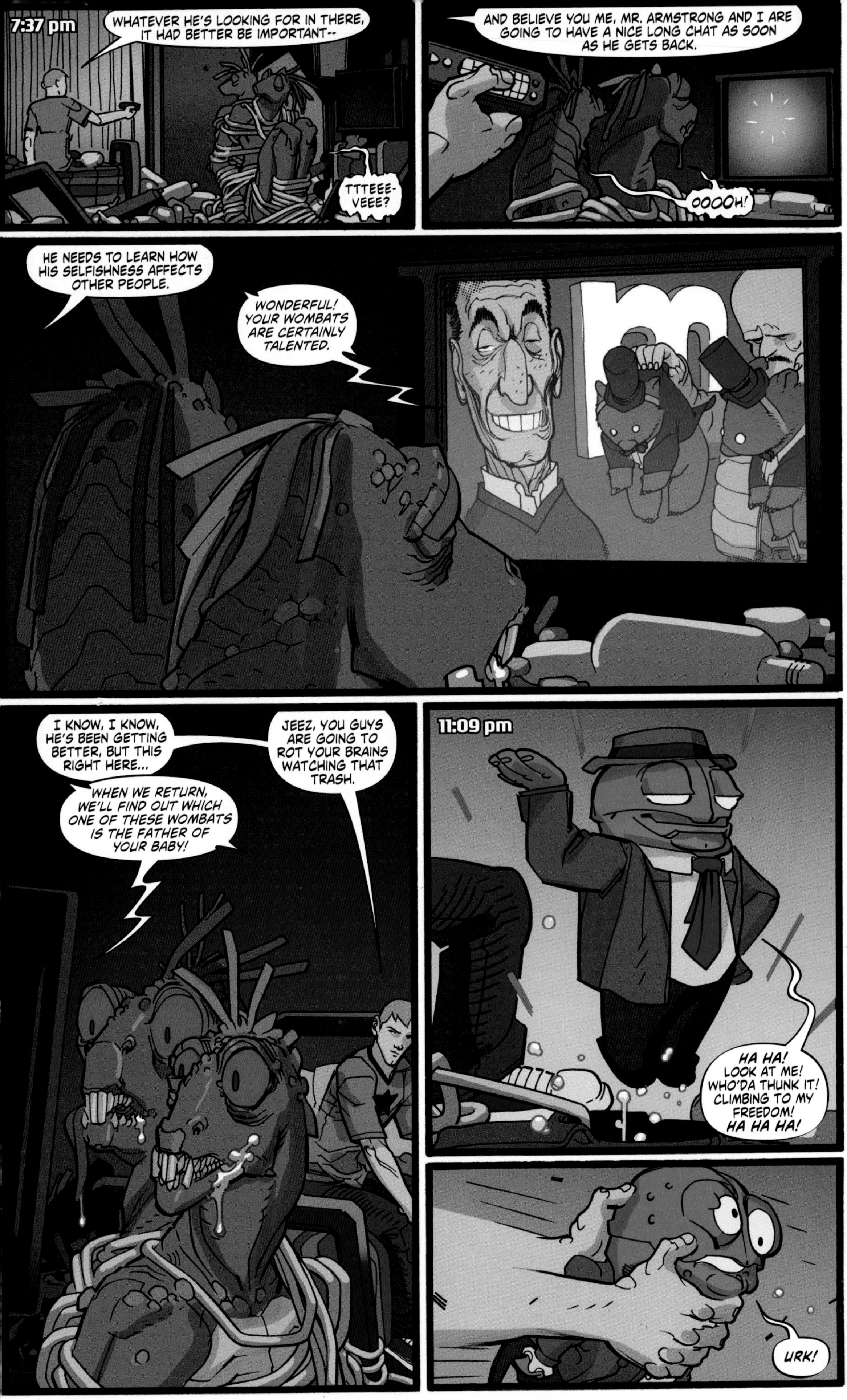
7:37 pm
WHATEVER HE'S LOOKING FOR IN THERE, IT HAD BETTER BE IMPORTANT--
TTTEEE-VEEE?
AND BELIEVE YOU ME, MR. ARMSTRONG AND I ARE GOING TO HAVE A NICE LONG CHAT AS SOON AS HE GETS BACK.
OOOOH!
HE NEEDS TO LEARN HOW HIS SELFISHNESS AFFECTS OTHER PEOPLE.
WONDERFUL! YOUR WOMBATS ARE CERTAINLY TALENTED.
I KNOW, I KNOW, HE'S BEEN GETTING BETTER, BUT THIS RIGHT HERE...
JEEZ, YOU GUYS ARE GOING TO ROT YOUR BRAINS WATCHING THAT TRASH.
WHEN WE RETURN, WE'LL FIND OUT WHICH ONE OF THESE WOMBATS IS THE FATHER OF YOUR BABY!
11:09 pm
HA HA! LOOK AT ME! WHO'DA THUNK IT! CLIMBING TO MY FREEDOM! HA HA HA!
URK!

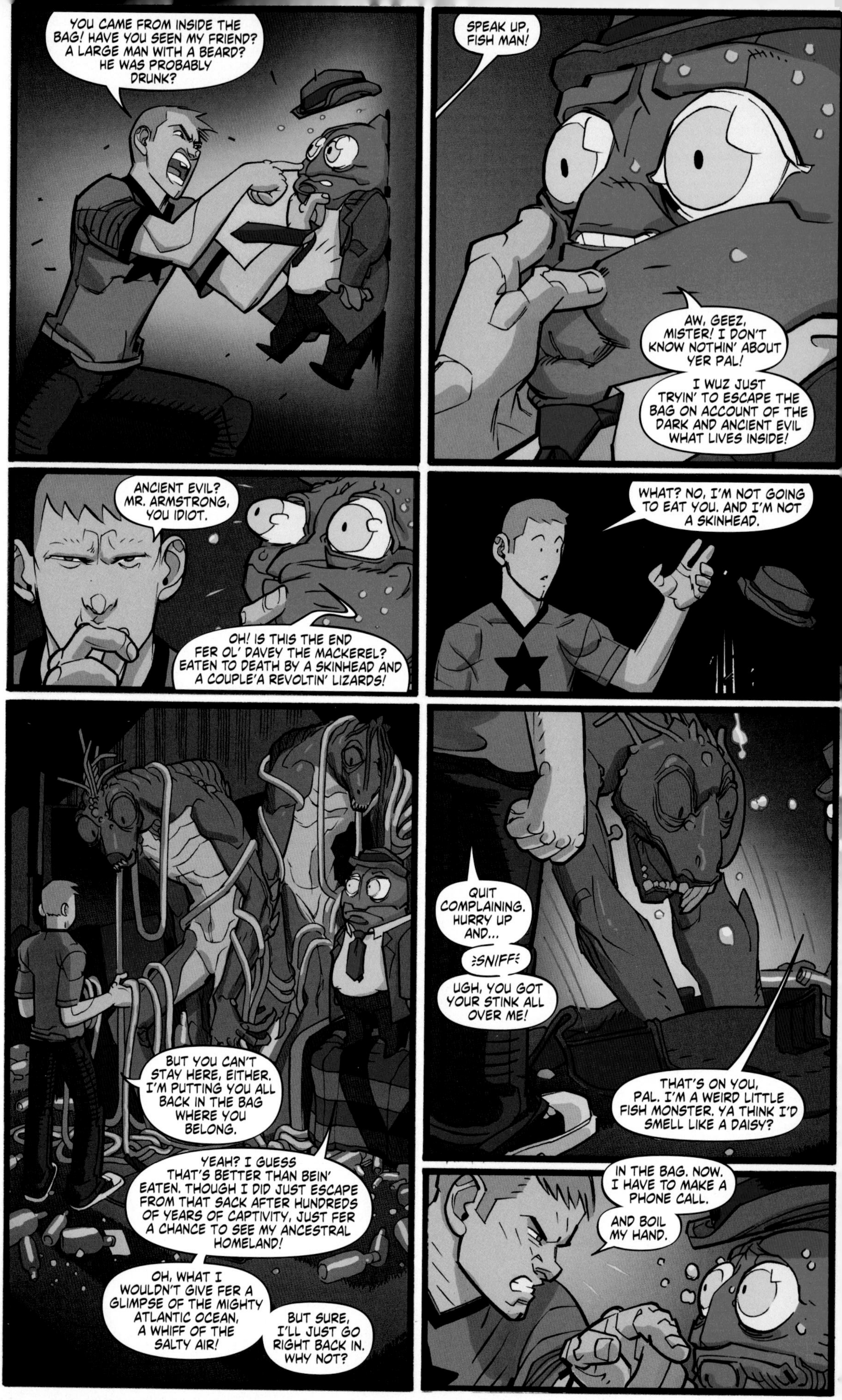
YOU CAME FROM INSIDE THE BAG! HAVE YOU SEEN MY FRIEND? A LARGE MAN WITH A BEARD? HE WAS PROBABLY DRUNK?
SPEAK UP, FISH MAN!
AW, GEEZ, MISTER! I DON'T KNOW NOTHIN' ABOUT YER PAL!
I WUZ JUST TRYIN' TO ESCAPE THE BAG ON ACCOUNT OF THE DARK AND ANCIENT EVIL WHAT LIVES INSIDE!
ANCIENT EVIL? MR. ARMSTRONG, YOU IDIOT.
OH! IS THIS THE END FER OL' DAVEY THE MACKEREL? EATEN TO DEATH BY A SKINHEAD AND A COUPLE'A REVOLTIN' LIZARDS!
WHAT? NO, I'M NOT GOING TO EAT YOU. AND I'M NOT A SKINHEAD.
BUT YOU CAN'T STAY HERE, EITHER. I'M PUTTING YOU ALL BACK IN THE BAG WHERE YOU BELONG.
YEAH? I GUESS THAT'S BETTER THAN BEIN' EATEN. THOUGH I DID JUST ESCAPE FROM THAT SACK AFTER HUNDREDS OF YEARS OF CAPTIVITY, JUST FER A CHANCE TO SEE MY ANCESTRAL HOMELAND!
OH, WHAT I WOULDN'T GIVE FER A GLIMPSE OF THE MIGHTY ATLANTIC OCEAN, A WHIFF OF THE SALTY AIR!
BUT SURE, I'LL JUST GO RIGHT BACK IN. WHY NOT?
QUIT COMPLAINING. HURRY UP AND...
SNIFF
UGH, YOU GOT YOUR STINK ALL OVER ME!
THAT'S ON YOU, PAL. I'M A WEIRD LITTLE FISH MONSTER. YA THINK I'D SMELL LIKE A DAISY?
IN THE BAG. NOW. I HAVE TO MAKE A PHONE CALL.
AND BOIL MY HAND.

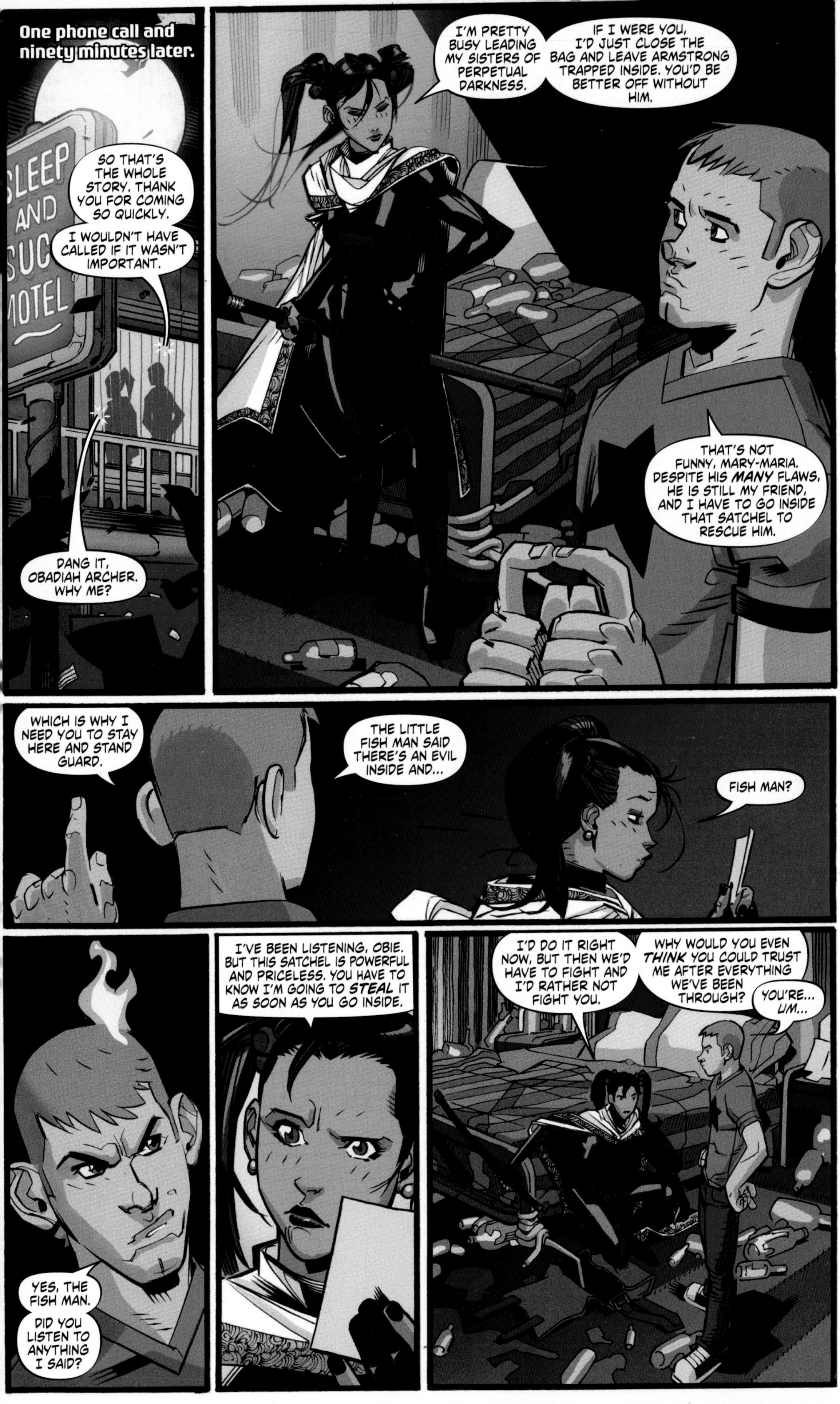

One phone call and ninety minutes later.
SLEEP AND SUC MOTEL
SO THAT'S THE WHOLE STORY. THANK YOU FOR COMING SO QUICKLY.
I WOULDN'T HAVE CALLED IF IT WASN'T IMPORTANT.
DANG IT, OBADIAH ARCHER. WHY ME?
I'M PRETTY BUSY LEADING MY SISTERS OF PERPETUAL DARKNESS.
IF I WERE YOU, I'D JUST CLOSE THE BAG AND LEAVE ARMSTRONG TRAPPED INSIDE. YOU'D BE BETTER OFF WITHOUT HIM.
THAT'S NOT FUNNY, MARY-MARIA. DESPITE HIS MANY FLAWS, HE IS STILL MY FRIEND, AND I HAVE TO GO INSIDE THAT SATCHEL TO RESCUE HIM.
WHICH IS WHY I NEED YOU TO STAY HERE AND STAND GUARD.
THE LITTLE FISH MAN SAID THERE'S AN EVIL INSIDE AND...
FISH MAN?
YES, THE FISH MAN.
DID YOU LISTEN TO ANYTHING I SAID?
I'VE BEEN LISTENING, OBIE. BUT THIS SATCHEL IS POWERFUL AND PRICELESS. YOU HAVE TO KNOW I'M GOING TO STEAL IT AS SOON AS YOU GO INSIDE.
I'D DO IT RIGHT NOW, BUT THEN WE'D HAVE TO FIGHT AND I'D RATHER NOT FIGHT YOU.
WHY WOULD YOU EVEN THINK YOU COULD TRUST ME AFTER EVERYTHING WE'VE BEEN THROUGH?
YOU'RE... UM...

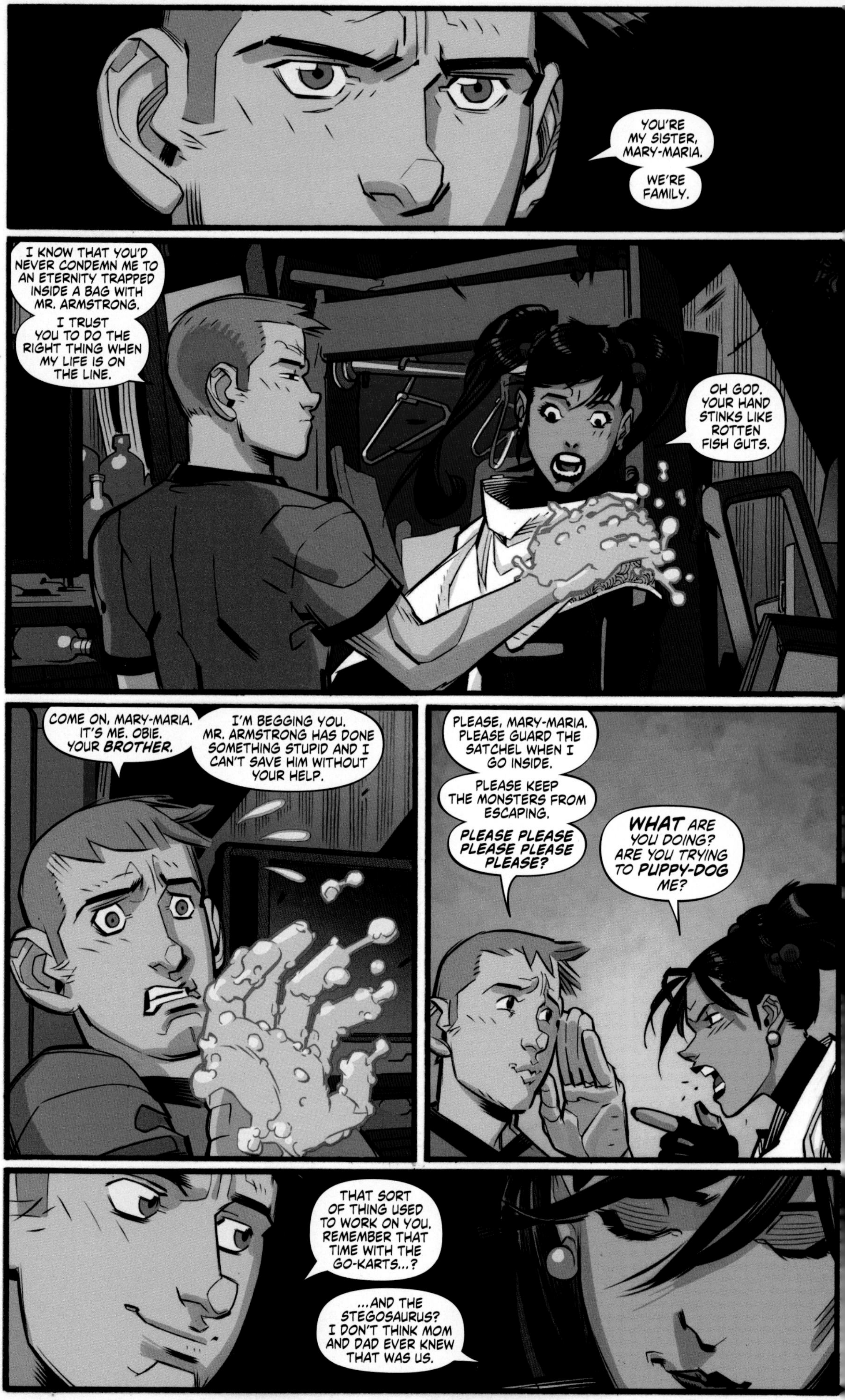
YOU'RE MY SISTER, MARY-MARIA.
WE'RE FAMILY.
I KNOW THAT YOU'D NEVER CONDEMN ME TO AN ETERNITY TRAPPED INSIDE A BAG WITH MR. ARMSTRONG.
I TRUST YOU TO DO THE RIGHT THING WHEN MY LIFE IS ON THE LINE.
OH GOD. YOUR HAND STINKS LIKE ROTTEN FISH GUTS.
COME ON, MARY-MARIA. IT'S ME. OBIE. YOUR BROTHER.
I'M BEGGING YOU. MR. ARMSTRONG HAS DONE SOMETHING STUPID AND I CAN'T SAVE HIM WITHOUT YOUR HELP.
PLEASE, MARY-MARIA. PLEASE GUARD THE SATCHEL WHEN I GO INSIDE.
PLEASE KEEP THE MONSTERS FROM ESCAPING.
PLEASE PLEASE PLEASE PLEASE PLEASE?
WHAT ARE YOU DOING? ARE YOU TRYING TO PUPPY-DOG ME?
THAT SORT OF THING USED TO WORK ON YOU. REMEMBER THAT TIME WITH THE GO-KARTS...?
...AND THE STEGOSAURUS? I DON'T THINK MOM AND DAD EVER KNEW THAT WAS US.

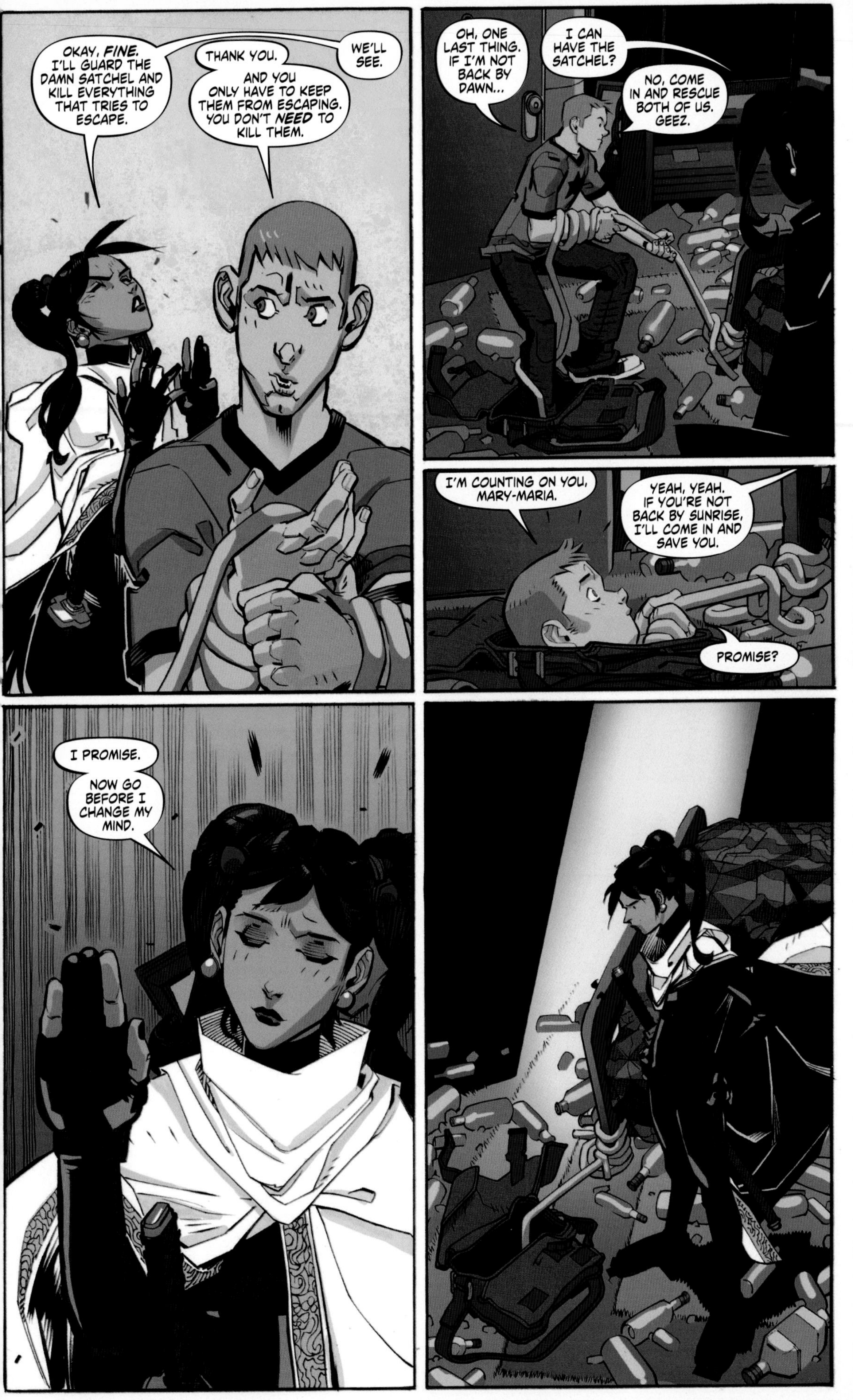
OKAY, *FINE.* I'LL GUARD THE DAMN SATCHEL AND KILL EVERYTHING THAT TRIES TO ESCAPE.
THANK YOU.
AND YOU ONLY HAVE TO KEEP THEM FROM ESCAPING. YOU DON'T *NEED* TO KILL THEM.
WE'LL SEE.
OH, ONE LAST THING. IF I'M NOT BACK BY DAWN...
I CAN HAVE THE SATCHEL?
NO, COME IN AND RESCUE BOTH OF US. GEEZ.
I'M COUNTING ON YOU, MARY-MARIA.
YEAH, YEAH. IF YOU'RE NOT BACK BY SUNRISE, I'LL COME IN AND SAVE YOU.
PROMISE?
I PROMISE.
NOW GO BEFORE I CHANGE MY MIND.

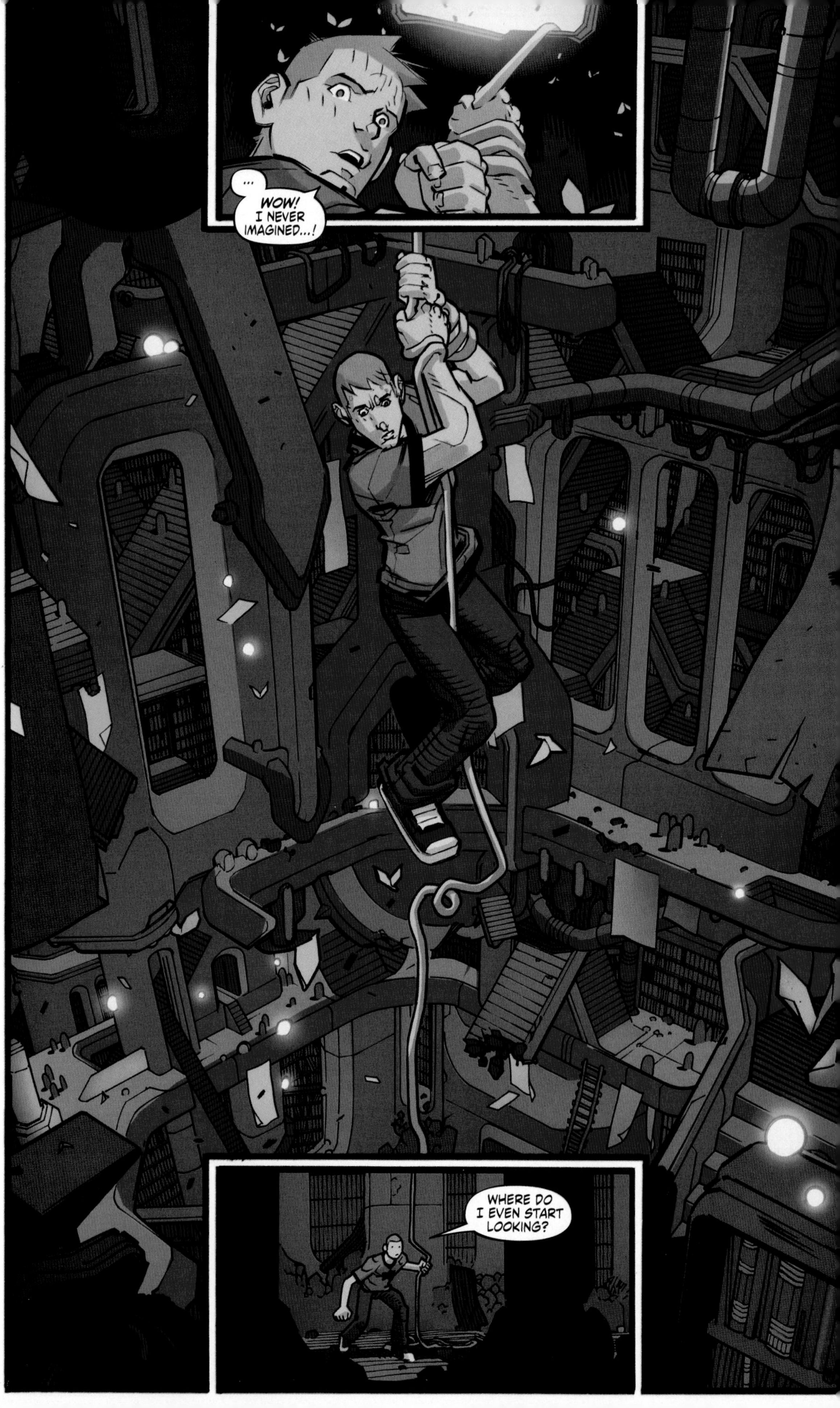
...
WOW! I NEVER IMAGINED...!
WHERE DO I EVEN START LOOKING?

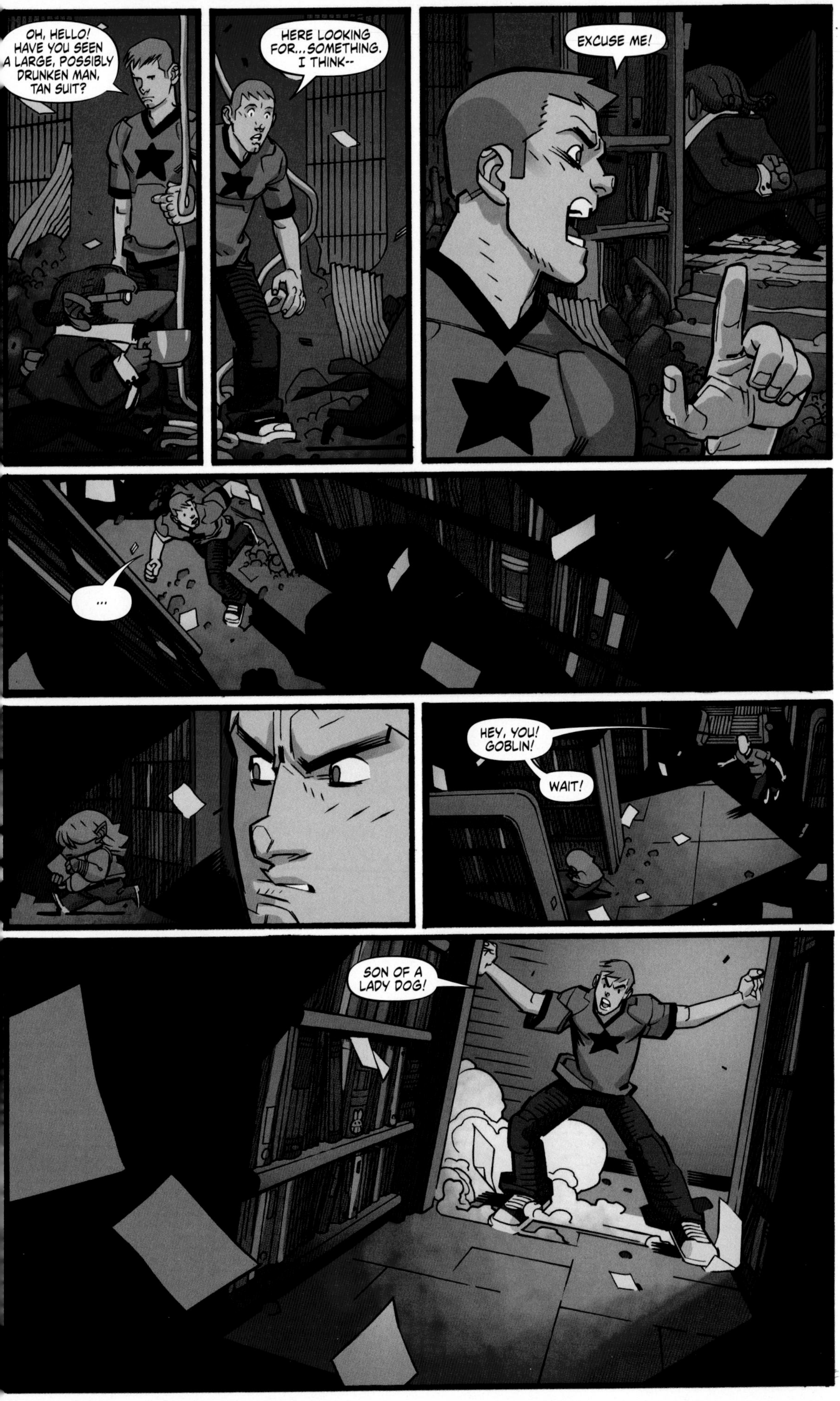
OH, HELLO! HAVE YOU SEEN A LARGE, POSSIBLY DRUNKEN MAN, TAN SUIT?
HERE LOOKING FOR...SOMETHING. I THINK--
EXCUSE ME!
...
HEY, YOU! GOBLIN!
WAIT!
SON OF A LADY DOG!

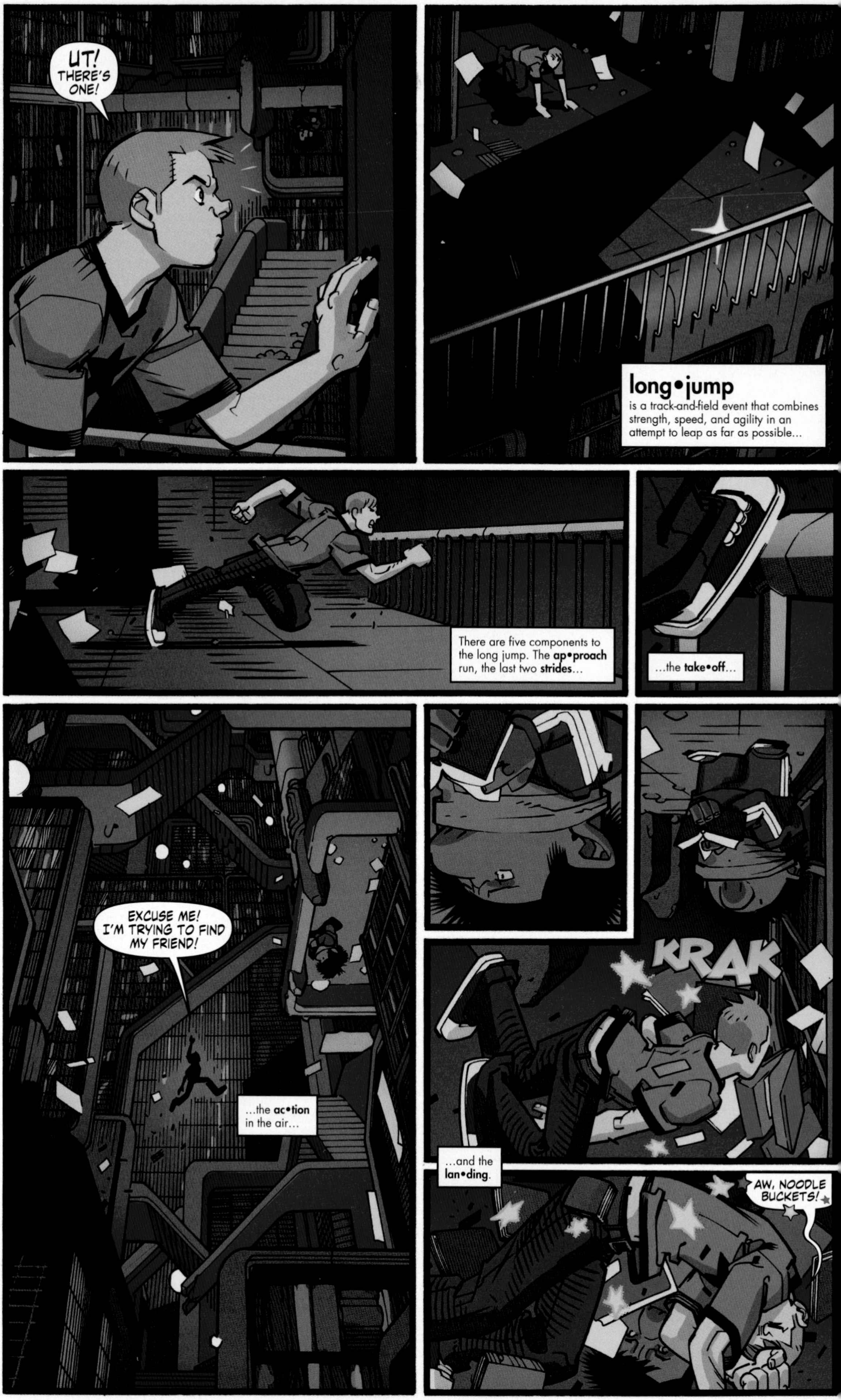

UT! THERE'S ONE!
long•jump
is a track-and-field event that combines strength, speed, and agility in an attempt to leap as far as possible...
There are five components to the long jump. The ap•proach run, the last two strides...
...the take•off...
EXCUSE ME! I'M TRYING TO FIND MY FRIEND!
...the ac•tion in the air...
KRAK
...and the lan•ding.
AW, NOODLE BUCKETS!

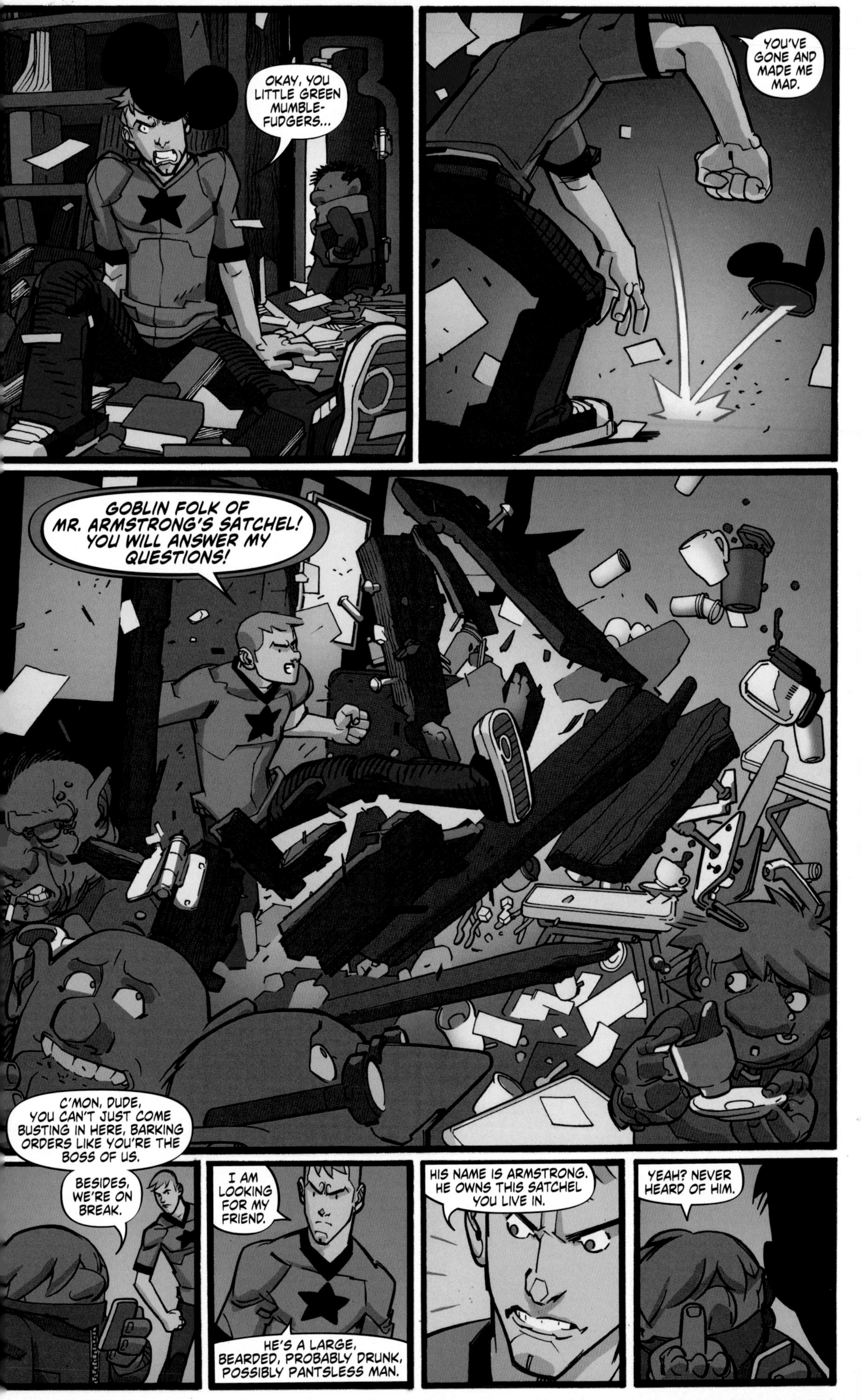

OKAY, YOU LITTLE GREEN MUMBLE-FUDGERS...
YOU'VE GONE AND MADE ME MAD.
GOBLIN FOLK OF MR. ARMSTRONG'S SATCHEL! YOU WILL ANSWER MY QUESTIONS!
C'MON, DUDE, YOU CAN'T JUST COME BUSTING IN HERE, BARKING ORDERS LIKE YOU'RE THE BOSS OF US.
BESIDES, WE'RE ON BREAK.
I AM LOOKING FOR MY FRIEND.
HE'S A LARGE, BEARDED, PROBABLY DRUNK, POSSIBLY PANTSLESS MAN.
HIS NAME IS ARMSTRONG. HE OWNS THIS SATCHEL YOU LIVE IN.
YEAH? NEVER HEARD OF HIM.

:SIGH: I DON'T HAVE TIME FOR YOUR LIES.

MR. ARMSTRONG IS LOOKING FOR SOMETHING IMPORTANT.

OWWWWWw!

WHERE DOES MR. ARMSTRONG KEEP HIS IMPORTANT STUFF?

TELL ME!

OWW, GEEZ! AWWW, *MAN!* I DON'T KNOW! I WORK IN THE COLLECTIBLE PORCELAIN FIGURINE SECTION. YOU KNOW, THOSE CREEPY DEAD-EYED BABIES?

COLLECTIBLE...WAIT, WHAT? MR. ARMSTRONG LIKES THOSE THINGS?

EXCUSE ME? ANGRY VIOLENT MAN?

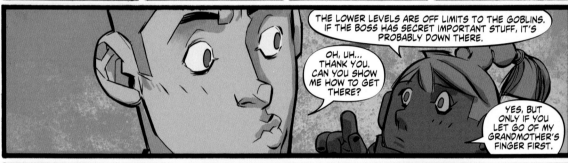

THE LOWER LEVELS ARE OFF LIMITS TO THE GOBLINS. IF THE BOSS HAS SECRET IMPORTANT STUFF, IT'S PROBABLY DOWN THERE.

OH, UH... THANK YOU. CAN YOU SHOW ME HOW TO GET THERE?

YES, BUT ONLY IF YOU LET GO OF MY GRANDMOTHER'S FINGER FIRST.

GRANDMOTHER? OH, GEEZ, I'M SORRY, MA'AM.

IT'S JUST... MY FRIEND MIGHT BE IN TROUBLE AND... GEEZ, I DON'T UNDERSTAND THIS PLACE AT ALL.

BITE ME.

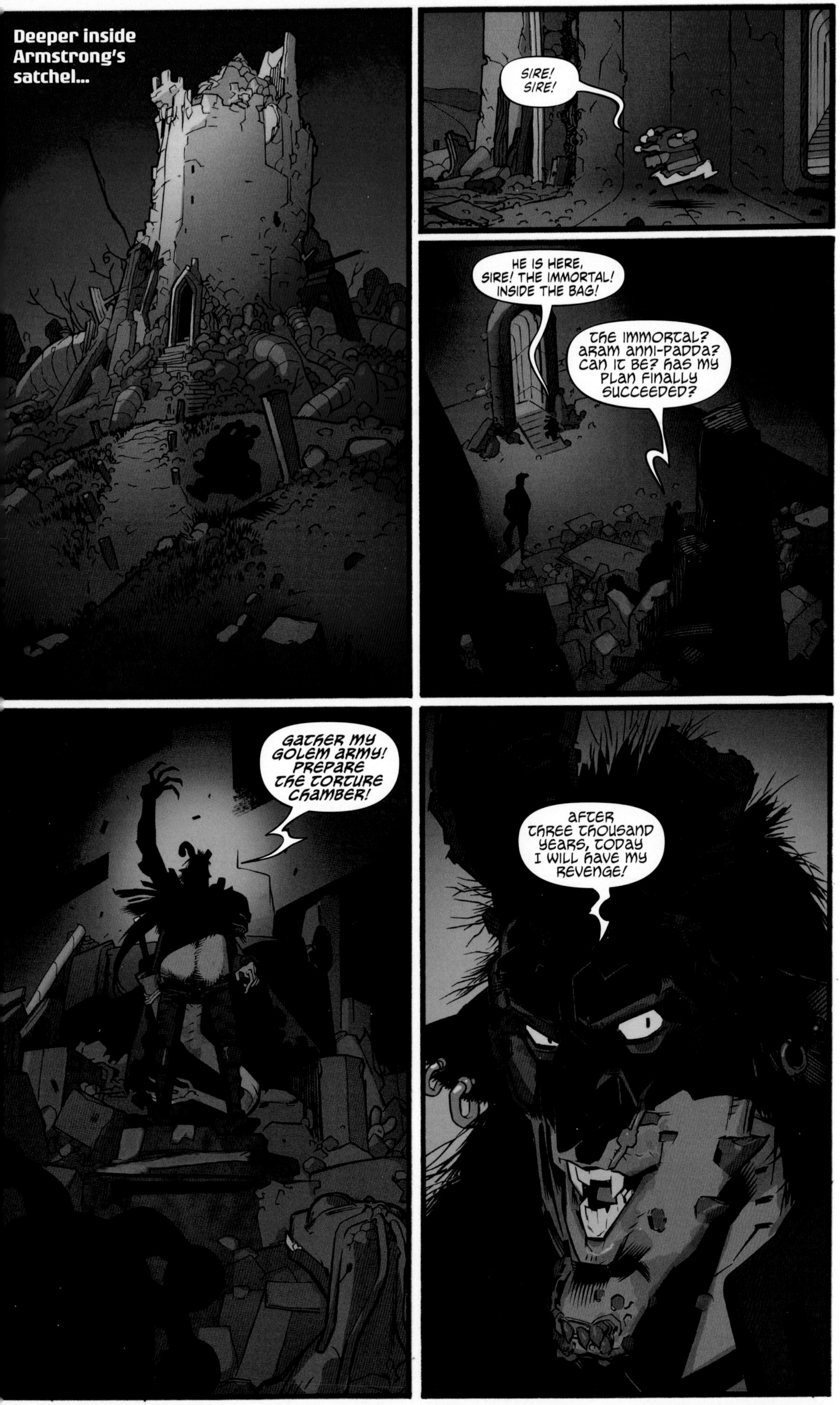
Deeper inside Armstrong's satchel...
SIRE! SIRE!
HE IS HERE, SIRE! THE IMMORTAL! INSIDE THE BAG!
THE IMMORTAL? ARAM ANNI-PADDA? CAN IT BE? HAS MY PLAN FINALLY SUCCEEDED?
GATHER MY GOLEM ARMY! PREPARE THE TORTURE CHAMBER!
AFTER THREE THOUSAND YEARS, TODAY I WILL HAVE MY REVENGE!

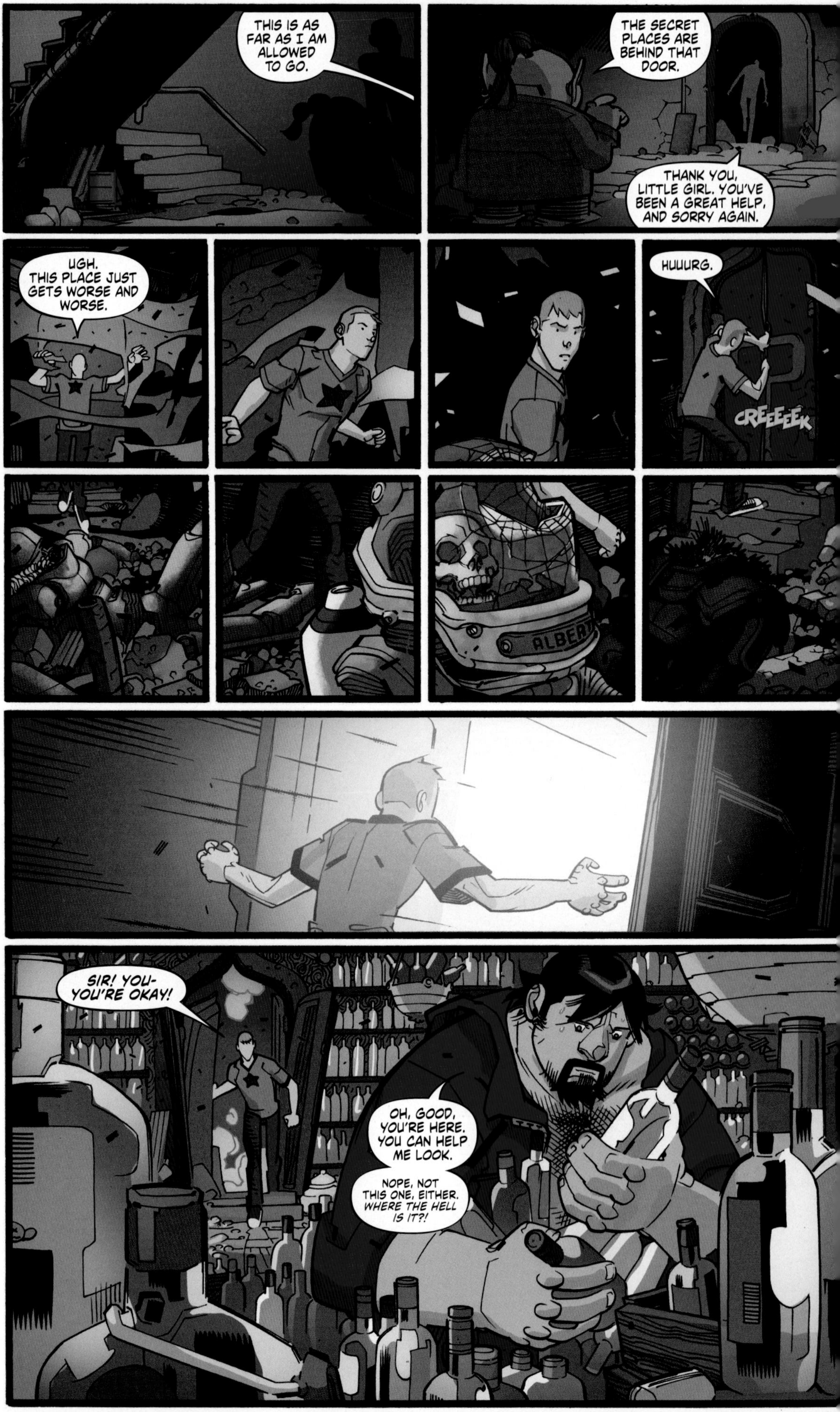
THIS IS AS FAR AS I AM ALLOWED TO GO.
THE SECRET PLACES ARE BEHIND THAT DOOR.
THANK YOU, LITTLE GIRL. YOU'VE BEEN A GREAT HELP, AND SORRY AGAIN.
UGH. THIS PLACE JUST GETS WORSE AND WORSE.
HUUURG.
CREEEEEK
ALBERT
SIR! YOU- YOU'RE OKAY!
OH, GOOD, YOU'RE HERE. YOU CAN HELP ME LOOK.
NOPE, NOT THIS ONE, EITHER. WHERE THE HELL IS IT?!

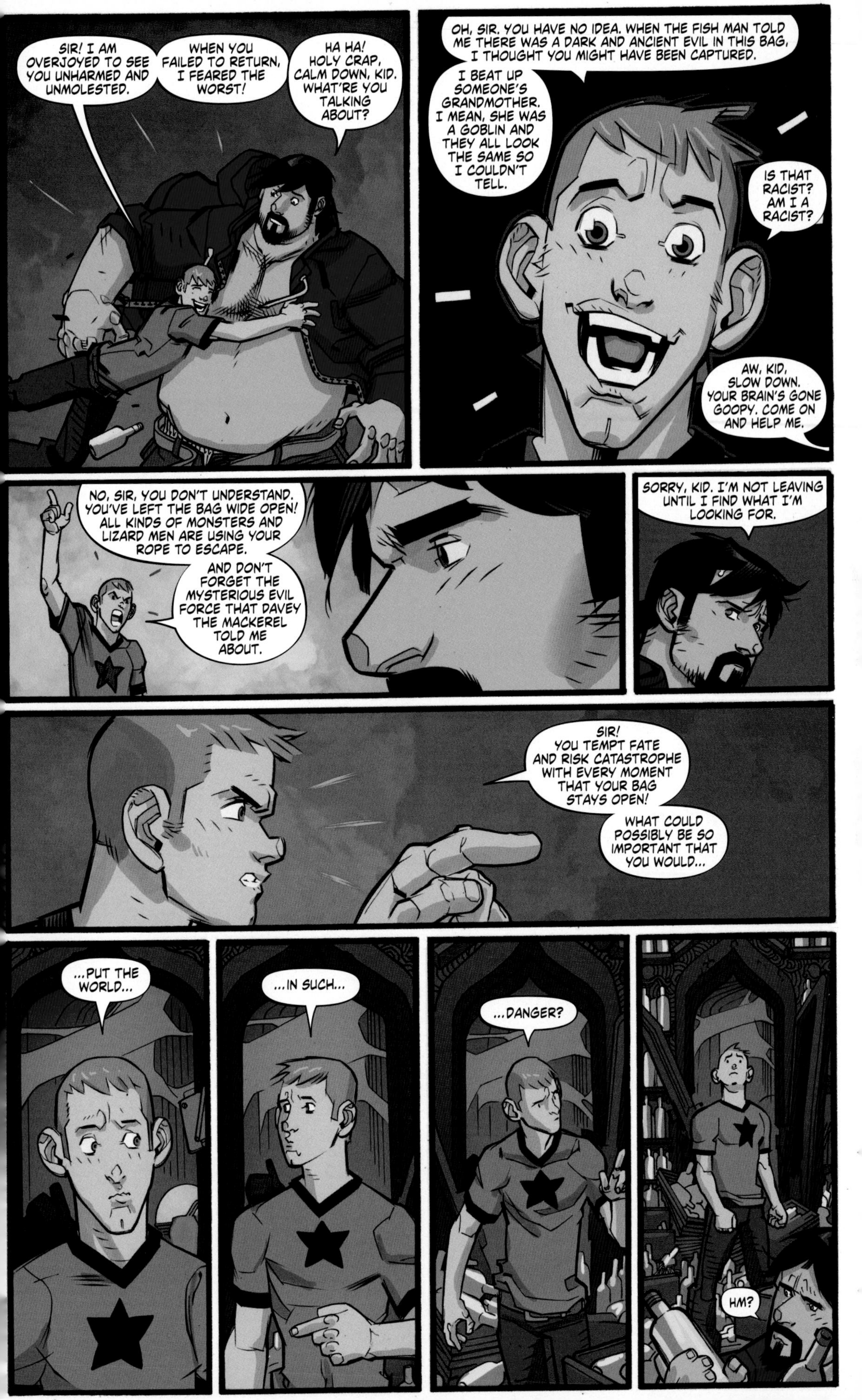
SIR! I AM OVERJOYED TO SEE YOU UNHARMED AND UNMOLESTED.
WHEN YOU FAILED TO RETURN, I FEARED THE WORST!
HA HA! HOLY CRAP, CALM DOWN, KID. WHAT'RE YOU TALKING ABOUT?
OH, SIR. YOU HAVE NO IDEA. WHEN THE FISH MAN TOLD ME THERE WAS A DARK AND ANCIENT EVIL IN THIS BAG, I THOUGHT YOU MIGHT HAVE BEEN CAPTURED.
I BEAT UP SOMEONE'S GRANDMOTHER. I MEAN, SHE WAS A GOBLIN AND THEY ALL LOOK THE SAME SO I COULDN'T TELL.
IS THAT RACIST? AM I A RACIST?
AW, KID, SLOW DOWN. YOUR BRAIN'S GONE GOOPY. COME ON AND HELP ME.
NO, SIR, YOU DON'T UNDERSTAND. YOU'VE LEFT THE BAG WIDE OPEN! ALL KINDS OF MONSTERS AND LIZARD MEN ARE USING YOUR ROPE TO ESCAPE.
AND DON'T FORGET THE MYSTERIOUS EVIL FORCE THAT DAVEY THE MACKEREL TOLD ME ABOUT.
SORRY, KID. I'M NOT LEAVING UNTIL I FIND WHAT I'M LOOKING FOR.
SIR! YOU TEMPT FATE AND RISK CATASTROPHE WITH EVERY MOMENT THAT YOUR BAG STAYS OPEN!
WHAT COULD POSSIBLY BE SO IMPORTANT THAT YOU WOULD...
...PUT THE WORLD...
...IN SUCH...
...DANGER?
HM?

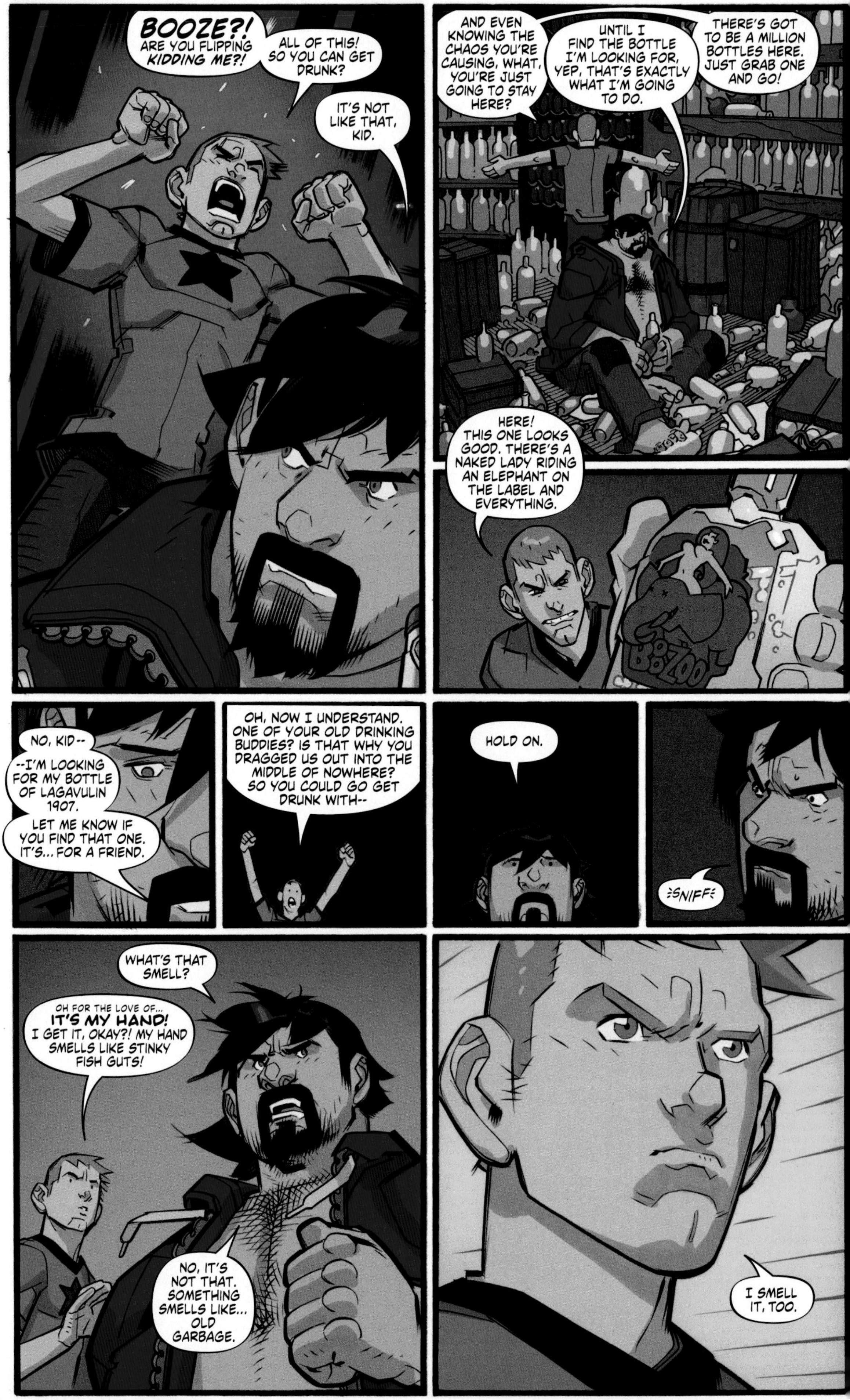
BOOZE?! ARE YOU FLIPPING KIDDING ME?!
ALL OF THIS! SO YOU CAN GET DRUNK?
IT'S NOT LIKE THAT, KID.
AND EVEN KNOWING THE CHAOS YOU'RE CAUSING, WHAT, YOU'RE JUST GOING TO STAY HERE?
UNTIL I FIND THE BOTTLE I'M LOOKING FOR, YEP, THAT'S EXACTLY WHAT I'M GOING TO DO.
THERE'S GOT TO BE A MILLION BOTTLES HERE. JUST GRAB ONE AND GO!
HERE! THIS ONE LOOKS GOOD. THERE'S A NAKED LADY RIDING AN ELEPHANT ON THE LABEL AND EVERYTHING.
NO, KID--
--I'M LOOKING FOR MY BOTTLE OF LAGAVULIN 1907.
LET ME KNOW IF YOU FIND THAT ONE. IT'S... FOR A FRIEND.
OH, NOW I UNDERSTAND. ONE OF YOUR OLD DRINKING BUDDIES? IS THAT WHY YOU DRAGGED US OUT INTO THE MIDDLE OF NOWHERE? SO YOU COULD GO GET DRUNK WITH--
HOLD ON.
SNIFF
WHAT'S THAT SMELL?
OH FOR THE LOVE OF... IT'S MY HAND! I GET IT, OKAY?! MY HAND SMELLS LIKE STINKY FISH GUTS!
NO, IT'S NOT THAT. SOMETHING SMELLS LIKE... OLD GARBAGE.
I SMELL IT, TOO.

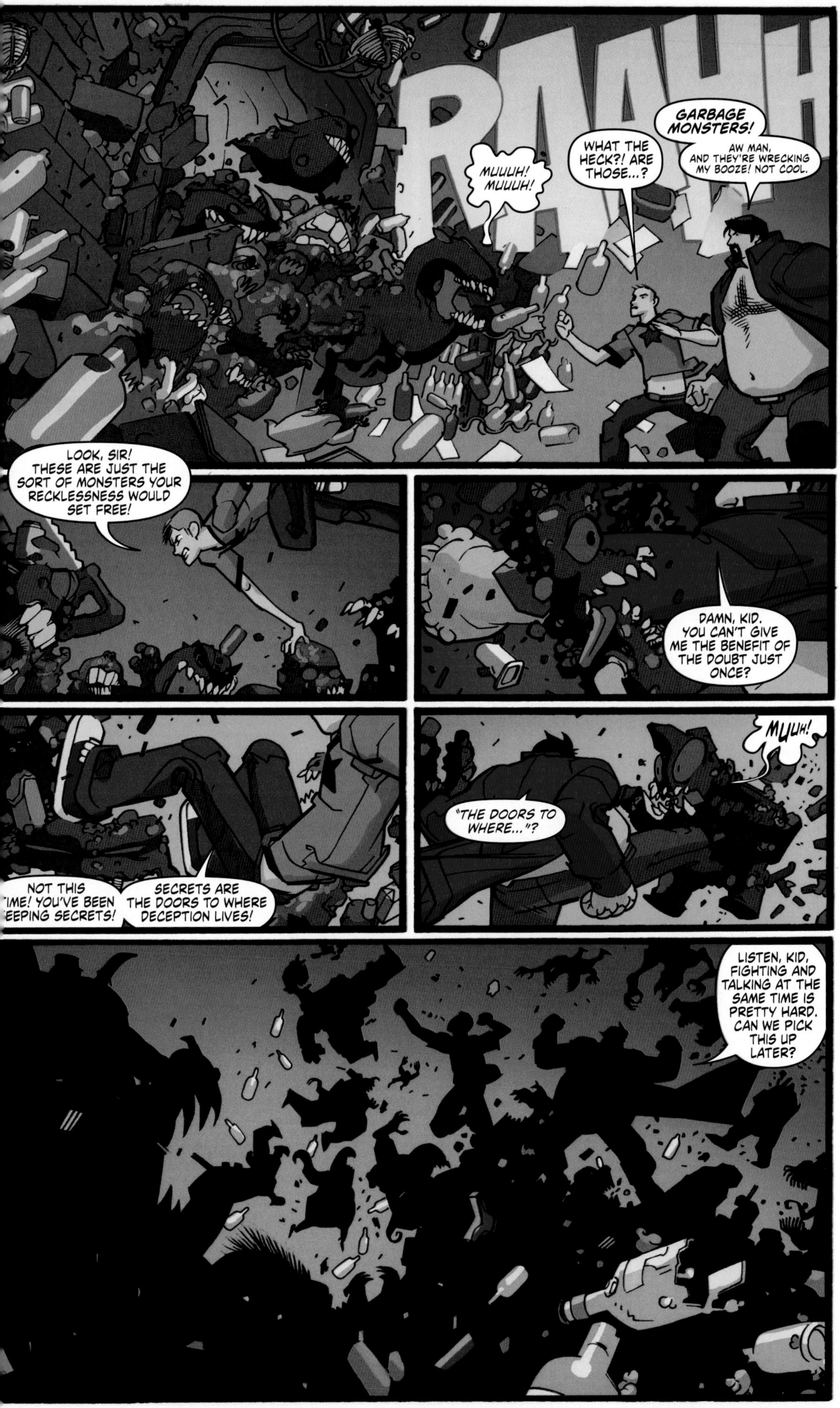
MUUUH! MUUUH!
WHAT THE HECK?! ARE THOSE...?
GARBAGE MONSTERS!
AW MAN, AND THEY'RE WRECKING MY BOOZE! NOT COOL.
LOOK, SIR! THESE ARE JUST THE SORT OF MONSTERS YOUR RECKLESSNESS WOULD SET FREE!
DAMN, KID. YOU CAN'T GIVE ME THE BENEFIT OF THE DOUBT JUST ONCE?
NOT THIS IME! YOU'VE BEEN EEPING SECRETS!
SECRETS ARE THE DOORS TO WHERE DECEPTION LIVES!
"THE DOORS TO WHERE..."?
MUUH!
LISTEN, KID, FIGHTING AND TALKING AT THE SAME TIME IS PRETTY HARD. CAN WE PICK THIS UP LATER?

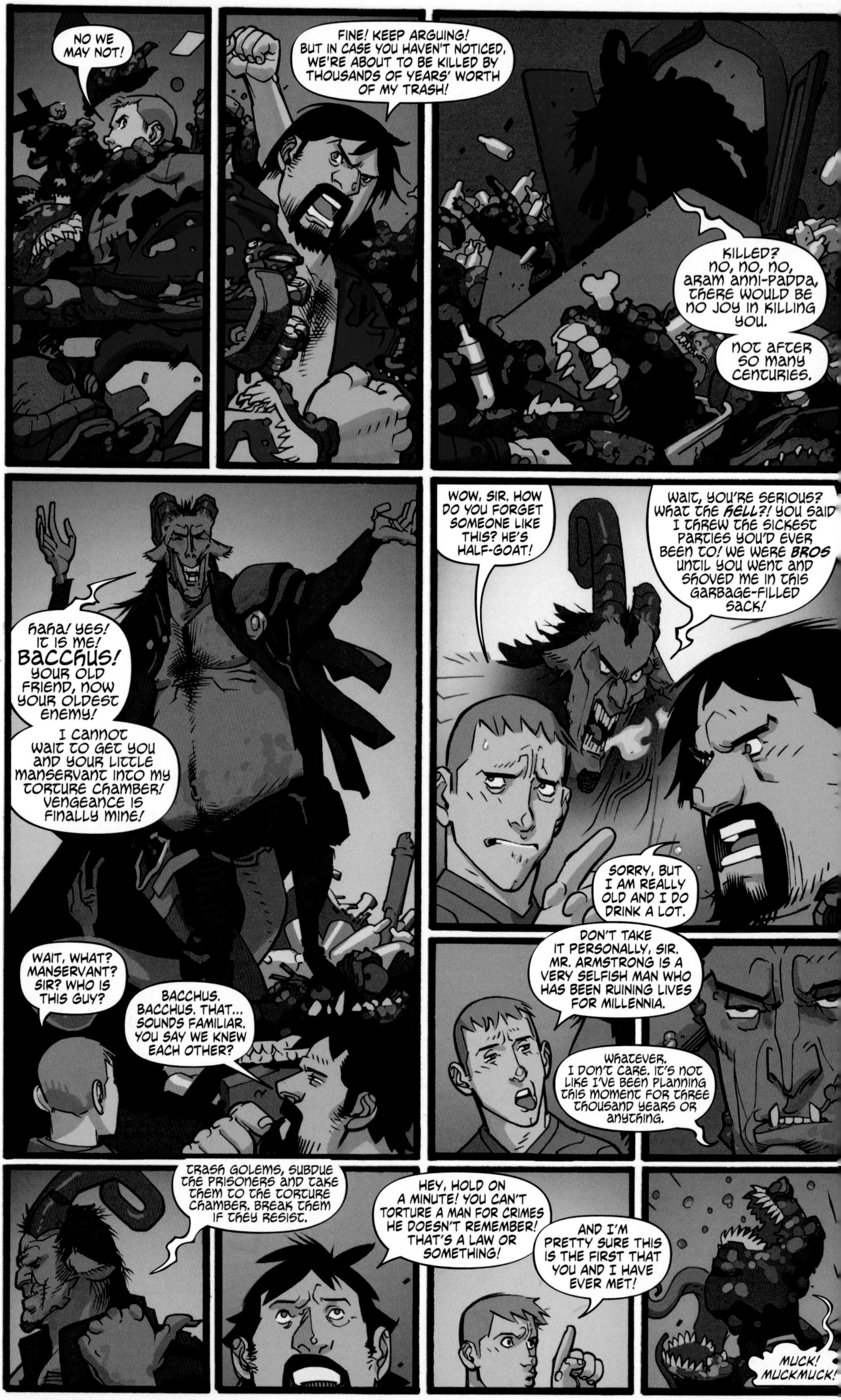
NO WE MAY NOT!
FINE! KEEP ARGUING! BUT IN CASE YOU HAVEN'T NOTICED, WE'RE ABOUT TO BE KILLED BY THOUSANDS OF YEARS' WORTH OF MY TRASH!
KILLED? NO, NO, NO, ARAM ANNI-PADDA, THERE WOULD BE NO JOY IN KILLING YOU.
NOT AFTER SO MANY CENTURIES.
HAHA! YES! IT IS ME! BACCHUS! YOUR OLD FRIEND, NOW YOUR OLDEST ENEMY!
I CANNOT WAIT TO GET YOU AND YOUR LITTLE MANSERVANT INTO MY TORTURE CHAMBER! VENGEANCE IS FINALLY MINE!
WAIT, WHAT? MANSERVANT? SIR? WHO IS THIS GUY?
BACCHUS. BACCHUS. THAT... SOUNDS FAMILIAR. YOU SAY WE KNEW EACH OTHER?
WOW, SIR. HOW DO YOU FORGET SOMEONE LIKE THIS? HE'S HALF-GOAT!
WAIT, YOU'RE SERIOUS? WHAT THE HELL?! YOU SAID I THREW THE SICKEST PARTIES YOU'D EVER BEEN TO! WE WERE BROS UNTIL YOU WENT AND SHOVED ME IN THIS GARBAGE-FILLED SACK!
SORRY, BUT I AM REALLY OLD AND I DO DRINK A LOT.
DON'T TAKE IT PERSONALLY, SIR. MR. ARMSTRONG IS A VERY SELFISH MAN WHO HAS BEEN RUINING LIVES FOR MILLENNIA.
WHATEVER. I DON'T CARE. IT'S NOT LIKE I'VE BEEN PLANNING THIS MOMENT FOR THREE THOUSAND YEARS OR ANYTHING.
TRASH GOLEMS, SUBDUE THE PRISONERS AND TAKE THEM TO THE TORTURE CHAMBER. BREAK THEM IF THEY RESIST.
HEY, HOLD ON A MINUTE! YOU CAN'T TORTURE A MAN FOR CRIMES HE DOESN'T REMEMBER! THAT'S A LAW OR SOMETHING!
AND I'M PRETTY SURE THIS IS THE FIRST THAT YOU AND I HAVE EVER MET!
MUCK! MUCKMUCK!

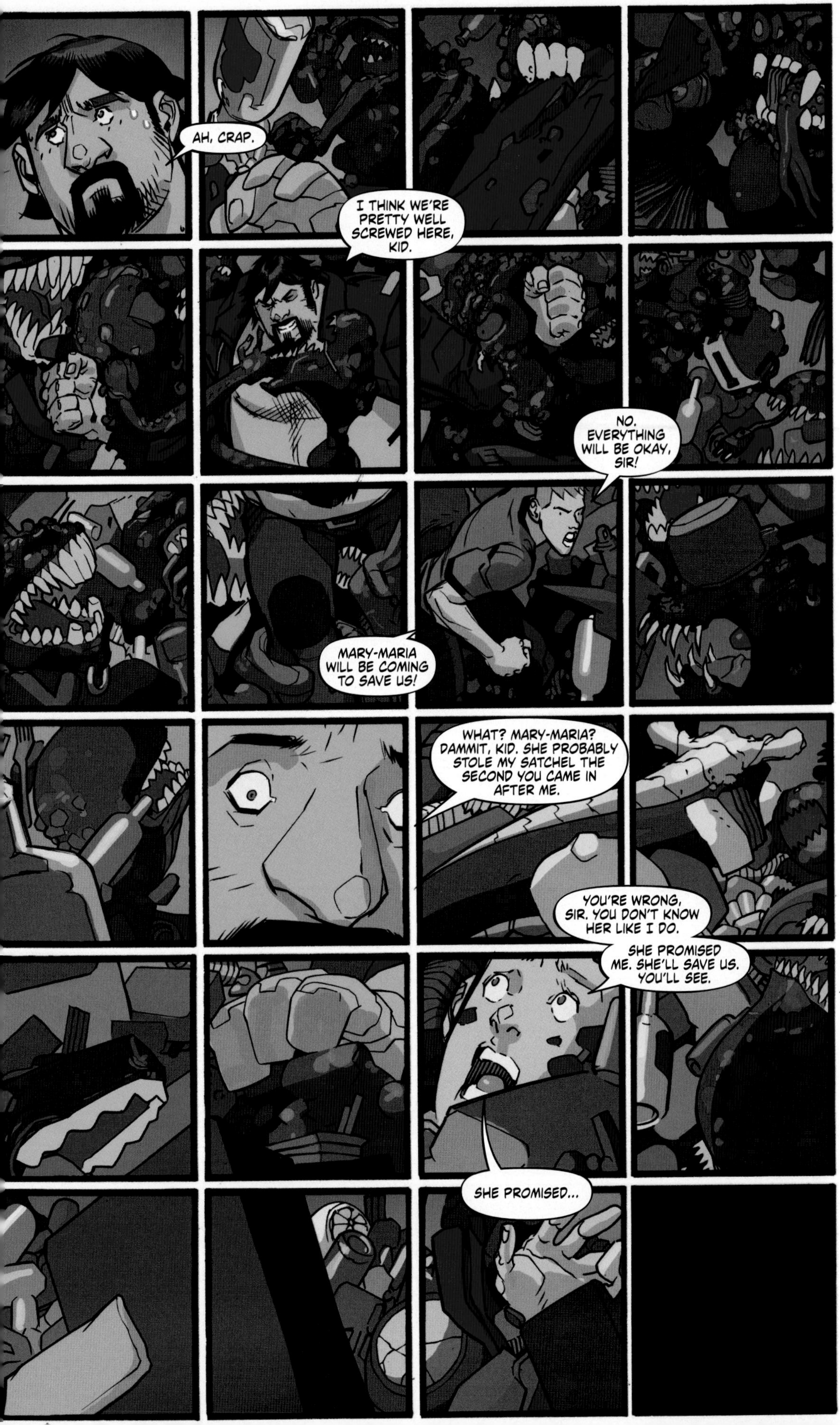
AH, CRAP.
I THINK WE'RE PRETTY WELL SCREWED HERE, KID.
NO. EVERYTHING WILL BE OKAY, SIR!
MARY-MARIA WILL BE COMING TO SAVE US!
WHAT? MARY-MARIA? DAMMIT, KID. SHE PROBABLY STOLE MY SATCHEL THE SECOND YOU CAME IN AFTER ME.
YOU'RE WRONG, SIR. YOU DON'T KNOW HER LIKE I DO.
SHE PROMISED ME. SHE'LL SAVE US. YOU'LL SEE.
SHE PROMISED...

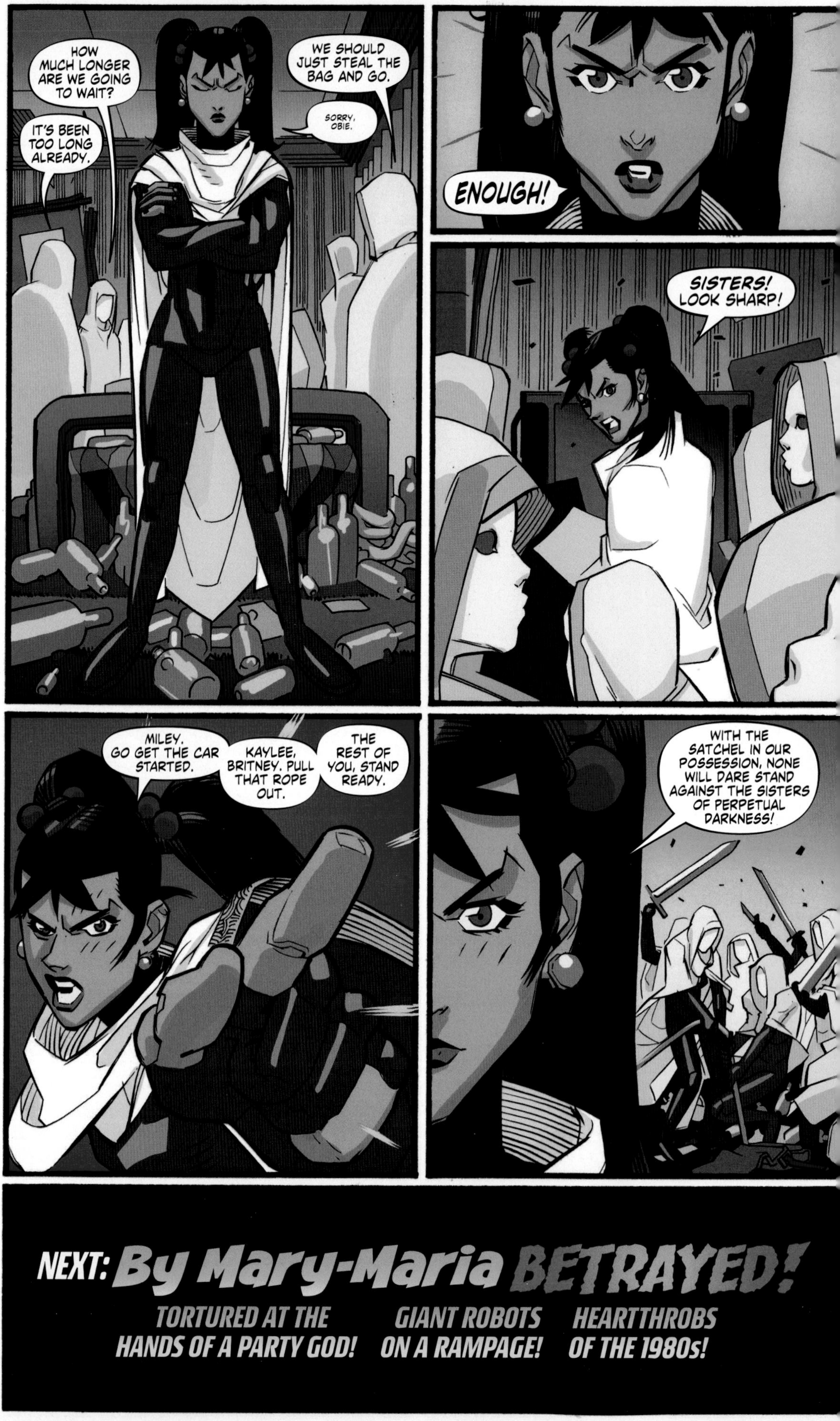
HOW MUCH LONGER ARE WE GOING TO WAIT?
IT'S BEEN TOO LONG ALREADY.
WE SHOULD JUST STEAL THE BAG AND GO.
SORRY, OBIE.
ENOUGH!
SISTERS! LOOK SHARP!
MILEY. GO GET THE CAR STARTED.
KAYLEE, BRITNEY. PULL THAT ROPE OUT.
THE REST OF YOU, STAND READY.
WITH THE SATCHEL IN OUR POSSESSION, NONE WILL DARE STAND AGAINST THE SISTERS OF PERPETUAL DARKNESS!

NEXT: By Mary-Maria BETRAYED!

TORTURED AT THE HANDS OF A PARTY GOD!

GIANT ROBOTS ON A RAMPAGE!

HEARTTHROBS OF THE 1980s!

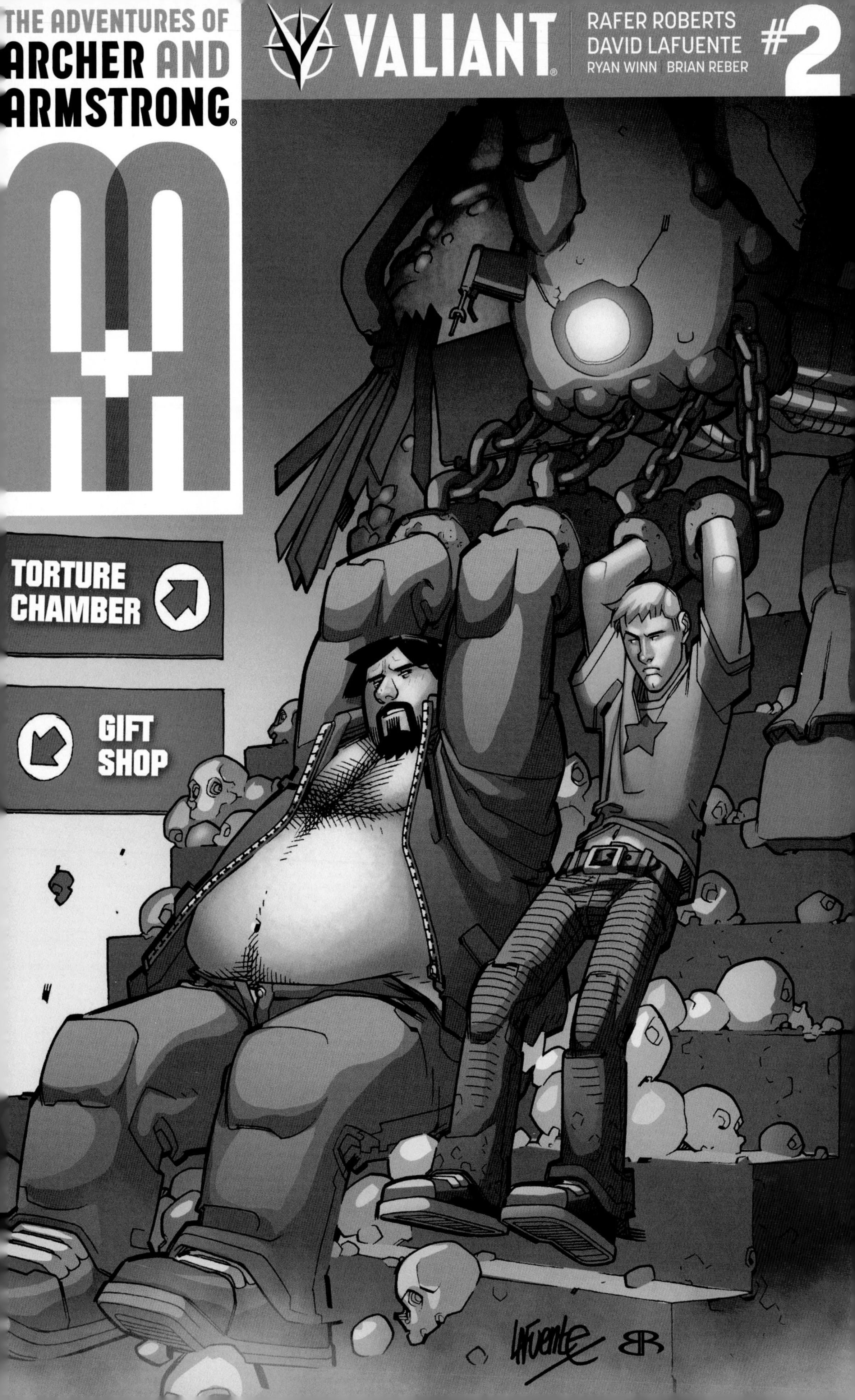
THE ADVENTURES OF
ARCHER AND ARMSTRONG
VALIANT
RAFER ROBERTS
DAVID LAFUENTE
RYAN WINN | BRIAN REBER
#2
TORTURE CHAMBER
GIFT SHOP
LAFUENTE
BR

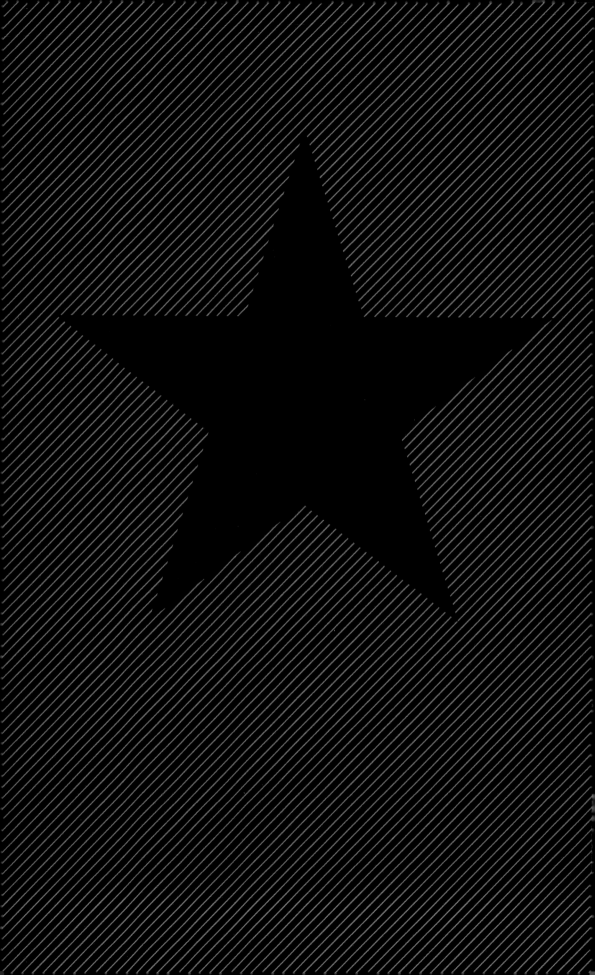

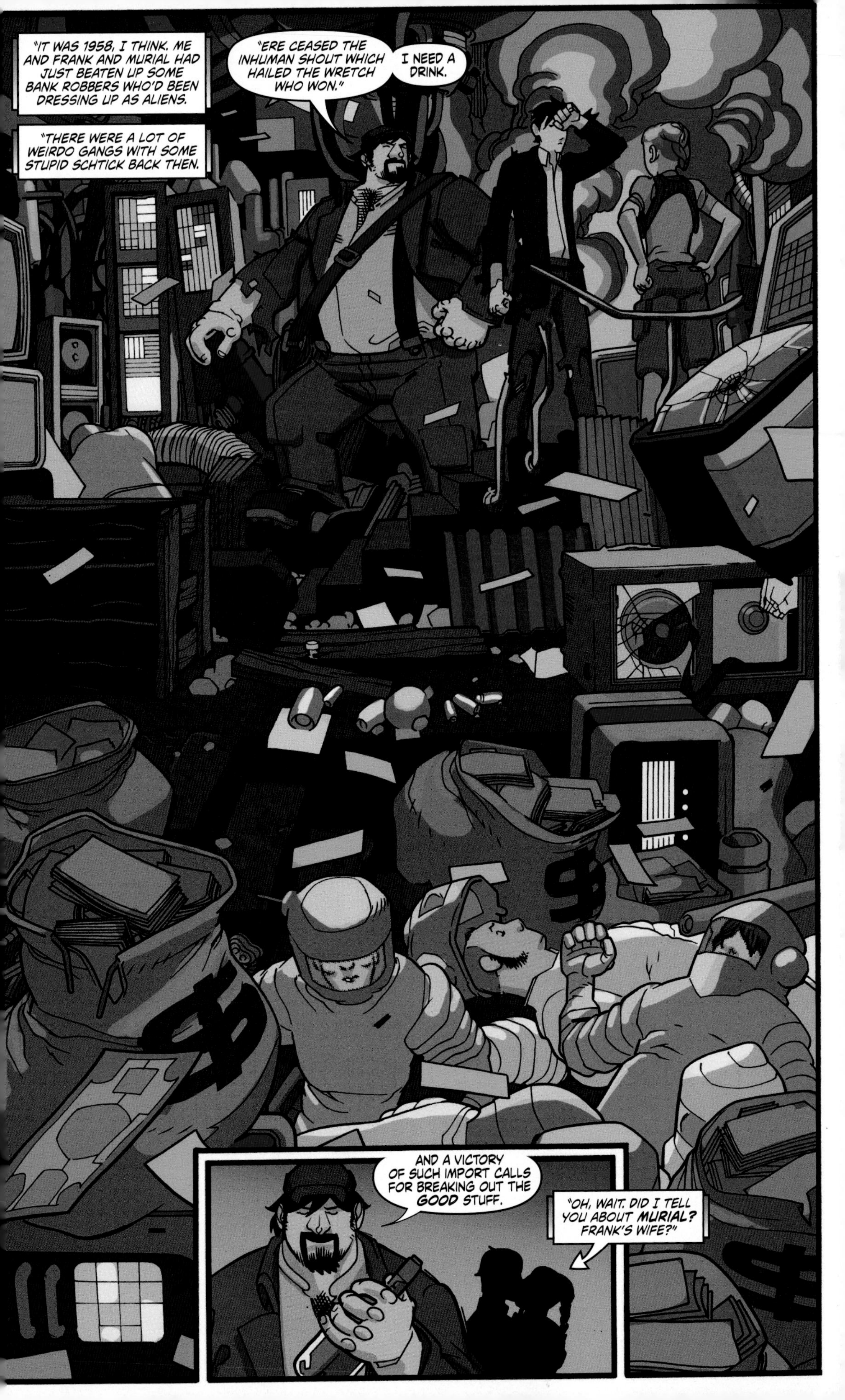
"IT WAS 1958, I THINK. ME AND FRANK AND MURIAL HAD JUST BEATEN UP SOME BANK ROBBERS WHO'D BEEN DRESSING UP AS ALIENS.
"THERE WERE A LOT OF WEIRDO GANGS WITH SOME STUPID SCHTICK BACK THEN.
"ERE CEASED THE INHUMAN SHOUT WHICH HAILED THE WRETCH WHO WON."
I NEED A DRINK.
AND A VICTORY OF SUCH IMPORT CALLS FOR BREAKING OUT THE **GOOD** STUFF.
"OH, WAIT. DID I TELL YOU ABOUT **MURIAL?** FRANK'S WIFE?"

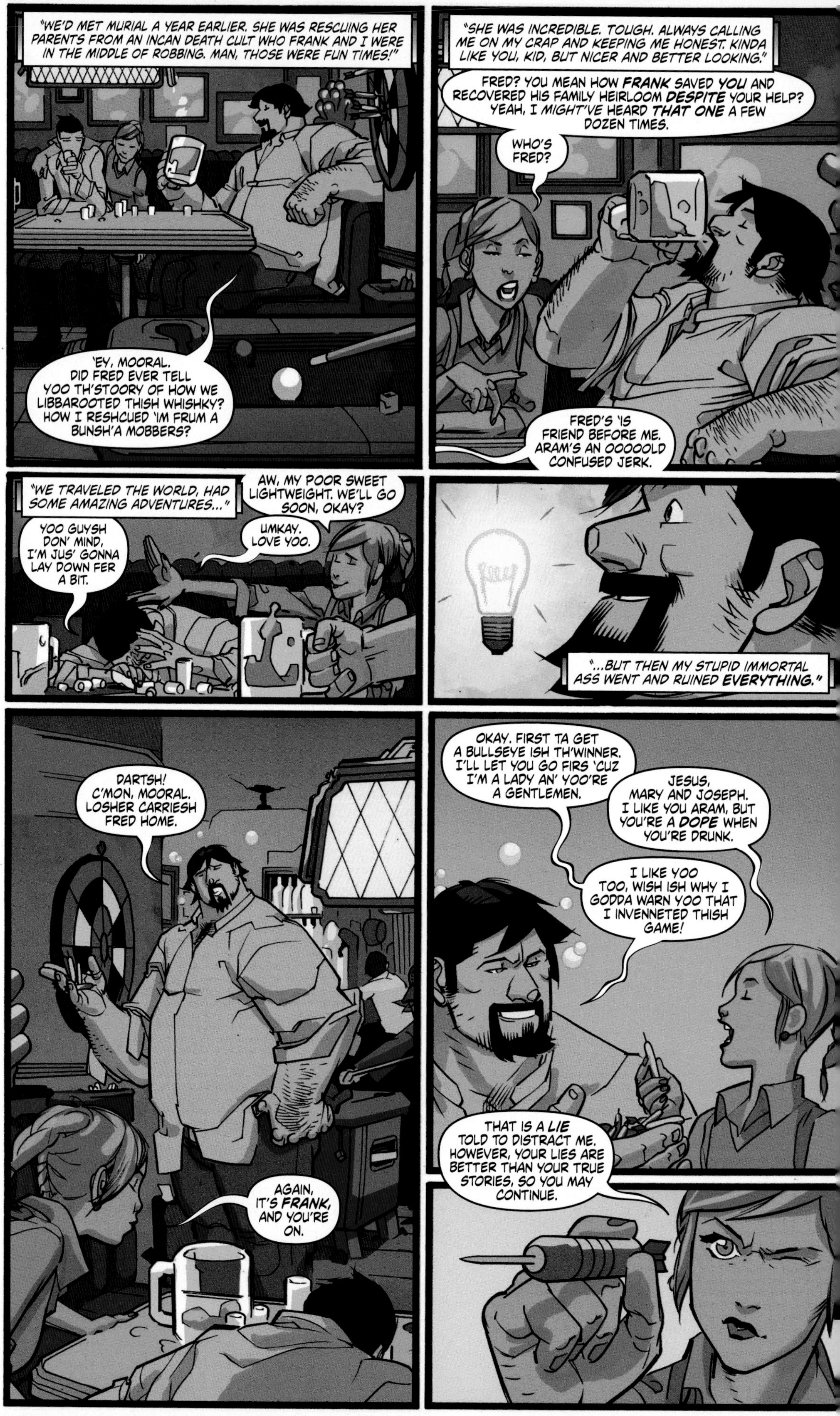
"WE'D MET MURIAL A YEAR EARLIER. SHE WAS RESCUING HER PARENTS FROM AN INCAN DEATH CULT WHO FRANK AND I WERE IN THE MIDDLE OF ROBBING. MAN, THOSE WERE FUN TIMES!"
'EY, MOORAL. DID FRED EVER TELL YOO TH'STOORY OF HOW WE LIBBAROOTED THISH WHISHKY? HOW I RESHCUED 'IM FRUM A BUNSH'A MOBBERS?
"SHE WAS INCREDIBLE. TOUGH. ALWAYS CALLING ME ON MY CRAP AND KEEPING ME HONEST. KINDA LIKE YOU, KID, BUT NICER AND BETTER LOOKING."
FRED? YOU MEAN HOW FRANK SAVED YOU AND RECOVERED HIS FAMILY HEIRLOOM DESPITE YOUR HELP? YEAH, I MIGHT'VE HEARD THAT ONE A FEW DOZEN TIMES.
WHO'S FRED?
FRED'S 'IS FRIEND BEFORE ME. ARAM'S AN OOOOOLD CONFUSED JERK.
"WE TRAVELED THE WORLD, HAD SOME AMAZING ADVENTURES..."
YOO GUYSH DON' MIND, I'M JUS' GONNA LAY DOWN FER A BIT.
AW, MY POOR SWEET LIGHTWEIGHT. WE'LL GO SOON, OKAY?
UMKAY. LOVE YOO.
"...BUT THEN MY STUPID IMMORTAL ASS WENT AND RUINED EVERYTHING."
DARTSH! C'MON, MOORAL. LOSHER CARRIESH FRED HOME.
AGAIN, IT'S FRANK, AND YOU'RE ON.
OKAY. FIRST TA GET A BULLSEYE ISH TH'WINNER. I'LL LET YOU GO FIRS 'CUZ I'M A LADY AN' YOO'RE A GENTLEMEN.
JESUS, MARY AND JOSEPH. I LIKE YOU ARAM, BUT YOU'RE A DOPE WHEN YOU'RE DRUNK.
I LIKE YOO TOO, WISH ISH WHY I GODDA WARN YOO THAT I INVENNETED THISH GAME!
THAT IS A LIE TOLD TO DISTRACT ME. HOWEVER, YOUR LIES ARE BETTER THAN YOUR TRUE STORIES, SO YOU MAY CONTINUE.

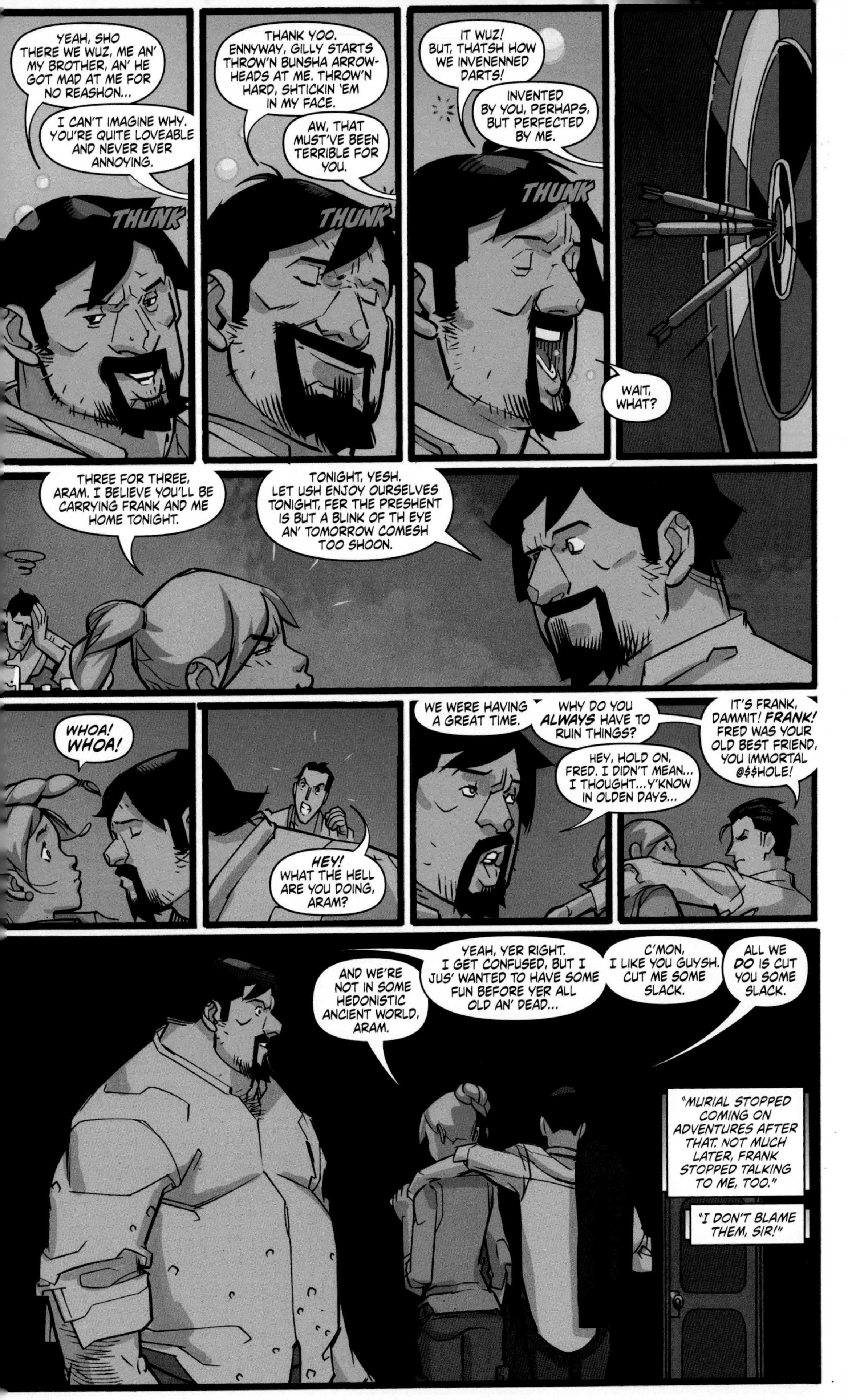
YEAH, SHO THERE WE WUZ, ME AN' MY BROTHER, AN' HE GOT MAD AT ME FOR NO REASHON...
I CAN'T IMAGINE WHY. YOU'RE QUITE LOVEABLE AND NEVER EVER ANNOYING.
THUNK
THANK YOO. ENNYWAY, GILLY STARTS THROW'N BUNSHA ARROW-HEADS AT ME. THROW'N HARD, SHTICKIN 'EM IN MY FACE.
AW, THAT MUST'VE BEEN TERRIBLE FOR YOU.
THUNK
IT WUZ! BUT, THATSH HOW WE INVENENNED DARTS!
INVENTED BY YOU, PERHAPS, BUT PERFECTED BY ME.
THUNK
WAIT, WHAT?
THREE FOR THREE, ARAM. I BELIEVE YOU'LL BE CARRYING FRANK AND ME HOME TONIGHT.
TONIGHT, YESH. LET USH ENJOY OURSELVES TONIGHT, FER THE PRESHENT IS BUT A BLINK OF TH EYE AN' TOMORROW COMESH TOO SHOON.
WHOA! WHOA!
HEY! WHAT THE HELL ARE YOU DOING, ARAM?
WE WERE HAVING A GREAT TIME.
WHY DO YOU ALWAYS HAVE TO RUIN THINGS?
HEY, HOLD ON, FRED. I DIDN'T MEAN... I THOUGHT...Y'KNOW IN OLDEN DAYS...
IT'S FRANK, DAMMIT! FRANK! FRED WAS YOUR OLD BEST FRIEND, YOU IMMORTAL @$$HOLE!
AND WE'RE NOT IN SOME HEDONISTIC ANCIENT WORLD, ARAM.
YEAH, YER RIGHT. I GET CONFUSED, BUT I JUS' WANTED TO HAVE SOME FUN BEFORE YER ALL OLD AN' DEAD...
C'MON, I LIKE YOU GUYSH. CUT ME SOME SLACK.
ALL WE DO IS CUT YOU SOME SLACK.
"MURIAL STOPPED COMING ON ADVENTURES AFTER THAT. NOT MUCH LATER, FRANK STOPPED TALKING TO ME, TOO."
"I DON'T BLAME THEM, SIR!"

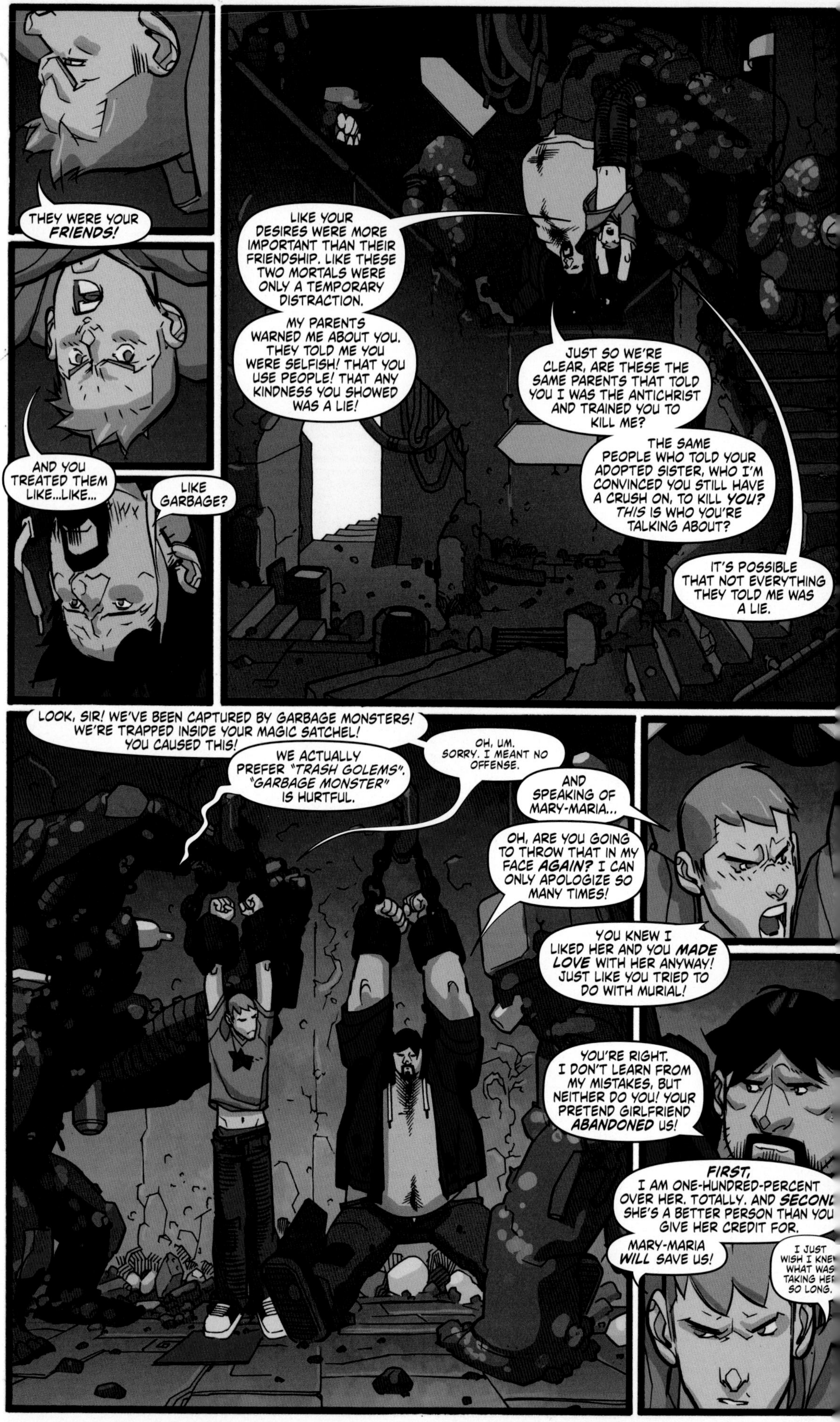

THEY WERE YOUR *FRIENDS!*
AND YOU TREATED THEM LIKE...LIKE...
LIKE GARBAGE?
LIKE YOUR DESIRES WERE MORE IMPORTANT THAN THEIR FRIENDSHIP. LIKE THESE TWO MORTALS WERE ONLY A TEMPORARY DISTRACTION.
MY PARENTS WARNED ME ABOUT YOU. THEY TOLD ME YOU WERE SELFISH! THAT YOU USE PEOPLE! THAT ANY KINDNESS YOU SHOWED WAS A LIE!
JUST SO WE'RE CLEAR, ARE THESE THE SAME PARENTS THAT TOLD YOU I WAS THE ANTICHRIST AND TRAINED YOU TO KILL ME?
THE SAME PEOPLE WHO TOLD YOUR ADOPTED SISTER, WHO I'M CONVINCED YOU STILL HAVE A CRUSH ON, TO KILL *YOU? THIS* IS WHO YOU'RE TALKING ABOUT?
IT'S POSSIBLE THAT NOT EVERYTHING THEY TOLD ME WAS A LIE.
LOOK, SIR! WE'VE BEEN CAPTURED BY GARBAGE MONSTERS! WE'RE TRAPPED INSIDE YOUR MAGIC SATCHEL! YOU CAUSED THIS!
WE ACTUALLY PREFER *"TRASH GOLEMS". "GARBAGE MONSTER"* IS HURTFUL.
OH, UM. SORRY. I MEANT NO OFFENSE.
AND SPEAKING OF MARY-MARIA...
OH, ARE YOU GOING TO THROW THAT IN MY FACE *AGAIN?* I CAN ONLY APOLOGIZE SO MANY TIMES!
YOU KNEW I LIKED HER AND YOU *MADE LOVE* WITH HER ANYWAY! JUST LIKE YOU TRIED TO DO WITH MURIAL!
YOU'RE RIGHT. I DON'T LEARN FROM MY MISTAKES, BUT NEITHER DO YOU! YOUR PRETEND GIRLFRIEND *ABANDONED* US!
FIRST, I AM ONE-HUNDRED-PERCENT OVER HER. TOTALLY. AND *SECON* SHE'S A BETTER PERSON THAN YOU GIVE HER CREDIT FOR.
MARY-MARIA *WILL* SAVE US!
I JUST WISH I KNE WHAT WAS TAKING HE SO LONG.

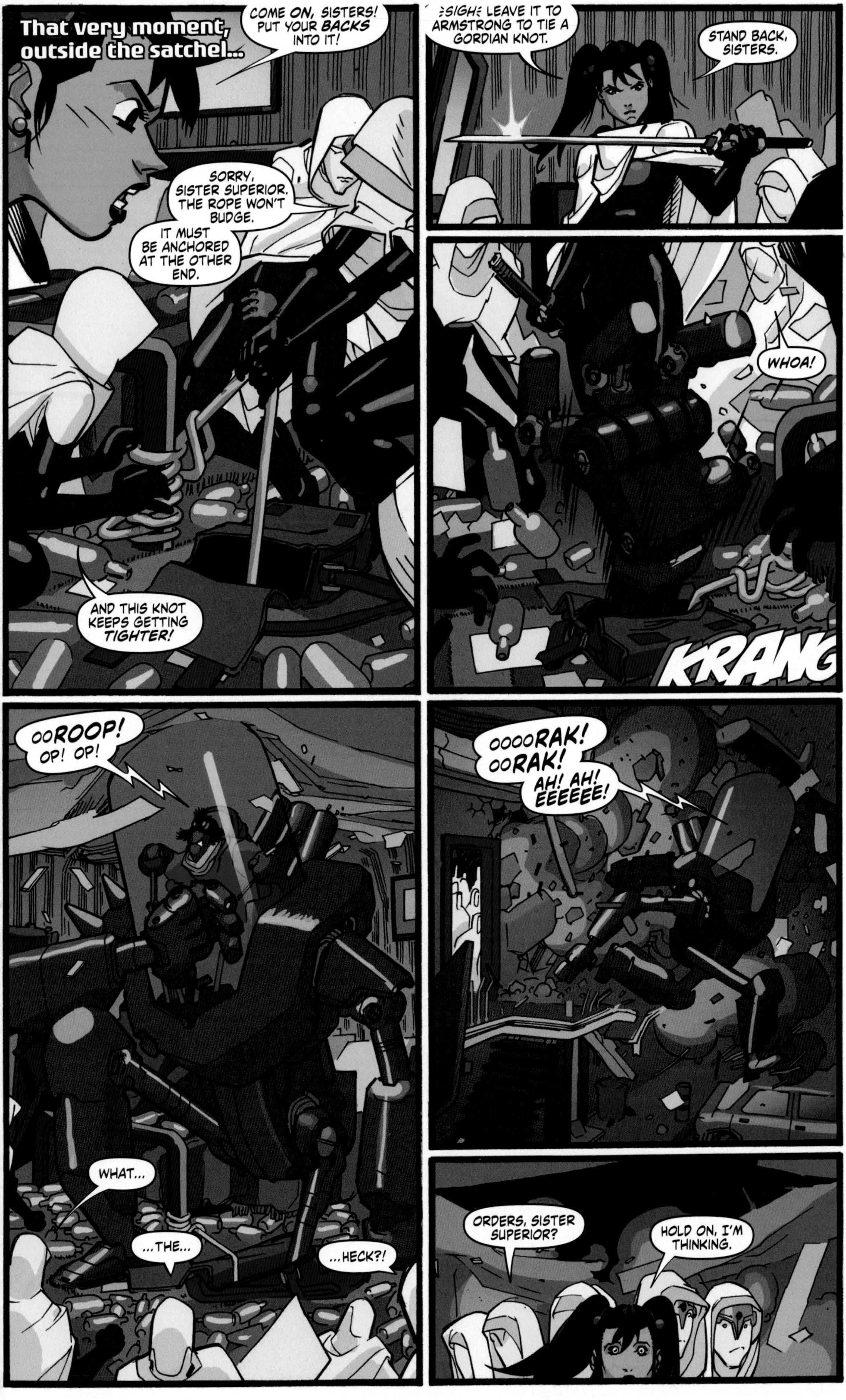

That very moment, outside the satchel...
COME ON, SISTERS! PUT YOUR BACKS INTO IT!
SORRY, SISTER SUPERIOR. THE ROPE WON'T BUDGE.
IT MUST BE ANCHORED AT THE OTHER END.
AND THIS KNOT KEEPS GETTING TIGHTER!
=SIGH= LEAVE IT TO ARMSTRONG TO TIE A GORDIAN KNOT.
STAND BACK, SISTERS.
WHOA!
KRANG
OOROOP! OP! OP!
WHAT...
...THE...
...HECK?!
OOOORAK! OORAK!
AH! AH! EEEEEE!
ORDERS, SISTER SUPERIOR?
HOLD ON, I'M THINKING.

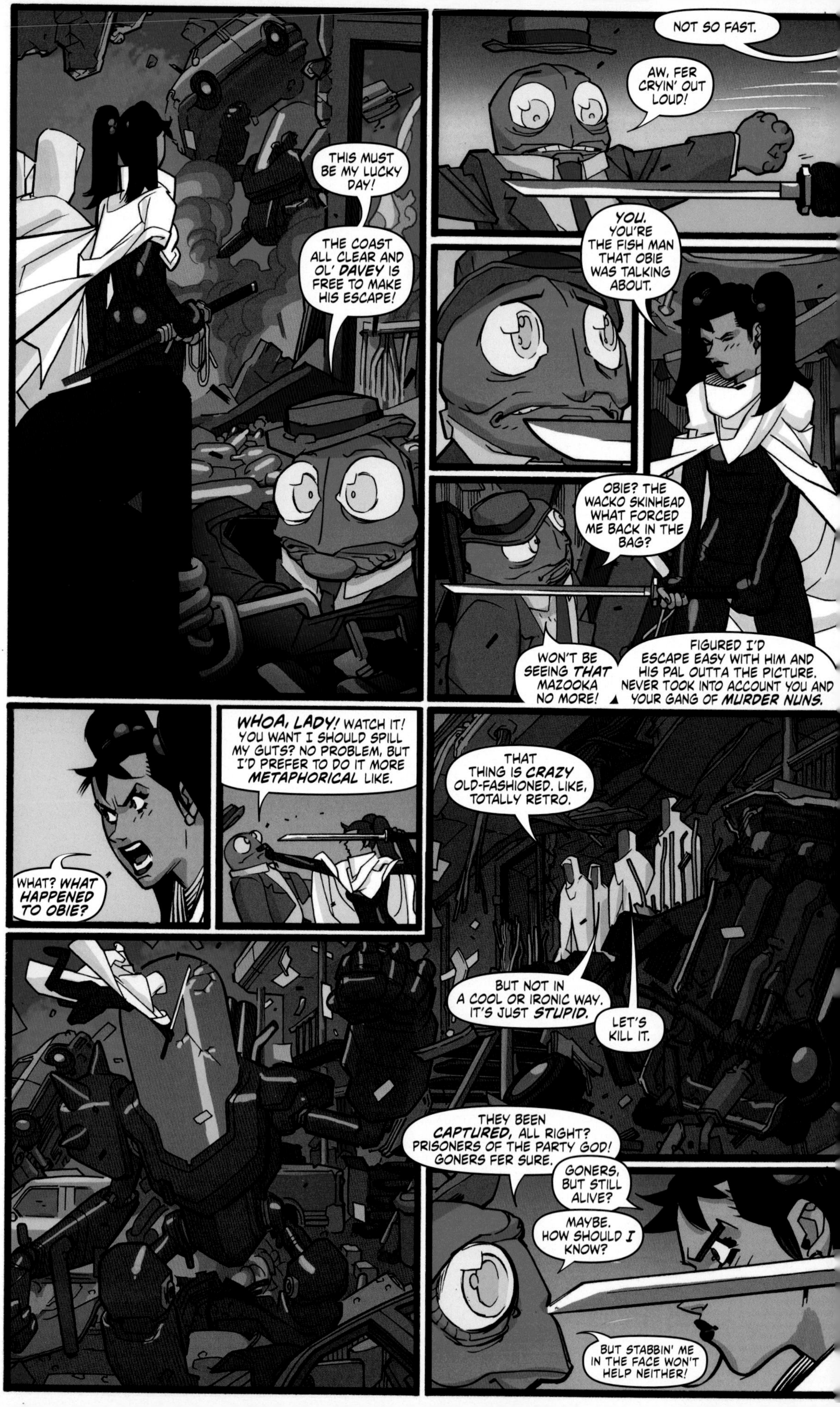
THIS MUST BE MY LUCKY DAY!
THE COAST ALL CLEAR AND OL' DAVEY IS FREE TO MAKE HIS ESCAPE!
NOT SO FAST.
AW, FER CRYIN' OUT LOUD!
YOU. YOU'RE THE FISH MAN THAT OBIE WAS TALKING ABOUT.
OBIE? THE WACKO SKINHEAD WHAT FORCED ME BACK IN THE BAG?
FIGURED I'D ESCAPE EASY WITH HIM AND HIS PAL OUTTA THE PICTURE. NEVER TOOK INTO ACCOUNT YOU AND YOUR GANG OF MURDER NUNS.
WON'T BE SEEING THAT MAZOOKA NO MORE!
WHAT? WHAT HAPPENED TO OBIE?
WHOA, LADY! WATCH IT! YOU WANT I SHOULD SPILL MY GUTS? NO PROBLEM, BUT I'D PREFER TO DO IT MORE METAPHORICAL LIKE.
THAT THING IS CRAZY OLD-FASHIONED. LIKE, TOTALLY RETRO.
BUT NOT IN A COOL OR IRONIC WAY. IT'S JUST STUPID.
LET'S KILL IT.
THEY BEEN CAPTURED, ALL RIGHT? PRISONERS OF THE PARTY GOD! GONERS FER SURE.
GONERS, BUT STILL ALIVE?
MAYBE. HOW SHOULD I KNOW?
BUT STABBIN' ME IN THE FACE WON'T HELP NEITHER!

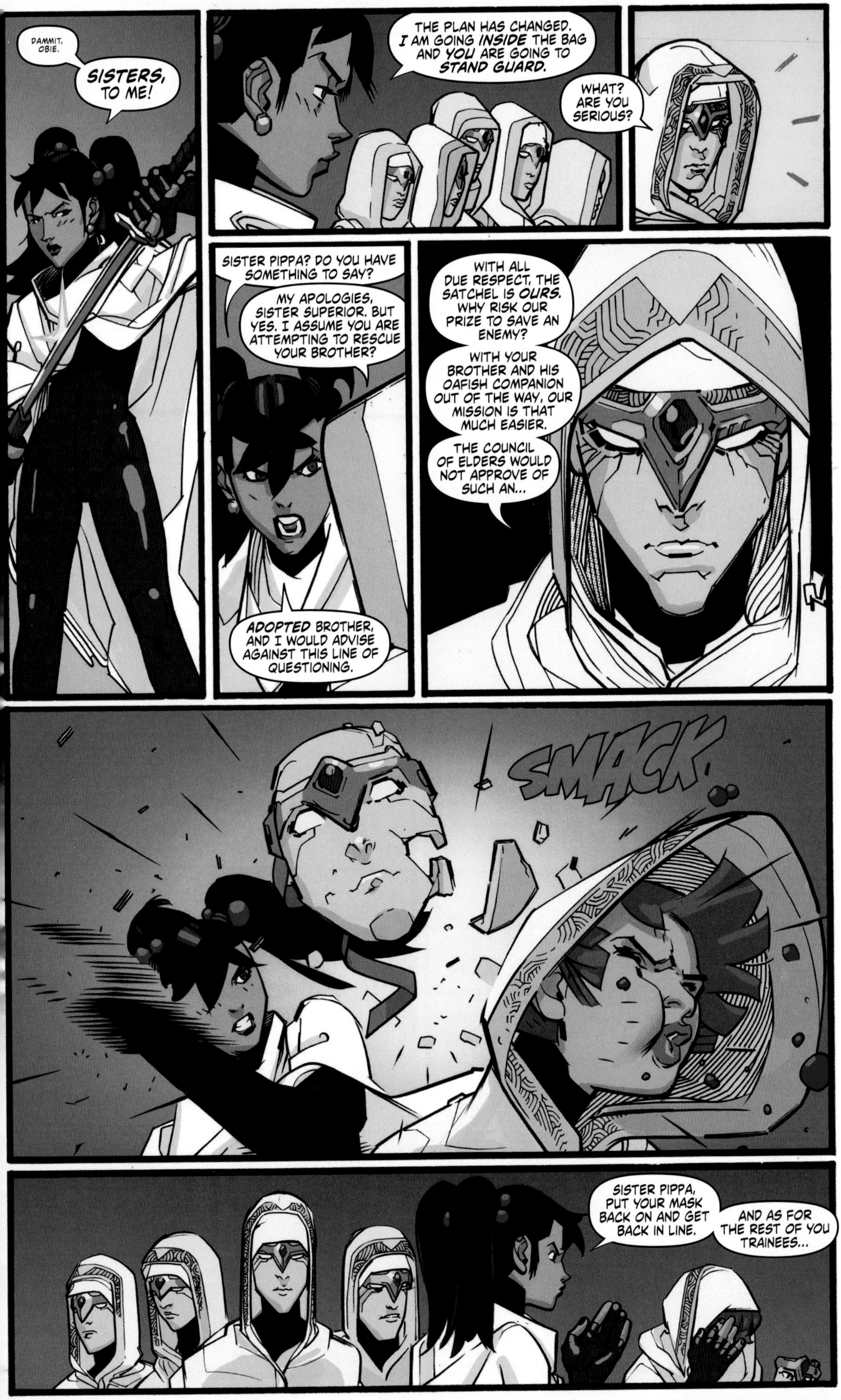
DAMMIT, OBIE.
SISTERS, TO ME!
THE PLAN HAS CHANGED. I AM GOING INSIDE THE BAG AND YOU ARE GOING TO STAND GUARD.
WHAT? ARE YOU SERIOUS?
SISTER PIPPA? DO YOU HAVE SOMETHING TO SAY?
MY APOLOGIES, SISTER SUPERIOR. BUT YES. I ASSUME YOU ARE ATTEMPTING TO RESCUE YOUR BROTHER?
ADOPTED BROTHER, AND I WOULD ADVISE AGAINST THIS LINE OF QUESTIONING.
WITH ALL DUE RESPECT, THE SATCHEL IS OURS. WHY RISK OUR PRIZE TO SAVE AN ENEMY?
WITH YOUR BROTHER AND HIS OAFISH COMPANION OUT OF THE WAY, OUR MISSION IS THAT MUCH EASIER.
THE COUNCIL OF ELDERS WOULD NOT APPROVE OF SUCH AN...
SMACK
SISTER PIPPA, PUT YOUR MASK BACK ON AND GET BACK IN LINE.
AND AS FOR THE REST OF YOU TRAINEES...

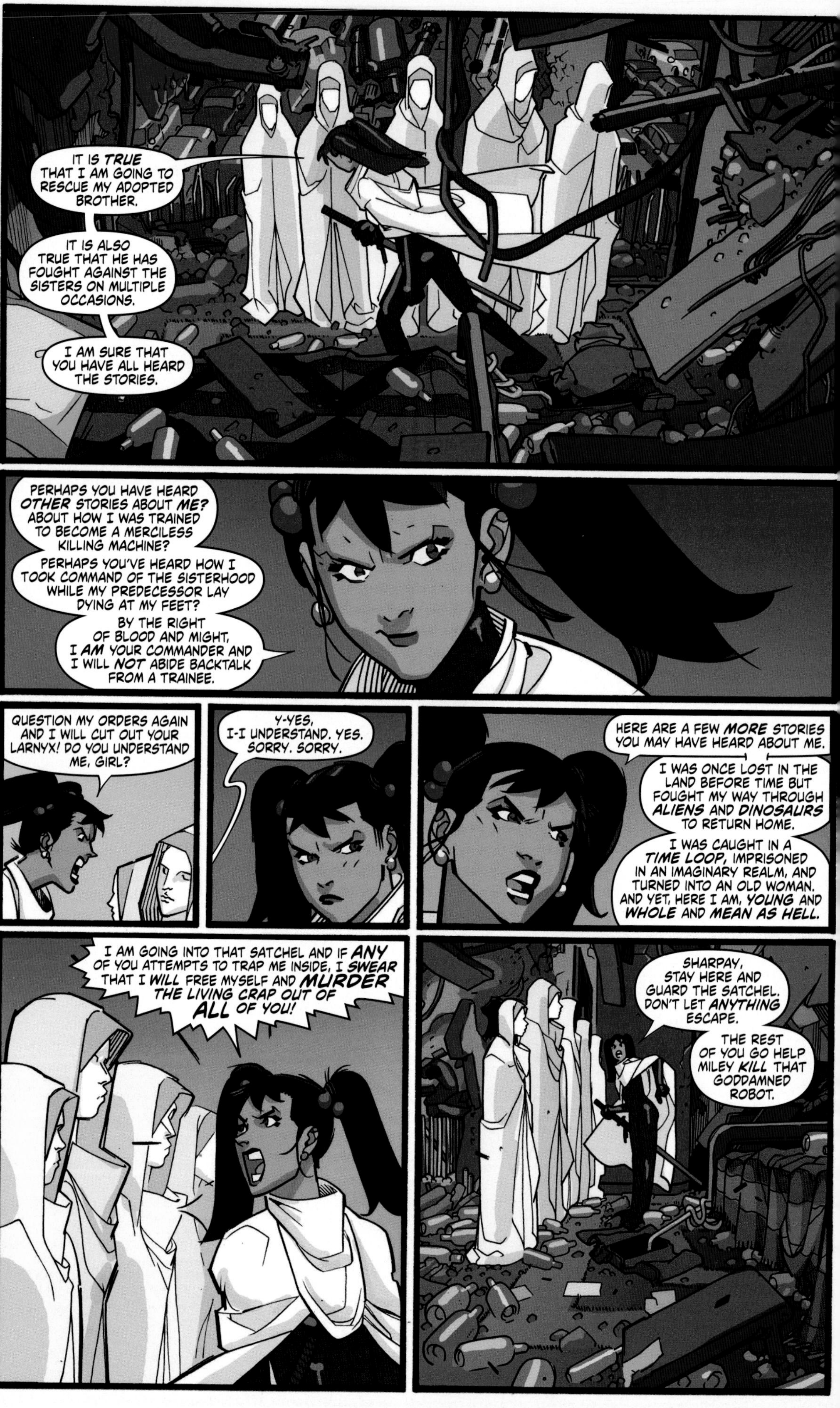
IT IS TRUE THAT I AM GOING TO RESCUE MY ADOPTED BROTHER.
IT IS ALSO TRUE THAT HE HAS FOUGHT AGAINST THE SISTERS ON MULTIPLE OCCASIONS.
I AM SURE THAT YOU HAVE ALL HEARD THE STORIES.
PERHAPS YOU HAVE HEARD OTHER STORIES ABOUT ME? ABOUT HOW I WAS TRAINED TO BECOME A MERCILESS KILLING MACHINE?
PERHAPS YOU'VE HEARD HOW I TOOK COMMAND OF THE SISTERHOOD WHILE MY PREDECESSOR LAY DYING AT MY FEET?
BY THE RIGHT OF BLOOD AND MIGHT, I AM YOUR COMMANDER AND I WILL NOT ABIDE BACKTALK FROM A TRAINEE.
QUESTION MY ORDERS AGAIN AND I WILL CUT OUT YOUR LARNYX! DO YOU UNDERSTAND ME, GIRL?
Y-YES, I-I UNDERSTAND. YES. SORRY. SORRY.
HERE ARE A FEW MORE STORIES YOU MAY HAVE HEARD ABOUT ME.
I WAS ONCE LOST IN THE LAND BEFORE TIME BUT FOUGHT MY WAY THROUGH ALIENS AND DINOSAURS TO RETURN HOME.
I WAS CAUGHT IN A TIME LOOP, IMPRISONED IN AN IMAGINARY REALM, AND TURNED INTO AN OLD WOMAN. AND YET, HERE I AM, YOUNG AND WHOLE AND MEAN AS HELL.
I AM GOING INTO THAT SATCHEL AND IF ANY OF YOU ATTEMPTS TO TRAP ME INSIDE, I SWEAR THAT I WILL FREE MYSELF AND MURDER THE LIVING CRAP OUT OF ALL OF YOU!
SHARPAY, STAY HERE AND GUARD THE SATCHEL. DON'T LET ANYTHING ESCAPE.
THE REST OF YOU GO HELP MILEY KILL THAT GODDAMNED ROBOT.

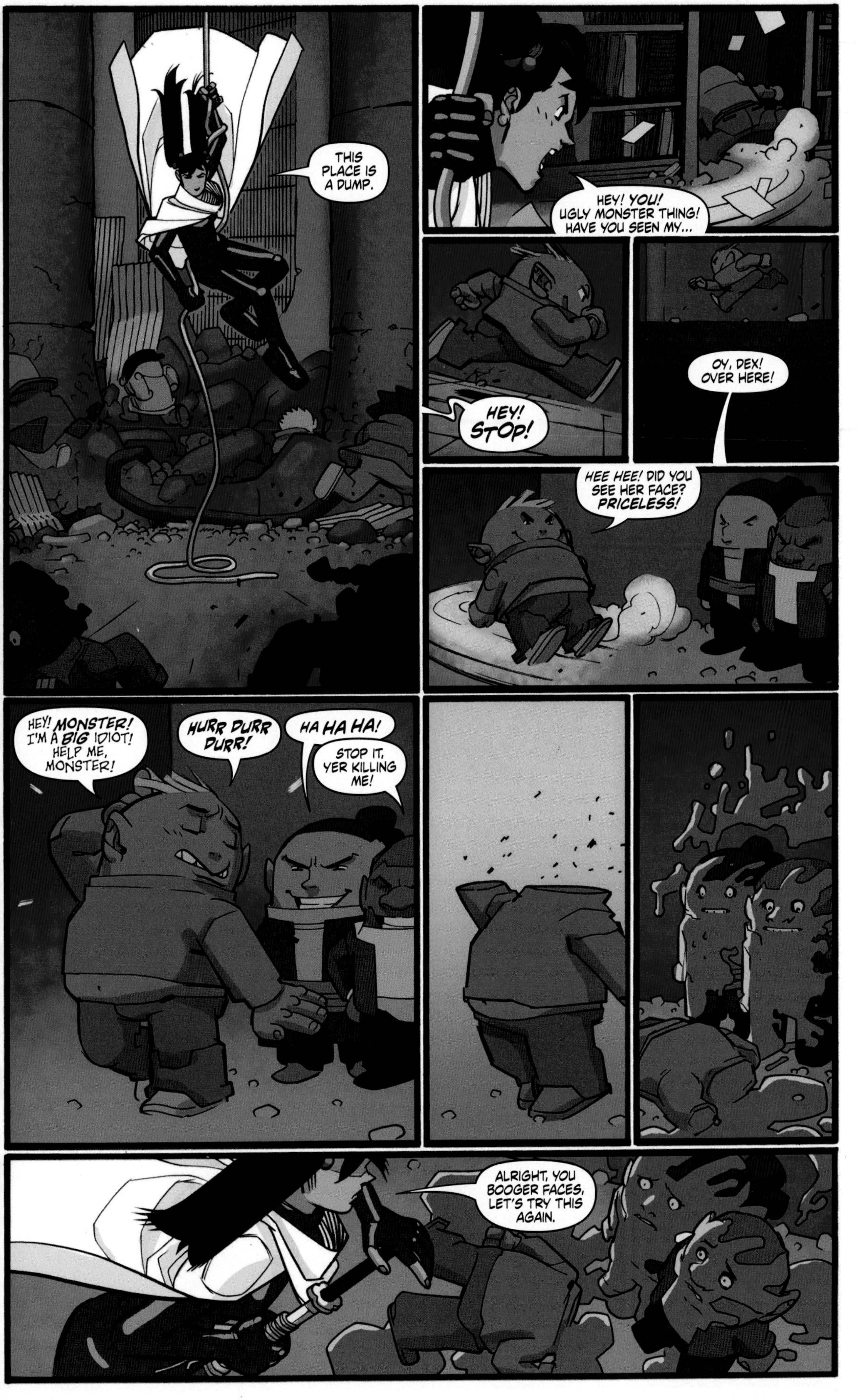
THIS PLACE IS A DUMP.
HEY! YOU! UGLY MONSTER THING! HAVE YOU SEEN MY...
HEY! STOP!
OY, DEX! OVER HERE!
HEE HEE! DID YOU SEE HER FACE? PRICELESS!
HEY! MONSTER! I'M A BIG IDIOT! HELP ME, MONSTER!
HURR DURR DURR!
HA HA HA!
STOP IT, YER KILLING ME!
ALRIGHT, YOU BOOGER FACES, LET'S TRY THIS AGAIN.

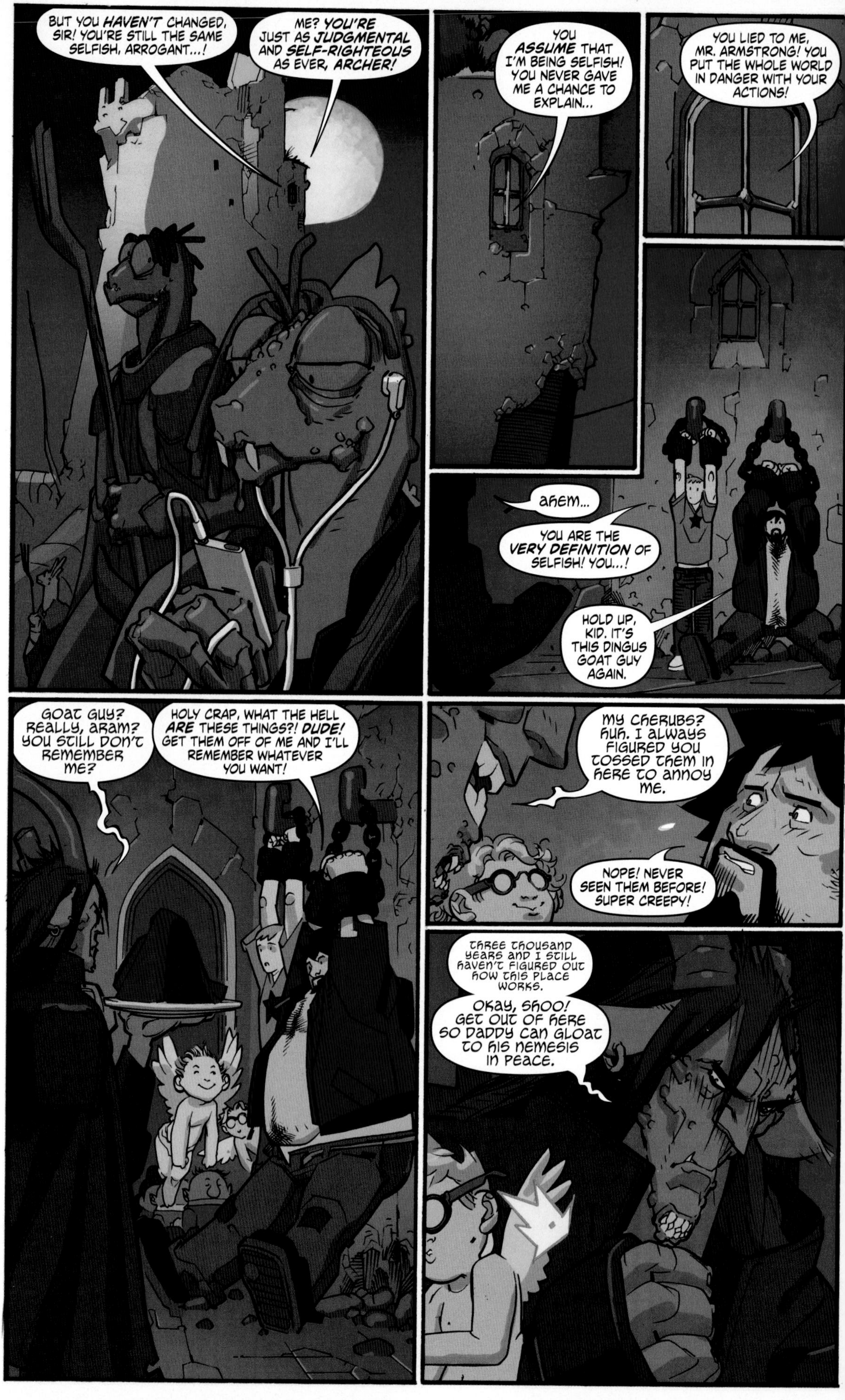
BUT YOU HAVEN'T CHANGED, SIR! YOU'RE STILL THE SAME SELFISH, ARROGANT...!
ME? YOU'RE JUST AS JUDGMENTAL AND SELF-RIGHTEOUS AS EVER, ARCHER!
YOU ASSUME THAT I'M BEING SELFISH! YOU NEVER GAVE ME A CHANCE TO EXPLAIN...
YOU LIED TO ME, MR. ARMSTRONG! YOU PUT THE WHOLE WORLD IN DANGER WITH YOUR ACTIONS!
AHEM...
YOU ARE THE VERY DEFINITION OF SELFISH! YOU...!
HOLD UP, KID. IT'S THIS DINGUS GOAT GUY AGAIN.
GOAT GUY? REALLY, ARAM? YOU STILL DON'T REMEMBER ME?
HOLY CRAP, WHAT THE HELL ARE THESE THINGS?! DUDE! GET THEM OFF OF ME AND I'LL REMEMBER WHATEVER YOU WANT!
MY CHERUBS? HUH. I ALWAYS FIGURED YOU TOSSED THEM IN HERE TO ANNOY ME.
NOPE! NEVER SEEN THEM BEFORE! SUPER CREEPY!
THREE THOUSAND YEARS AND I STILL HAVEN'T FIGURED OUT HOW THIS PLACE WORKS.
OKAY, SHOO! GET OUT OF HERE SO DADDY CAN GLOAT TO HIS NEMESIS IN PEACE.

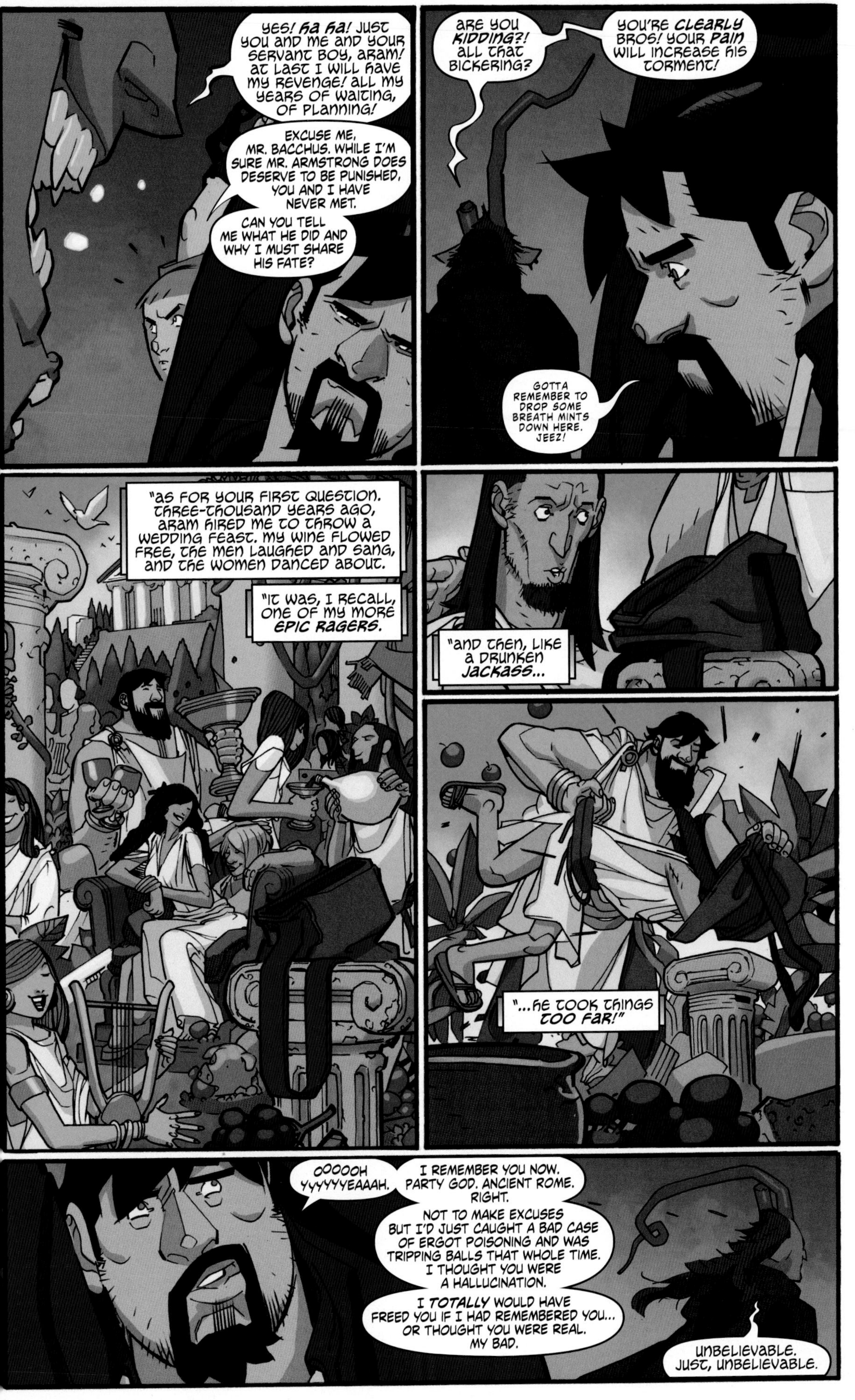

YES! HA HA! JUST YOU AND ME AND YOUR SERVANT BOY, ARAM! AT LAST I WILL HAVE MY REVENGE! ALL MY YEARS OF WAITING, OF PLANNING!
EXCUSE ME, MR. BACCHUS. WHILE I'M SURE MR. ARMSTRONG DOES DESERVE TO BE PUNISHED, YOU AND I HAVE NEVER MET.
CAN YOU TELL ME WHAT HE DID AND WHY I MUST SHARE HIS FATE?
ARE YOU KIDDING?! ALL THAT BICKERING?
YOU'RE CLEARLY BROS! YOUR PAIN WILL INCREASE HIS TORMENT!
GOTTA REMEMBER TO DROP SOME BREATH MINTS DOWN HERE. JEEZ!
"AS FOR YOUR FIRST QUESTION. THREE-THOUSAND YEARS AGO, ARAM HIRED ME TO THROW A WEDDING FEAST. MY WINE FLOWED FREE, THE MEN LAUGHED AND SANG, AND THE WOMEN DANCED ABOUT.
"IT WAS, I RECALL, ONE OF MY MORE EPIC RAGERS.
"AND THEN, LIKE A DRUNKEN JACKASS...
"...HE TOOK THINGS TOO FAR!"
OOOOOH YYYYYYEAAAH.
I REMEMBER YOU NOW. PARTY GOD. ANCIENT ROME. RIGHT.
NOT TO MAKE EXCUSES BUT I'D JUST CAUGHT A BAD CASE OF ERGOT POISONING AND WAS TRIPPING BALLS THAT WHOLE TIME. I THOUGHT YOU WERE A HALLUCINATION.
I TOTALLY WOULD HAVE FREED YOU IF I HAD REMEMBERED YOU... OR THOUGHT YOU WERE REAL. MY BAD.
UNBELIEVABLE. JUST, UNBELIEVABLE.

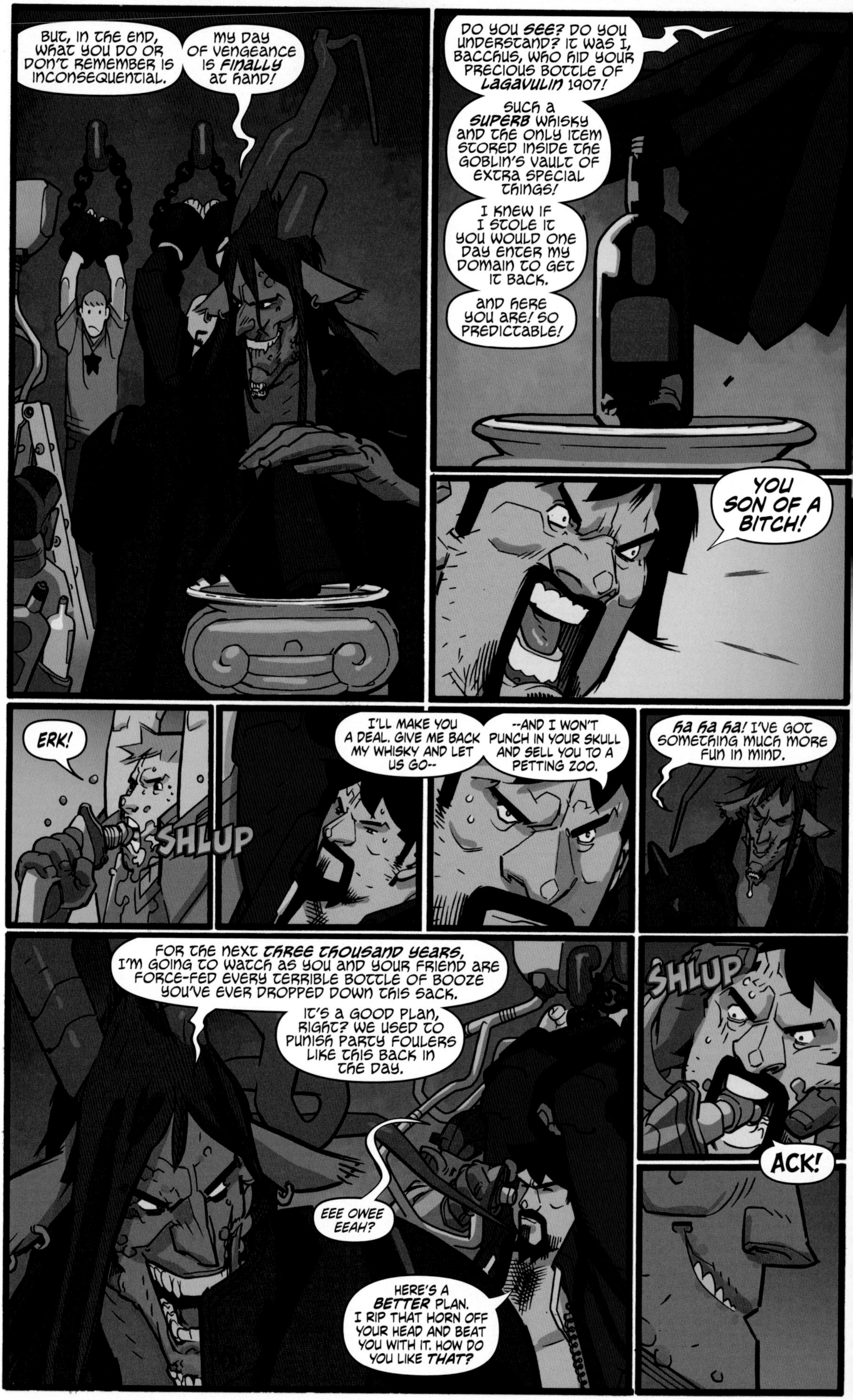
BUT, IN THE END, WHAT YOU DO OR DON'T REMEMBER IS INCONSEQUENTIAL.
MY DAY OF VENGEANCE IS FINALLY AT HAND!
DO YOU SEE? DO YOU UNDERSTAND? IT WAS I, BACCHUS, WHO HID YOUR PRECIOUS BOTTLE OF LAGAVULIN 1907!
SUCH A SUPERB WHISKY AND THE ONLY ITEM STORED INSIDE THE GOBLIN'S VAULT OF EXTRA SPECIAL THINGS!
I KNEW IF I STOLE IT YOU WOULD ONE DAY ENTER MY DOMAIN TO GET IT BACK.
AND HERE YOU ARE! SO PREDICTABLE!
YOU SON OF A BITCH!
ERK!
SHLUP
I'LL MAKE YOU A DEAL. GIVE ME BACK MY WHISKY AND LET US GO--
--AND I WON'T PUNCH IN YOUR SKULL AND SELL YOU TO A PETTING ZOO.
HA HA HA! I'VE GOT SOMETHING MUCH MORE FUN IN MIND.
FOR THE NEXT THREE THOUSAND YEARS, I'M GOING TO WATCH AS YOU AND YOUR FRIEND ARE FORCE-FED EVERY TERRIBLE BOTTLE OF BOOZE YOU'VE EVER DROPPED DOWN THIS SACK.
IT'S A GOOD PLAN, RIGHT? WE USED TO PUNISH PARTY FOULERS LIKE THIS BACK IN THE DAY.
EEE OWEE EEAH?
HERE'S A BETTER PLAN. I RIP THAT HORN OFF YOUR HEAD AND BEAT YOU WITH IT. HOW DO YOU LIKE THAT?
SHLUP
ACK!

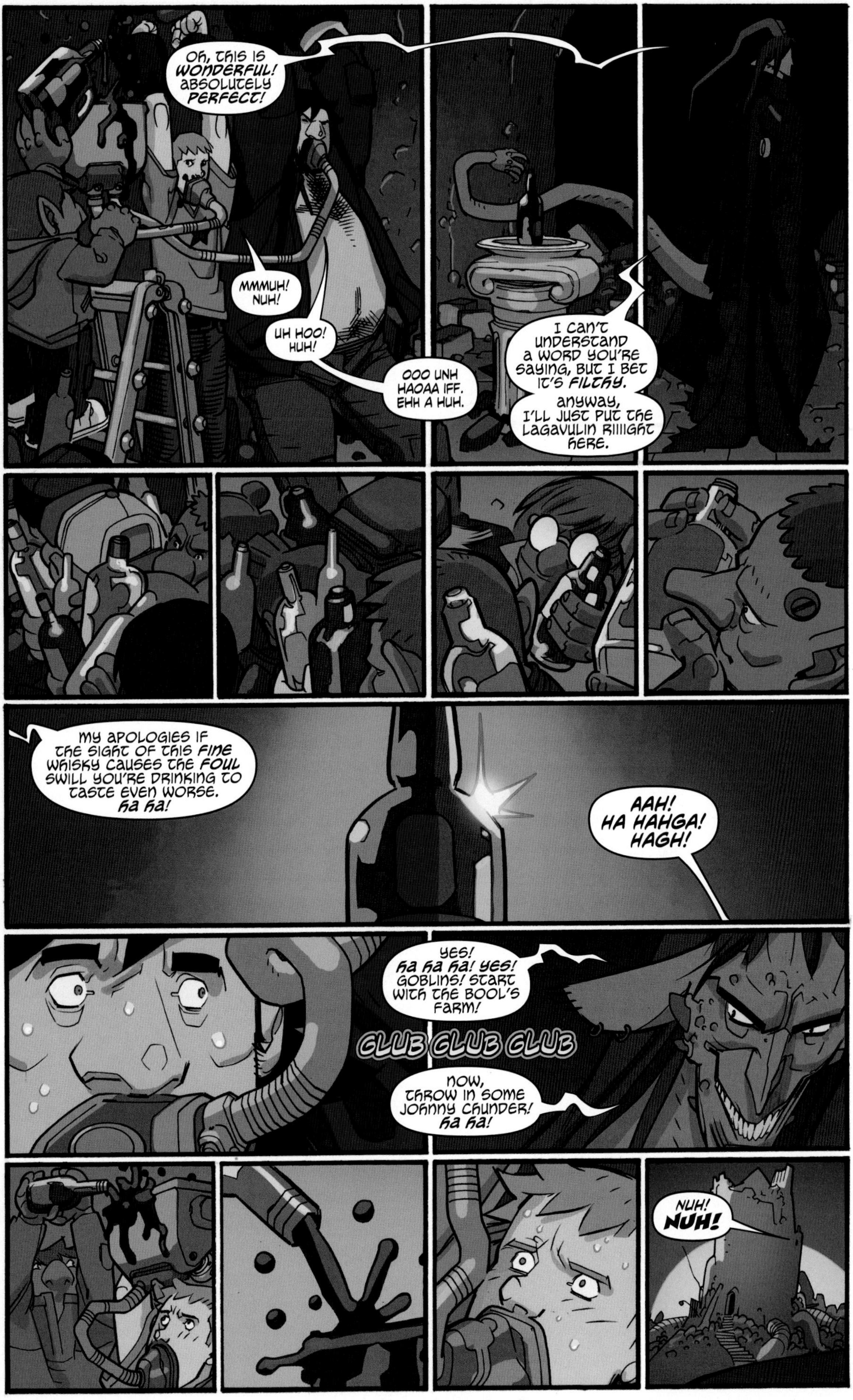
OH, THIS IS WONDERFUL! ABSOLUTELY PERFECT!
MMMUH! NUH!
UH HOO! HUH!
OOO UNH HAOAA IFF. EHH A HUH.
I CAN'T UNDERSTAND A WORD YOU'RE SAYING, BUT I BET IT'S FILTHY.
ANYWAY, I'LL JUST PUT THE LAGAVULIN RIIIIGHT HERE.
MY APOLOGIES IF THE SIGHT OF THIS FINE WHISKY CAUSES THE FOUL SWILL YOU'RE DRINKING TO TASTE EVEN WORSE. HA HA!
AAH! HA HAHGA! HAGH!
YES! HA HA HA! YES! GOBLINS! START WITH THE BOOL'S FARM!
GLUB GLUB GLUB
NOW, THROW IN SOME JOHNNY CHUNDER! HA HA!
NUH! NUH!

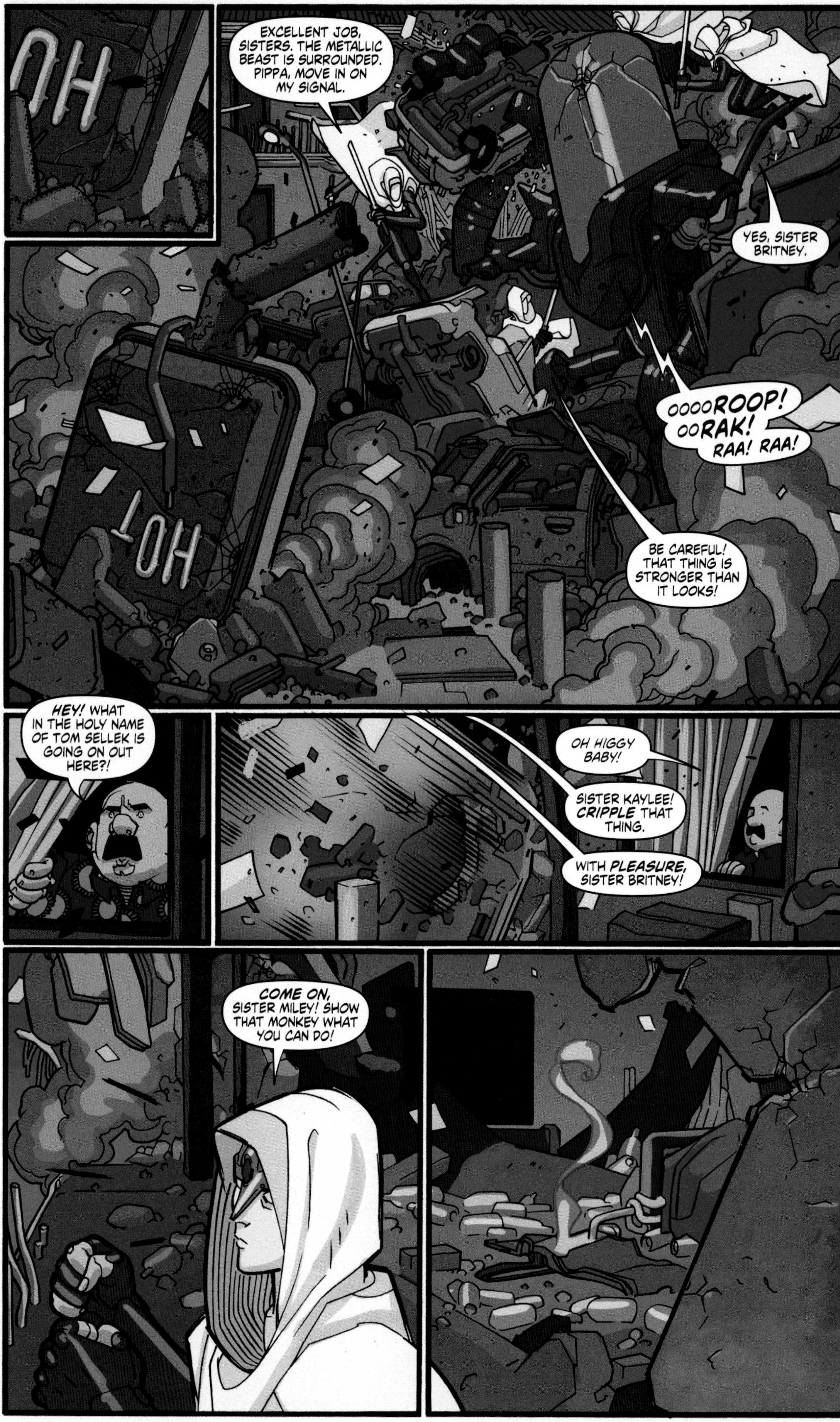

OH
EXCELLENT JOB, SISTERS. THE METALLIC BEAST IS SURROUNDED. PIPPA, MOVE IN ON MY SIGNAL.
YES, SISTER BRITNEY.
OOOOROOP! OORAK! RAA! RAA!
HOT
BE CAREFUL! THAT THING IS STRONGER THAN IT LOOKS!
HEY! WHAT IN THE HOLY NAME OF TOM SELLEK IS GOING ON OUT HERE?!
OH HIGGY BABY!
SISTER KAYLEE! CRIPPLE THAT THING.
WITH PLEASURE, SISTER BRITNEY!
COME ON, SISTER MILEY! SHOW THAT MONKEY WHAT YOU CAN DO!

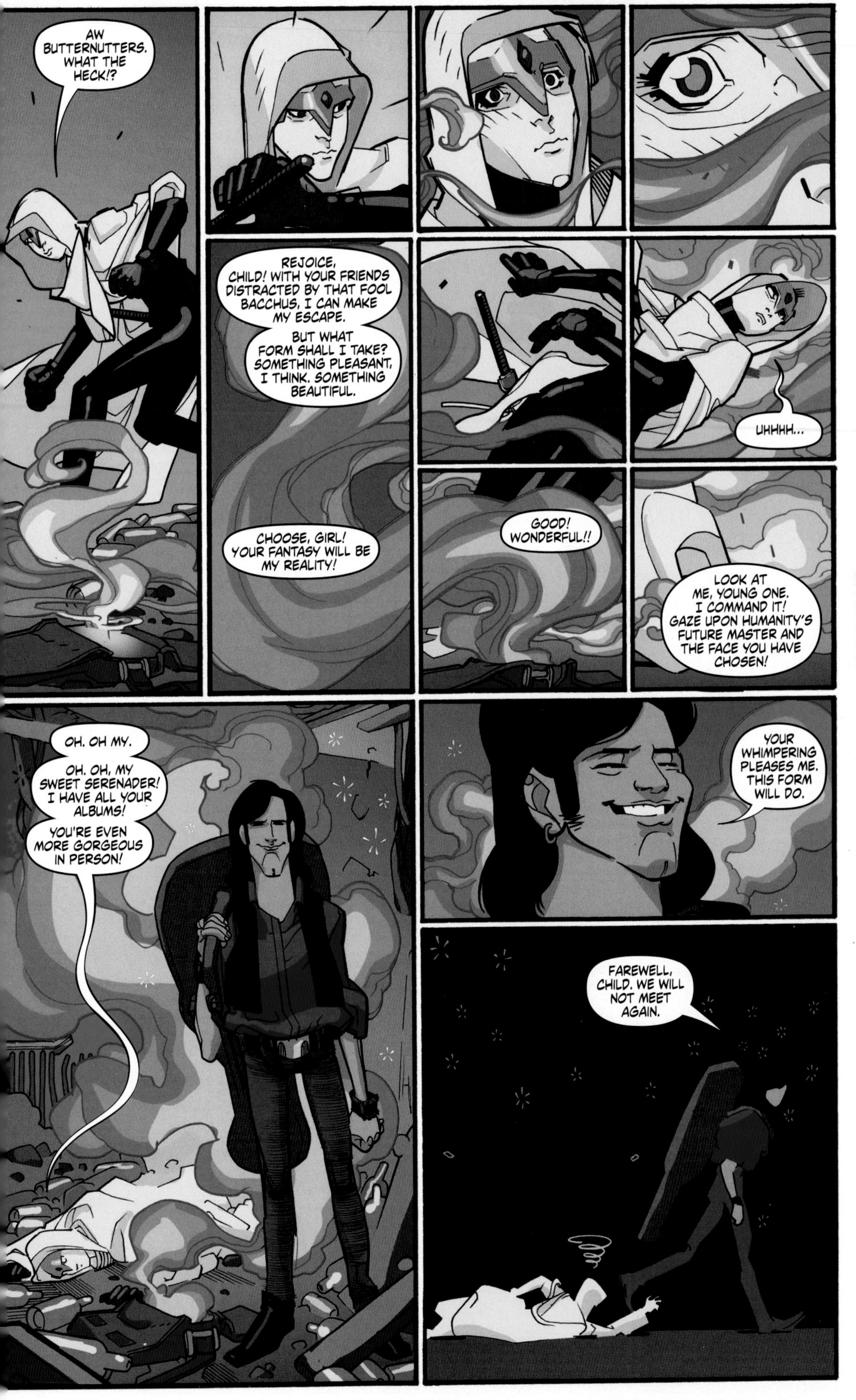
AW BUTTERNUTTERS. WHAT THE HECK!?
REJOICE, CHILD! WITH YOUR FRIENDS DISTRACTED BY THAT FOOL BACCHUS, I CAN MAKE MY ESCAPE.
BUT WHAT FORM SHALL I TAKE? SOMETHING PLEASANT, I THINK. SOMETHING BEAUTIFUL.
UHHHH...
CHOOSE, GIRL! YOUR FANTASY WILL BE MY REALITY!
GOOD! WONDERFUL!!
LOOK AT ME, YOUNG ONE. I COMMAND IT! GAZE UPON HUMANITY'S FUTURE MASTER AND THE FACE YOU HAVE CHOSEN!
OH. OH MY.
OH. OH, MY SWEET SERENADER! I HAVE ALL YOUR ALBUMS!
YOU'RE EVEN MORE GORGEOUS IN PERSON!
YOUR WHIMPERING PLEASES ME. THIS FORM WILL DO.
FAREWELL, CHILD. WE WILL NOT MEET AGAIN.

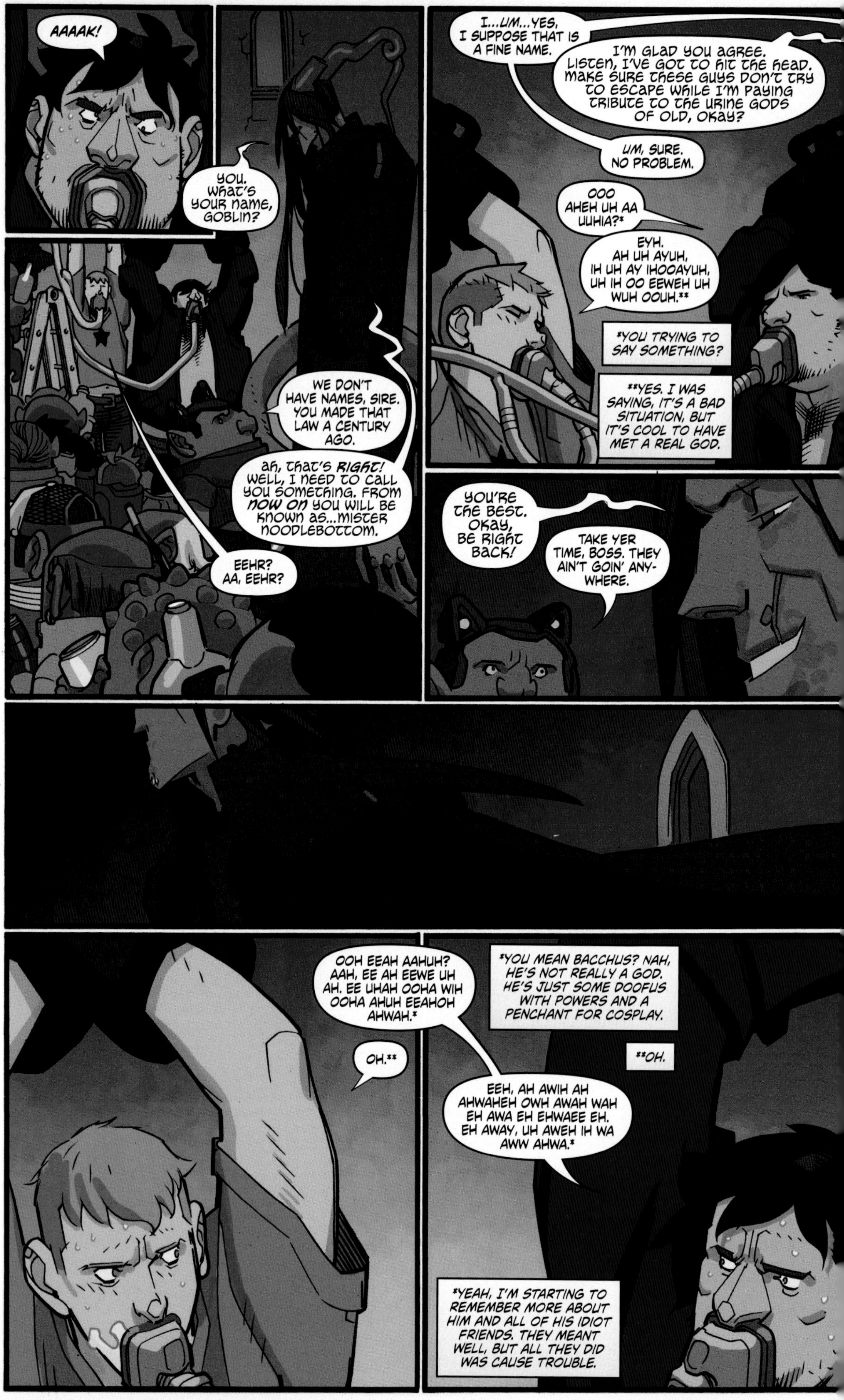
AAAAK!
YOU. WHAT'S YOUR NAME, GOBLIN?
I...UM...YES, I SUPPOSE THAT IS A FINE NAME.
I'M GLAD YOU AGREE. LISTEN, I'VE GOT TO HIT THE HEAD. MAKE SURE THESE GUYS DON'T TRY TO ESCAPE WHILE I'M PAYING TRIBUTE TO THE URINE GODS OF OLD, OKAY?
UM, SURE. NO PROBLEM.
WE DON'T HAVE NAMES, SIRE. YOU MADE THAT LAW A CENTURY AGO.
AH, THAT'S RIGHT! WELL, I NEED TO CALL YOU SOMETHING. FROM NOW ON YOU WILL BE KNOWN AS...MISTER NOODLEBOTTOM.
EEHR? AA, EEHR?
OOO AHEH UH AA UUHIA?*
EYH. AH UH AYUH, IH UH AY IHOOAYUH, UH IH OO EEWEH UH WUH OOUH.**
*YOU TRYING TO SAY SOMETHING?
**YES. I WAS SAYING, IT'S A BAD SITUATION, BUT IT'S COOL TO HAVE MET A REAL GOD.
YOU'RE THE BEST. OKAY, BE RIGHT BACK!
TAKE YER TIME, BOSS. THEY AIN'T GOIN' ANY-WHERE.
OOH EEAH AAHUH? AAH, EE AH EEWE UH AH. EE UHAH OOHA WIH OOHA AHUH EEAHOH AHWAH.*
*YOU MEAN BACCHUS? NAH, HE'S NOT REALLY A GOD. HE'S JUST SOME DOOFUS WITH POWERS AND A PENCHANT FOR COSPLAY.
OH.**
**OH.
EEH, AH AWIH AH AHWAHEH OWH AWAH WAH EH AWA EH EHWAEE EH. EH AWAY, UH AWEH IH WA AWW AHWA.*
*YEAH, I'M STARTING TO REMEMBER MORE ABOUT HIM AND ALL OF HIS IDIOT FRIENDS. THEY MEANT WELL, BUT ALL THEY DID WAS CAUSE TROUBLE.

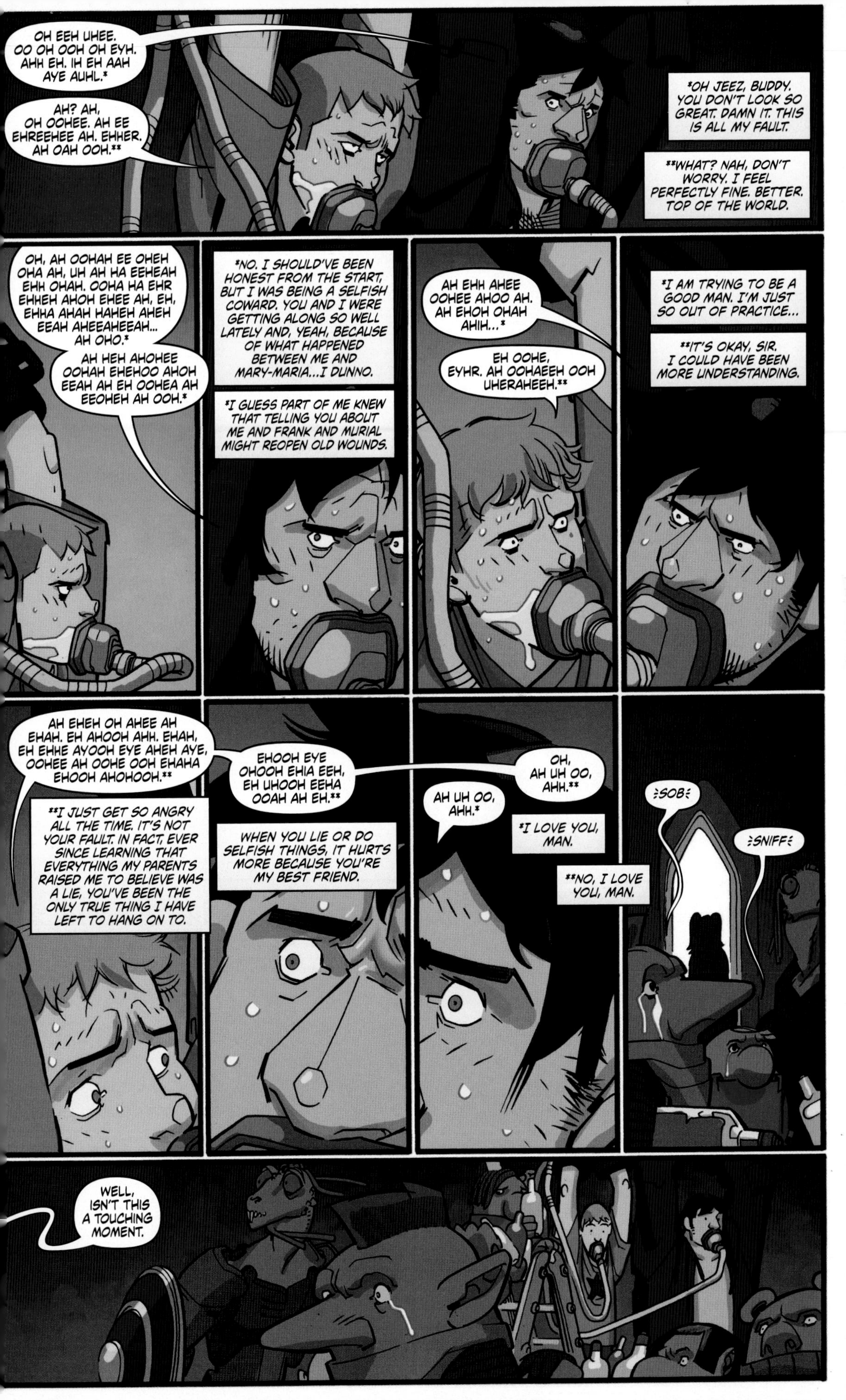
OH EEH UHEE. OO OH OOH OH EYH. AHH EH. IH EH AAH AYE AUHL.*
AH? AH, OH OOHEE. AH EE EHREEHEE AH. EHHER. AH OAH OOH.**
*OH JEEZ, BUDDY. YOU DON'T LOOK SO GREAT. DAMN IT. THIS IS ALL MY FAULT.
**WHAT? NAH, DON'T WORRY. I FEEL PERFECTLY FINE. BETTER. TOP OF THE WORLD.
OH, AH OOHAH EE OHEH OHA AH, UH AH HA EEHEAH EHH OHAH. OOHA HA EHR EHHEH AHOH EHEE AH, EH, EHHA AHAH HAHEH AHEH EEAH AHEEAHEEAH... AH OHO.*
AH HEH AHOHEE OOHAH EHEHOO AHOH EEAH AH EH OOHEA AH EEOHEH AH OOH.*
*NO. I SHOULD'VE BEEN HONEST FROM THE START, BUT I WAS BEING A SELFISH COWARD. YOU AND I WERE GETTING ALONG SO WELL LATELY AND, YEAH, BECAUSE OF WHAT HAPPENED BETWEEN ME AND MARY-MARIA...I DUNNO.
*I GUESS PART OF ME KNEW THAT TELLING YOU ABOUT ME AND FRANK AND MURIAL MIGHT REOPEN OLD WOUNDS.
AH EHH AHEE OOHEE AHOO AH. AH EHOH OHAH AHIH...*
EH OOHE, EYHR. AH OOHAEEH OOH UHERAHEEH.**
*I AM TRYING TO BE A GOOD MAN. I'M JUST SO OUT OF PRACTICE...
**IT'S OKAY, SIR. I COULD HAVE BEEN MORE UNDERSTANDING.
AH EHEH OH AHEE AH EHAH. EH AHOOH AHH. EHAH, EH EHHE AYOOH EYE AHEH AYE, OOHEE AH OOHE OOH EHAHA EHOOH AHOHOOH.**
**I JUST GET SO ANGRY ALL THE TIME. IT'S NOT YOUR FAULT. IN FACT, EVER SINCE LEARNING THAT EVERYTHING MY PARENTS RAISED ME TO BELIEVE WAS A LIE, YOU'VE BEEN THE ONLY TRUE THING I HAVE LEFT TO HANG ON TO.
EHOOH EYE OHOOH EHIA EEH, EH UHOOH EEHA OOAH AH EH.**
WHEN YOU LIE OR DO SELFISH THINGS, IT HURTS MORE BECAUSE YOU'RE MY BEST FRIEND.
AH UH OO, AHH.*
OH, AH UH OO, AHH.**
*I LOVE YOU, MAN.
**NO, I LOVE YOU, MAN.
SOB
SNIFF
WELL, ISN'T THIS A TOUCHING MOMENT.

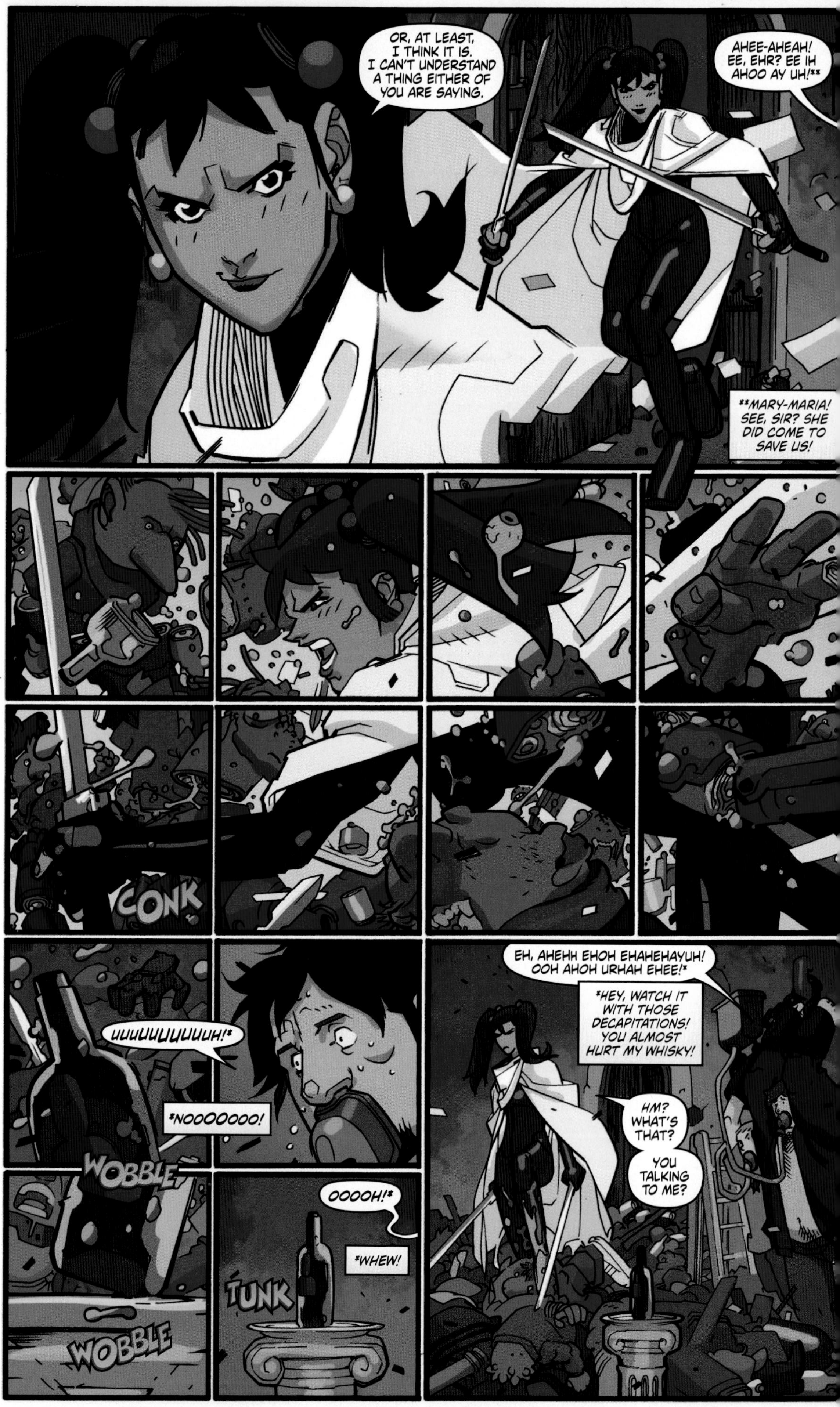

OR, AT LEAST, I THINK IT IS. I CAN'T UNDERSTAND A THING EITHER OF YOU ARE SAYING.
AHEE-AHEAH! EE, EHR? EE IH AHOO AY UH!**
**MARY-MARIA! SEE, SIR? SHE DID COME TO SAVE US!
CONK
UUUUUUUUUUUH!*
*NOOOOOOO!
WOBBLE
WOBBLE
OOOOH!*
*WHEW!
TUNK
EH, AHEHH EHOH EHAHEHAYUH! OOH AHOH URHAH EHEE!*
*HEY, WATCH IT WITH THOSE DECAPITATIONS! YOU ALMOST HURT MY WHISKY!
HM? WHAT'S THAT?
YOU TALKING TO ME?

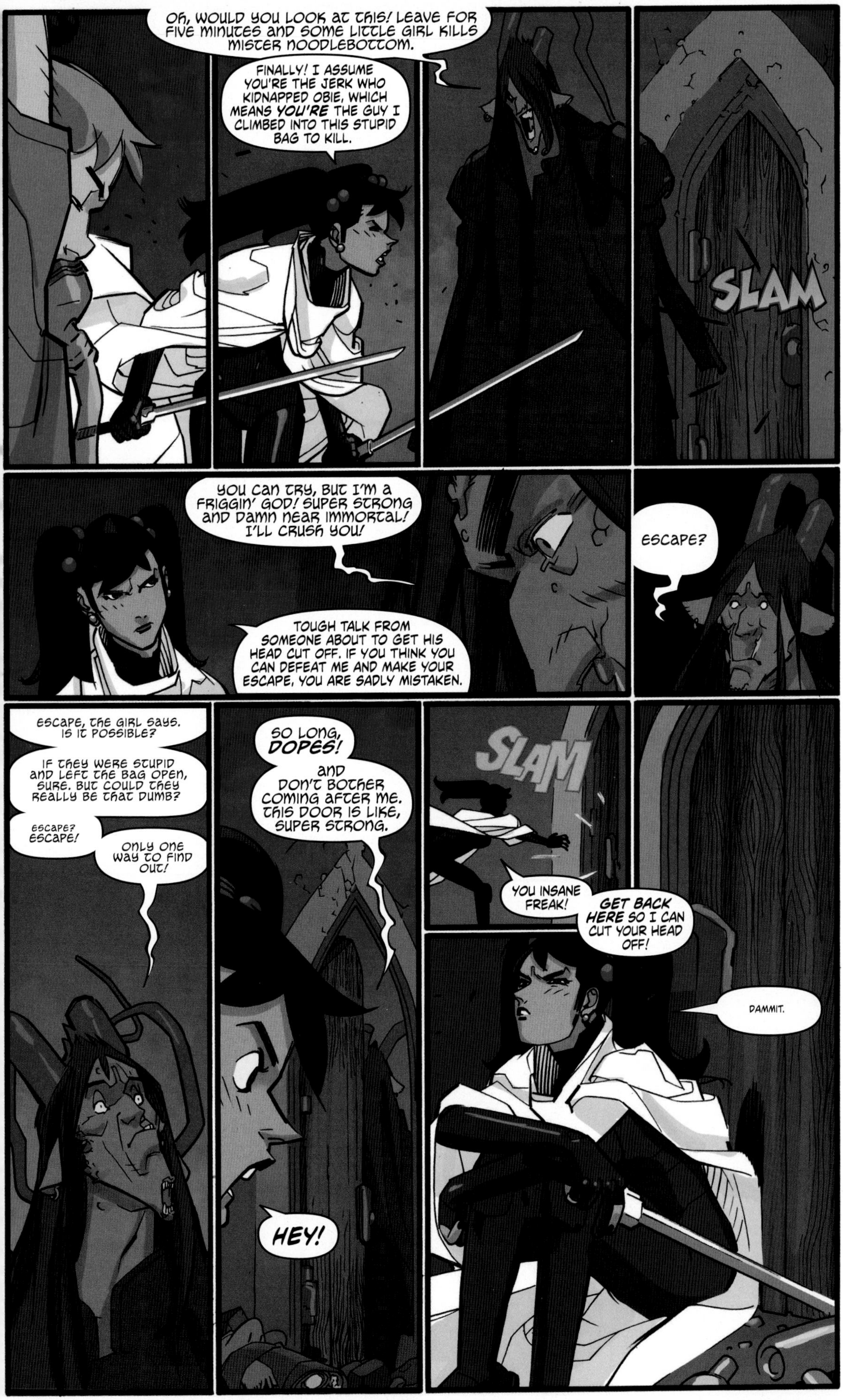
OH, WOULD YOU LOOK AT THIS! LEAVE FOR FIVE MINUTES AND SOME LITTLE GIRL KILLS MISTER NOODLEBOTTOM.
FINALLY! I ASSUME YOU'RE THE JERK WHO KIDNAPPED OBIE, WHICH MEANS YOU'RE THE GUY I CLIMBED INTO THIS STUPID BAG TO KILL.
SLAM
YOU CAN TRY, BUT I'M A FRIGGIN' GOD! SUPER STRONG AND DAMN NEAR IMMORTAL! I'LL CRUSH YOU!
TOUGH TALK FROM SOMEONE ABOUT TO GET HIS HEAD CUT OFF. IF YOU THINK YOU CAN DEFEAT ME AND MAKE YOUR ESCAPE, YOU ARE SADLY MISTAKEN.
ESCAPE?
ESCAPE, THE GIRL SAYS. IS IT POSSIBLE?
IF THEY WERE STUPID AND LEFT THE BAG OPEN, SURE. BUT COULD THEY REALLY BE THAT DUMB?
ESCAPE? ESCAPE!
ONLY ONE WAY TO FIND OUT!
SO LONG, DOPES!
AND DON'T BOTHER COMING AFTER ME. THIS DOOR IS LIKE, SUPER STRONG.
HEY!
SLAM
YOU INSANE FREAK!
GET BACK HERE SO I CAN CUT YOUR HEAD OFF!
DAMMIT.

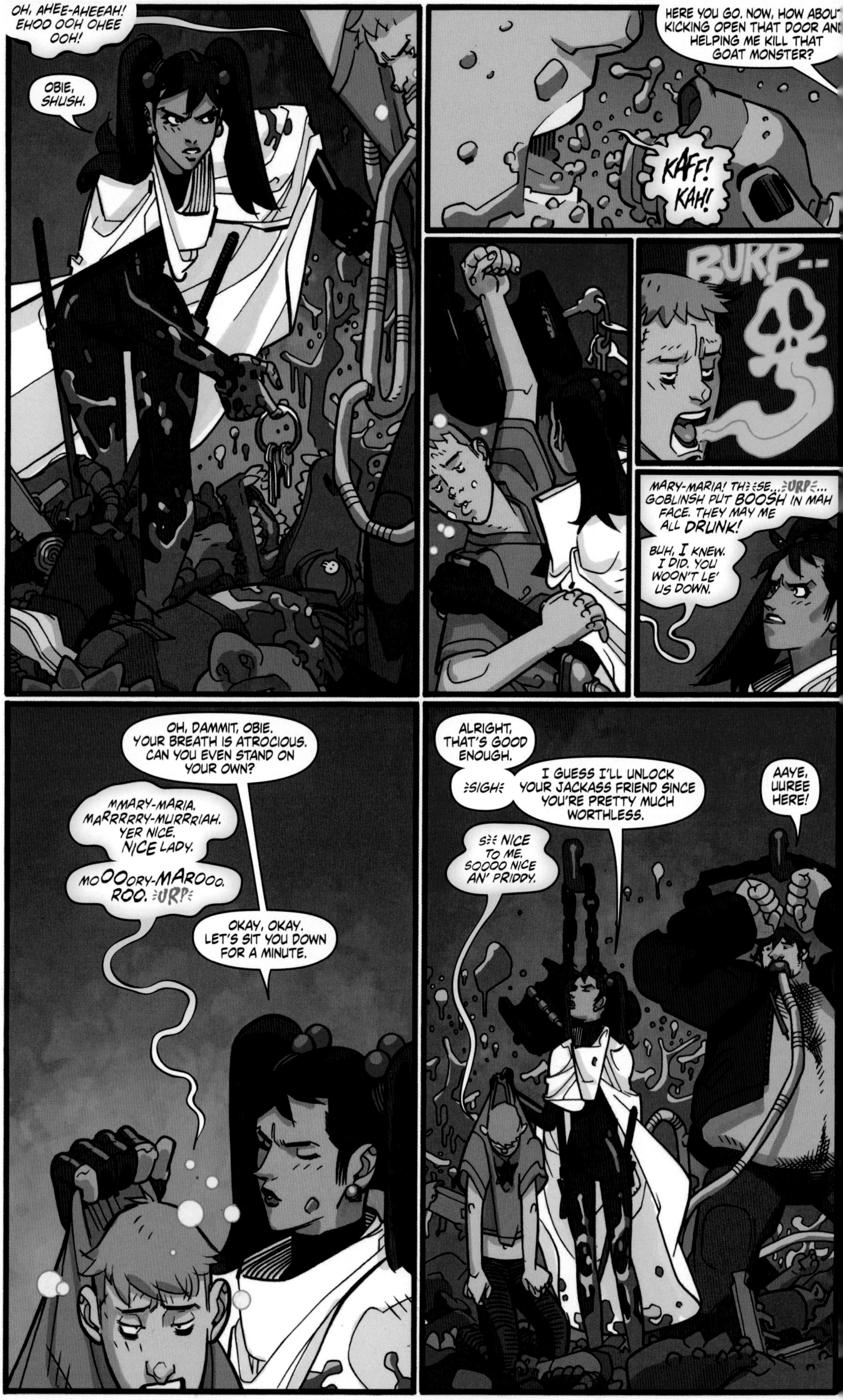
OH, AHEE-AHEEAH! EHOO OOH OHEE OOH!
OBIE, SHUSH.
HERE YOU GO. NOW, HOW ABOUT KICKING OPEN THAT DOOR AND HELPING ME KILL THAT GOAT MONSTER?
KAFF! KAH!
BURP--
MARY-MARIA! THESE... URP... GOBLINSH PUT BOOSH IN MAH FACE. THEY MAY ME ALL DRUNK!
BUH, I KNEW. I DID. YOU WOON'T LE' US DOWN.
OH, DAMMIT, OBIE. YOUR BREATH IS ATROCIOUS. CAN YOU EVEN STAND ON YOUR OWN?
MMARY-MARIA. MARRRRRY-MURRRIAH. YER NICE. NICE LADY.
MOOOORY-MAROOO. ROO. URP
OKAY, OKAY. LET'S SIT YOU DOWN FOR A MINUTE.
ALRIGHT, THAT'S GOOD ENOUGH.
SIGH
I GUESS I'LL UNLOCK YOUR JACKASS FRIEND SINCE YOU'RE PRETTY MUCH WORTHLESS.
AAYE, UUREE HERE!
SHE NICE TO ME. SOOOO NICE AN' PRIDDY.

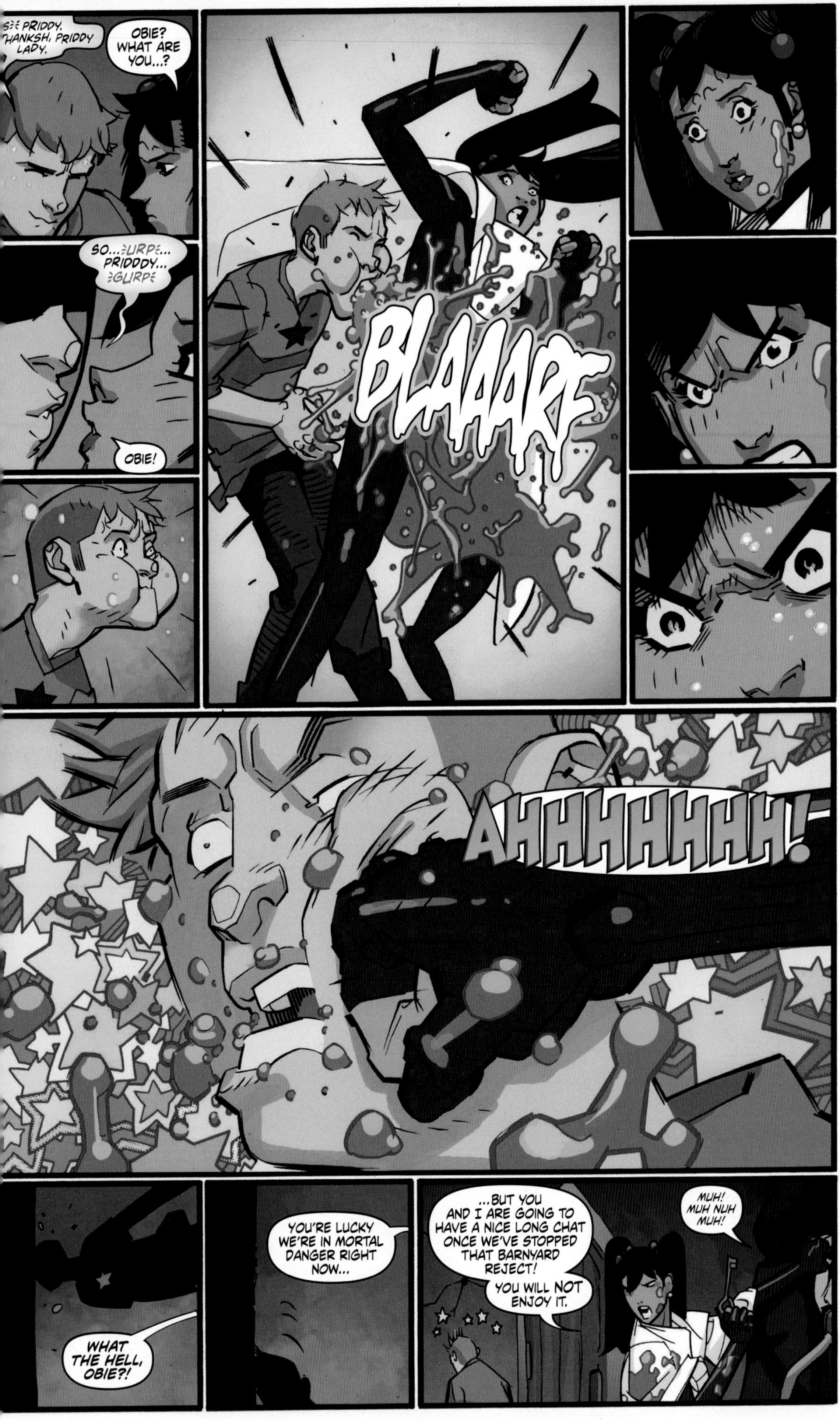
S... PRIDDY. THANKSH, PRIDDY LADY.
OBIE? WHAT ARE YOU...?
SO... URP... PRIDDDY... GURP
OBIE!
BLAAARF
AHHHHHHH!
WHAT THE HELL, OBIE?!
YOU'RE LUCKY WE'RE IN MORTAL DANGER RIGHT NOW...
...BUT YOU AND I ARE GOING TO HAVE A NICE LONG CHAT ONCE WE'VE STOPPED THAT BARNYARD REJECT!
YOU WILL NOT ENJOY IT.
MUH! MUH NUH MUH!

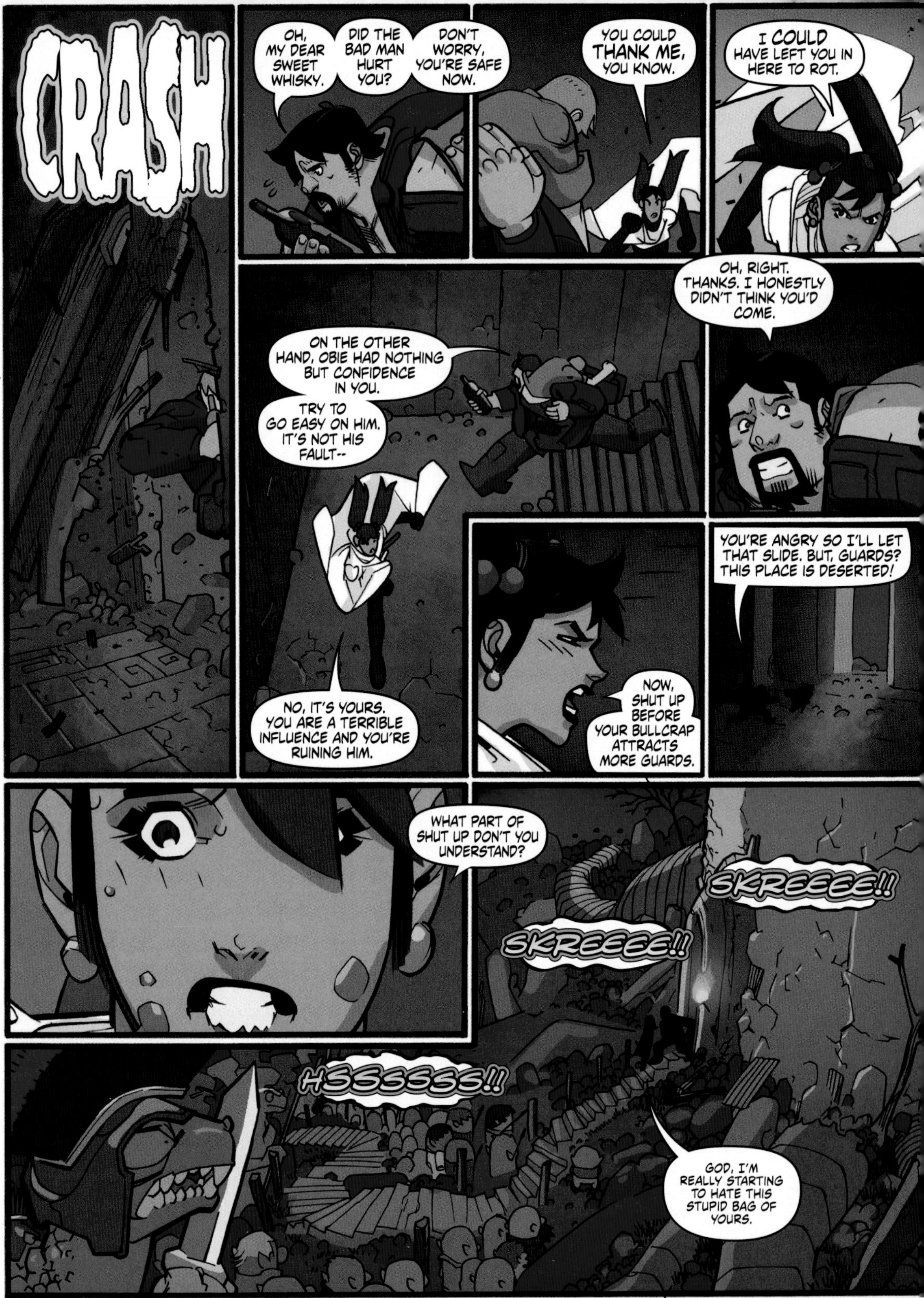
CRASH
OH, MY DEAR SWEET WHISKY.
DID THE BAD MAN HURT YOU?
DON'T WORRY, YOU'RE SAFE NOW.
YOU COULD THANK ME, YOU KNOW.
I COULD HAVE LEFT YOU IN HERE TO ROT.
OH, RIGHT. THANKS. I HONESTLY DIDN'T THINK YOU'D COME.
ON THE OTHER HAND, OBIE HAD NOTHING BUT CONFIDENCE IN YOU.
TRY TO GO EASY ON HIM. IT'S NOT HIS FAULT--
NO, IT'S YOURS. YOU ARE A TERRIBLE INFLUENCE AND YOU'RE RUINING HIM.
NOW, SHUT UP BEFORE YOUR BULLCRAP ATTRACTS MORE GUARDS.
YOU'RE ANGRY SO I'LL LET THAT SLIDE. BUT, GUARDS? THIS PLACE IS DESERTED!
WHAT PART OF SHUT UP DON'T YOU UNDERSTAND?
SKREEEEE!!
SKREEEEE!!
HSSSSSSS!!
GOD, I'M REALLY STARTING TO HATE THIS STUPID BAG OF YOURS.

NEXT: Battle Royale!

RAGE OF THE PARTY GOD! HANGOVER OF THE CENTURY! BUTTS!

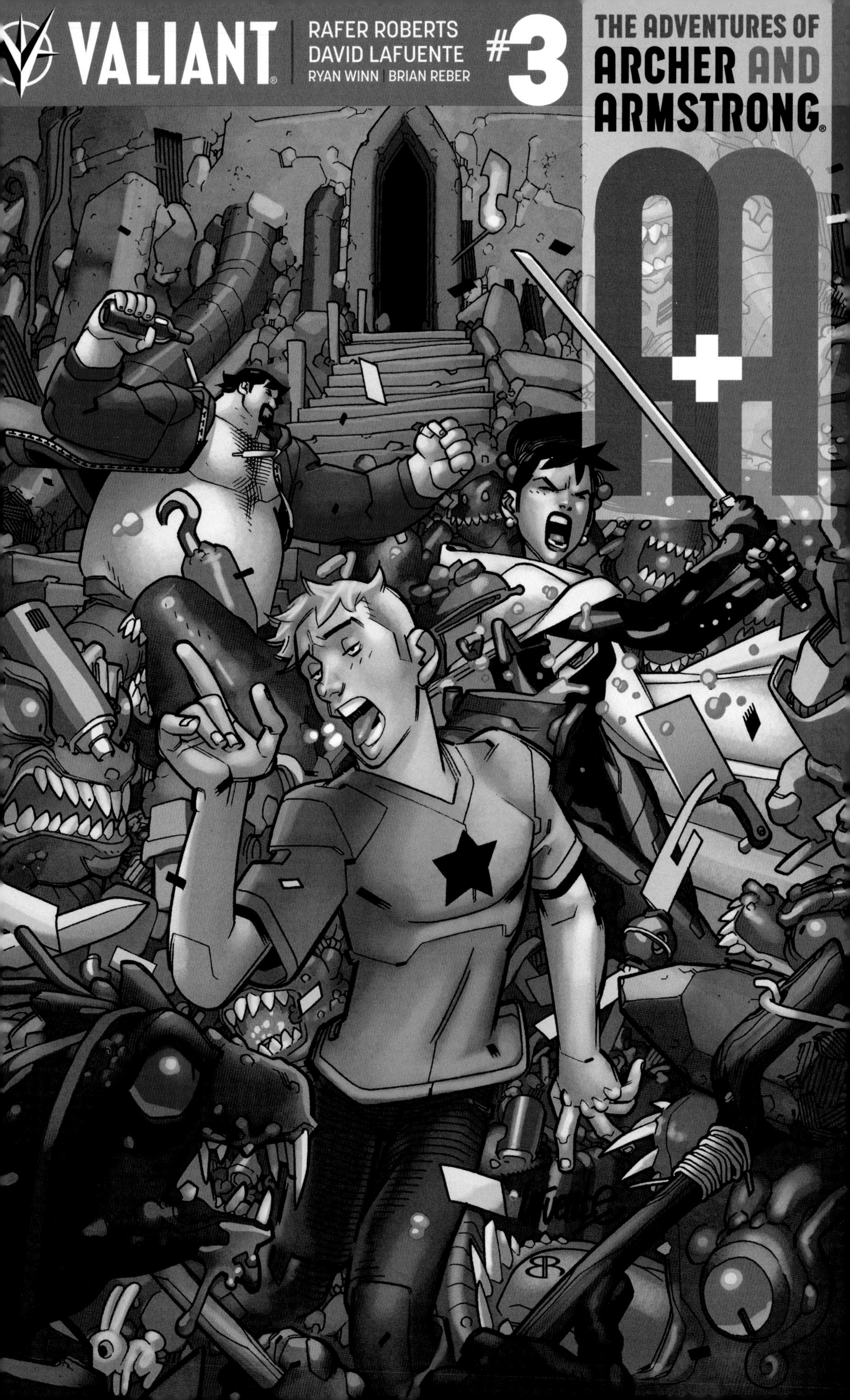
VALIANT
RAFER ROBERTS
DAVID LAFUENTE
RYAN WINN | BRIAN REBER
#3
THE ADVENTURES OF
ARCHER AND
ARMSTRONG
A+A

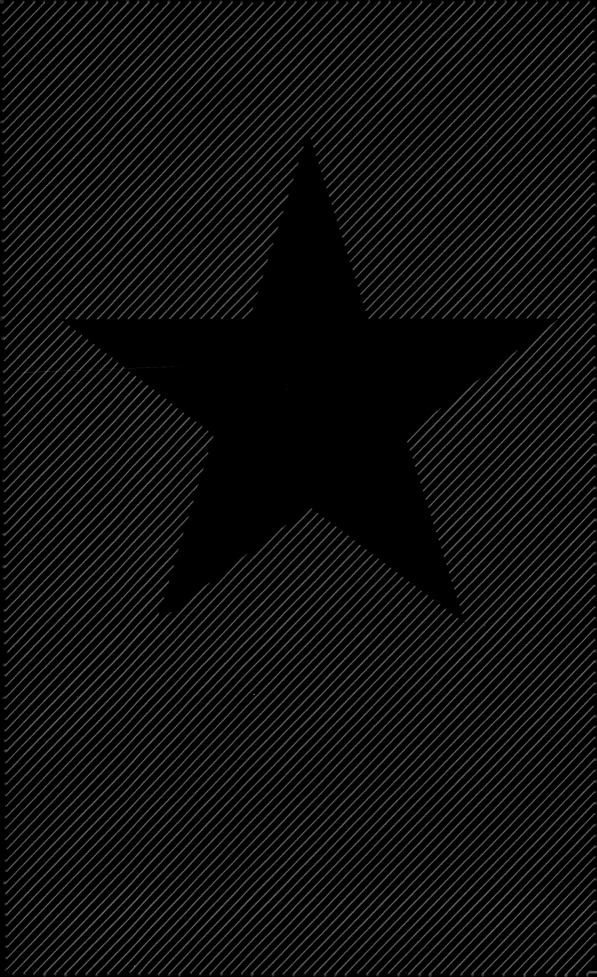

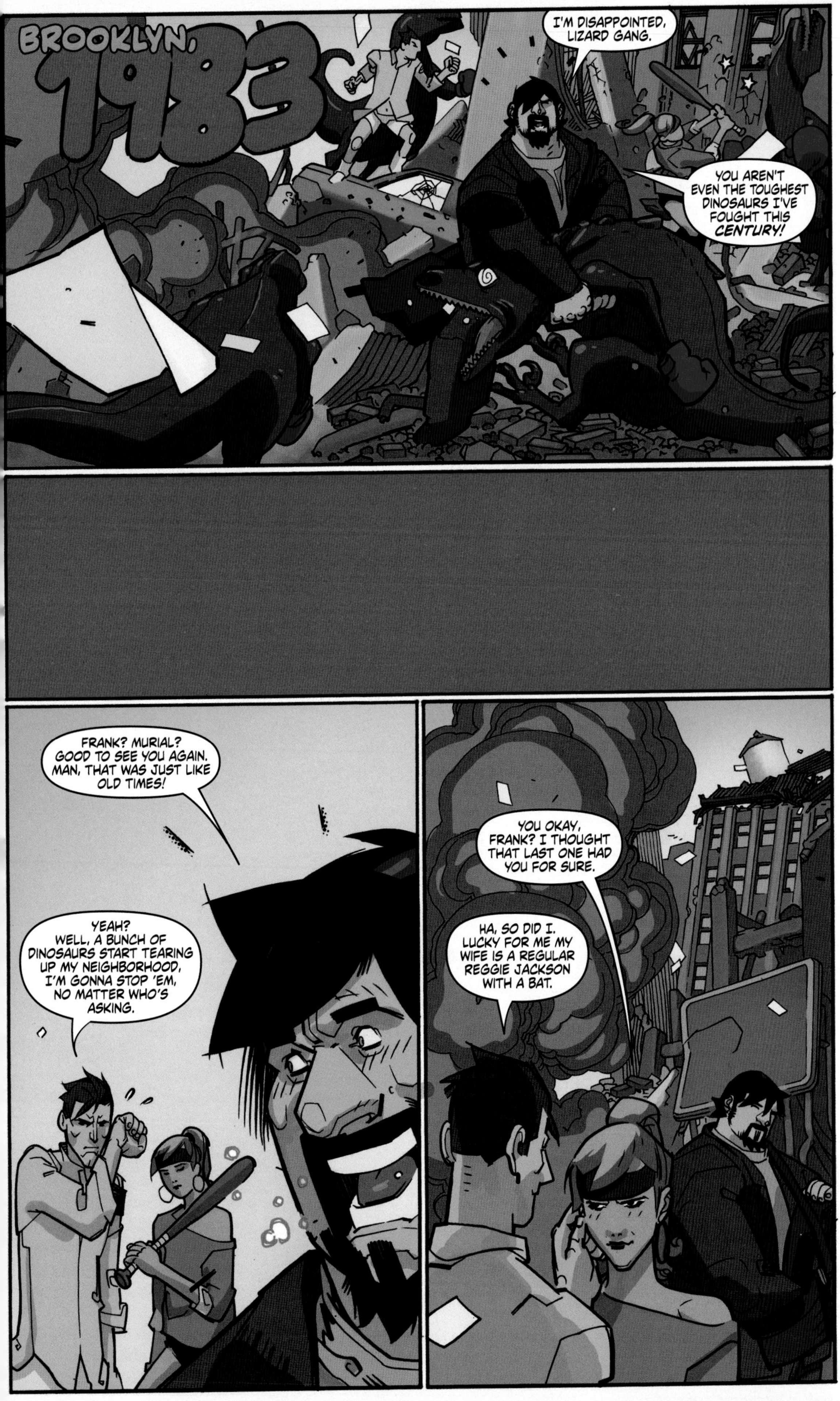
BROOKLYN, 1983
I'M DISAPPOINTED, LIZARD GANG.
YOU AREN'T EVEN THE TOUGHEST DINOSAURS I'VE FOUGHT THIS *CENTURY!*
FRANK? MURIAL? GOOD TO SEE YOU AGAIN. MAN, THAT WAS JUST LIKE OLD TIMES!
YEAH? WELL, A BUNCH OF DINOSAURS START TEARING UP MY NEIGHBORHOOD, I'M GONNA STOP 'EM, NO MATTER WHO'S ASKING.
YOU OKAY, FRANK? I THOUGHT THAT LAST ONE HAD YOU FOR SURE.
HA, SO DID I. LUCKY FOR ME MY WIFE IS A REGULAR REGGIE JACKSON WITH A BAT.

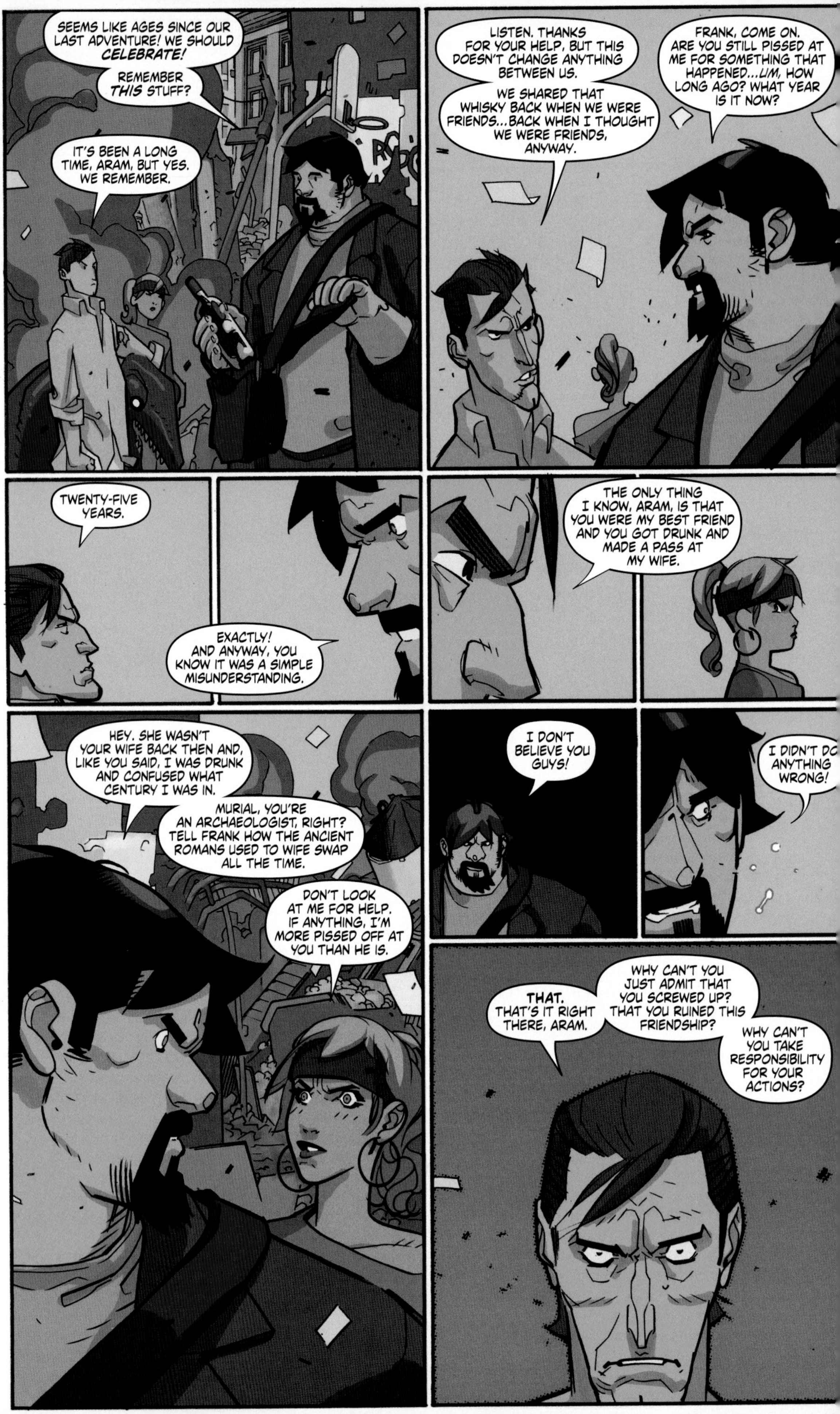
SEEMS LIKE AGES SINCE OUR LAST ADVENTURE! WE SHOULD *CELEBRATE!*
REMEMBER *THIS* STUFF?
IT'S BEEN A LONG TIME, ARAM, BUT YES. WE REMEMBER.
LISTEN. THANKS FOR YOUR HELP, BUT THIS DOESN'T CHANGE ANYTHING BETWEEN US.
WE SHARED THAT WHISKY BACK WHEN WE WERE FRIENDS...BACK WHEN I THOUGHT WE WERE FRIENDS, ANYWAY.
FRANK, COME ON. ARE YOU STILL PISSED AT ME FOR SOMETHING THAT HAPPENED...*UM,* HOW LONG AGO? WHAT YEAR IS IT NOW?
TWENTY-FIVE YEARS.
EXACTLY! AND ANYWAY, YOU KNOW IT WAS A SIMPLE MISUNDERSTANDING.
THE ONLY THING I KNOW, ARAM, IS THAT YOU WERE MY BEST FRIEND AND YOU GOT DRUNK AND MADE A PASS AT MY WIFE.
HEY. SHE WASN'T YOUR WIFE BACK THEN AND, LIKE YOU SAID, I WAS DRUNK AND CONFUSED WHAT CENTURY I WAS IN.
MURIAL, YOU'RE AN ARCHAEOLOGIST, RIGHT? TELL FRANK HOW THE ANCIENT ROMANS USED TO WIFE SWAP ALL THE TIME.
DON'T LOOK AT ME FOR HELP. IF ANYTHING, I'M MORE PISSED OFF AT YOU THAN HE IS.
I DON'T BELIEVE YOU GUYS!
I DIDN'T DO ANYTHING WRONG!
THAT. THAT'S IT RIGHT THERE, ARAM.
WHY CAN'T YOU JUST ADMIT THAT YOU SCREWED UP? THAT YOU RUINED THIS FRIENDSHIP?
WHY CAN'T YOU TAKE RESPONSIBILITY FOR YOUR ACTIONS?

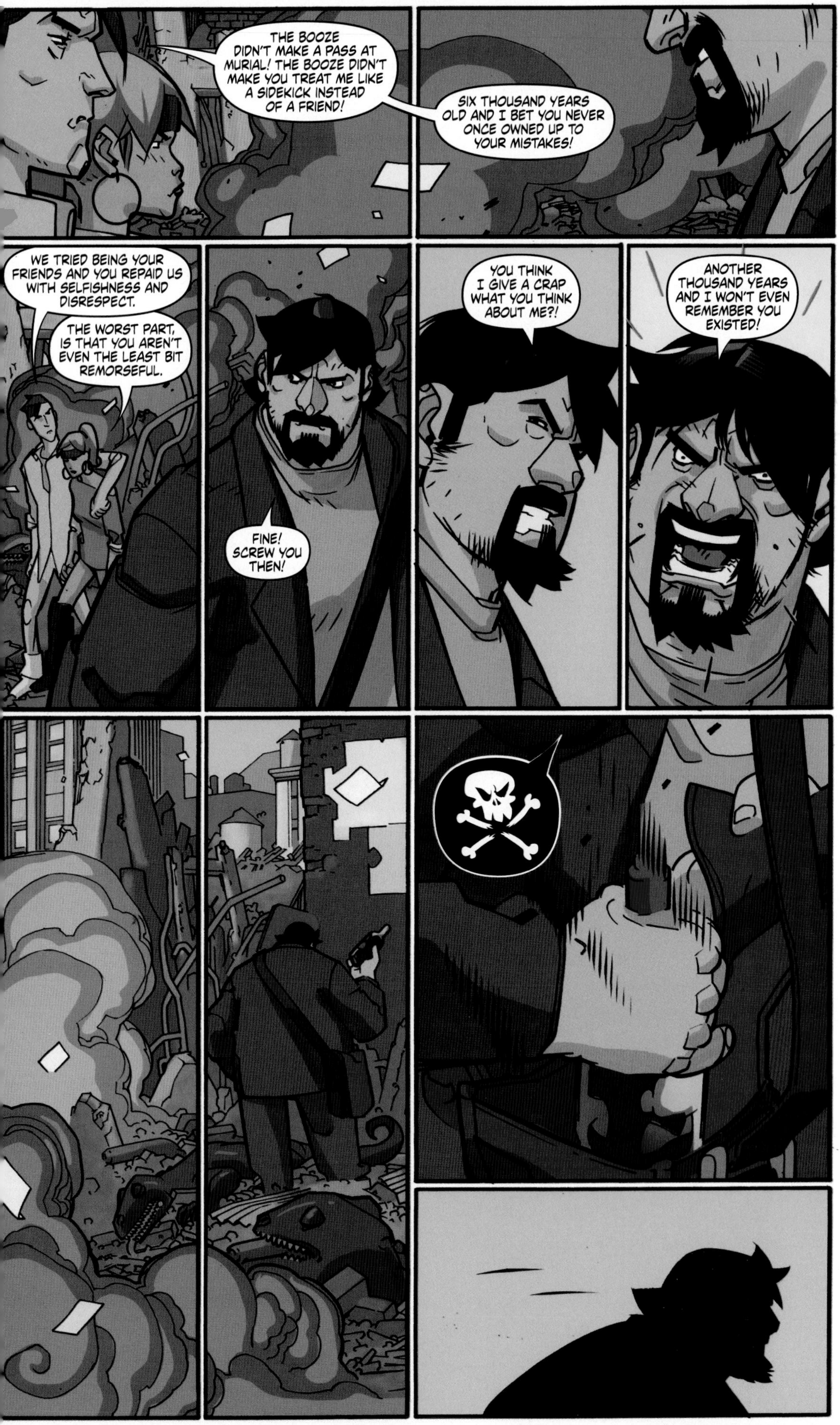
THE BOOZE DIDN'T MAKE A PASS AT MURIAL! THE BOOZE DIDN'T MAKE YOU TREAT ME LIKE A SIDEKICK INSTEAD OF A FRIEND!
SIX THOUSAND YEARS OLD AND I BET YOU NEVER ONCE OWNED UP TO YOUR MISTAKES!
WE TRIED BEING YOUR FRIENDS AND YOU REPAID US WITH SELFISHNESS AND DISRESPECT.
THE WORST PART, IS THAT YOU AREN'T EVEN THE LEAST BIT REMORSEFUL.
FINE! SCREW YOU THEN!
YOU THINK I GIVE A CRAP WHAT YOU THINK ABOUT ME?!
ANOTHER THOUSAND YEARS AND I WON'T EVEN REMEMBER YOU EXISTED!

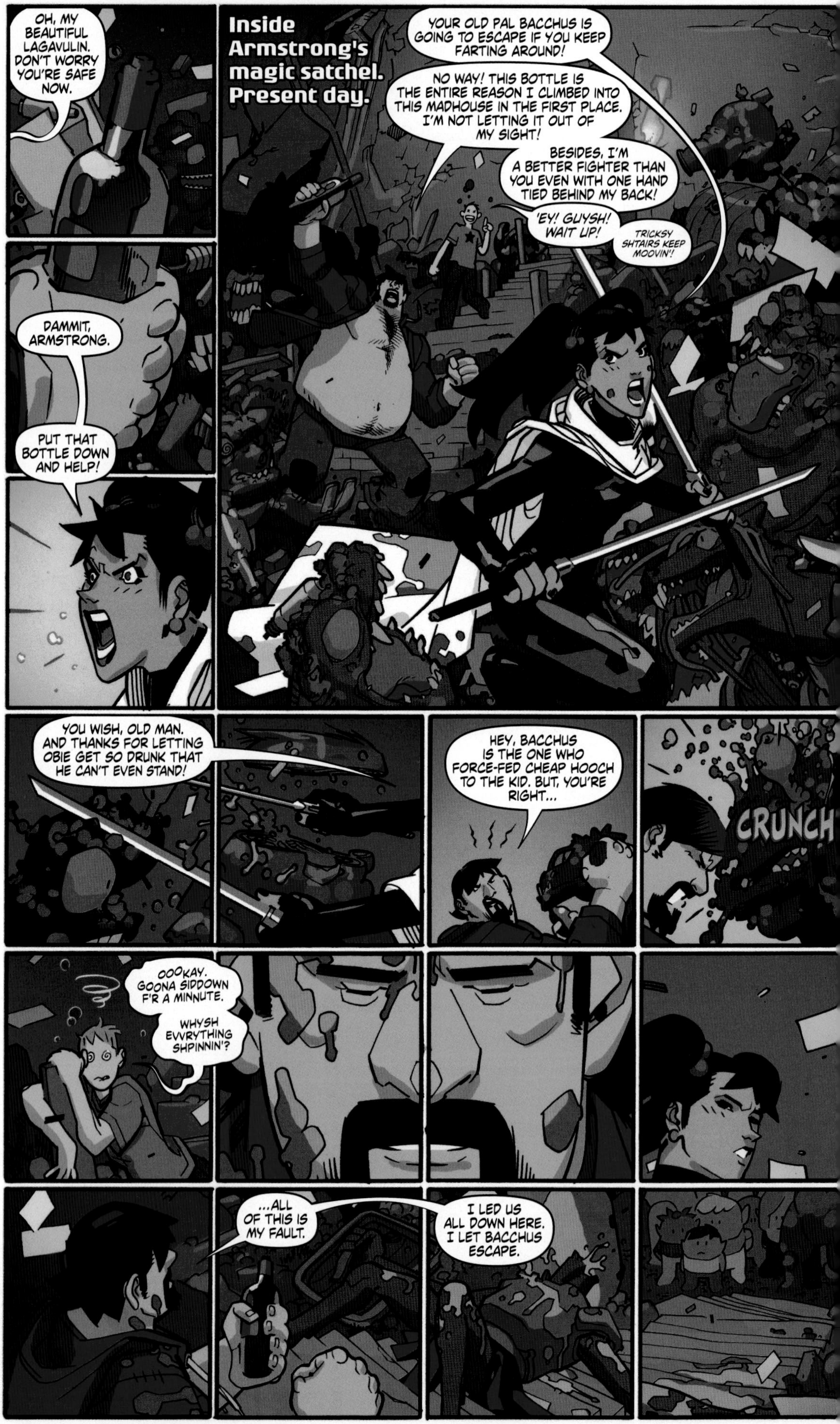
OH, MY BEAUTIFUL LAGAVULIN. DON'T WORRY YOU'RE SAFE NOW.
Inside Armstrong's magic satchel. Present day.
YOUR OLD PAL BACCHUS IS GOING TO ESCAPE IF YOU KEEP FARTING AROUND!
NO WAY! THIS BOTTLE IS THE ENTIRE REASON I CLIMBED INTO THIS MADHOUSE IN THE FIRST PLACE. I'M NOT LETTING IT OUT OF MY SIGHT!
BESIDES, I'M A BETTER FIGHTER THAN YOU EVEN WITH ONE HAND TIED BEHIND MY BACK!
'EY! GUYSH! WAIT UP!
TRICKSY SHTAIRS KEEP MOOVIN'!
DAMMIT, ARMSTRONG.
PUT THAT BOTTLE DOWN AND HELP!
YOU WISH, OLD MAN. AND THANKS FOR LETTING OBIE GET SO DRUNK THAT HE CAN'T EVEN STAND!
HEY, BACCHUS IS THE ONE WHO FORCE-FED CHEAP HOOCH TO THE KID. BUT, YOU'RE RIGHT...
CRUNCH
OOOKAY. GOONA SIDDOWN F'R A MINNUTE.
WHYSH EVVRYTHING SHPINNIN'?
...ALL OF THIS IS MY FAULT.
I LED US ALL DOWN HERE. I LET BACCHUS ESCAPE.

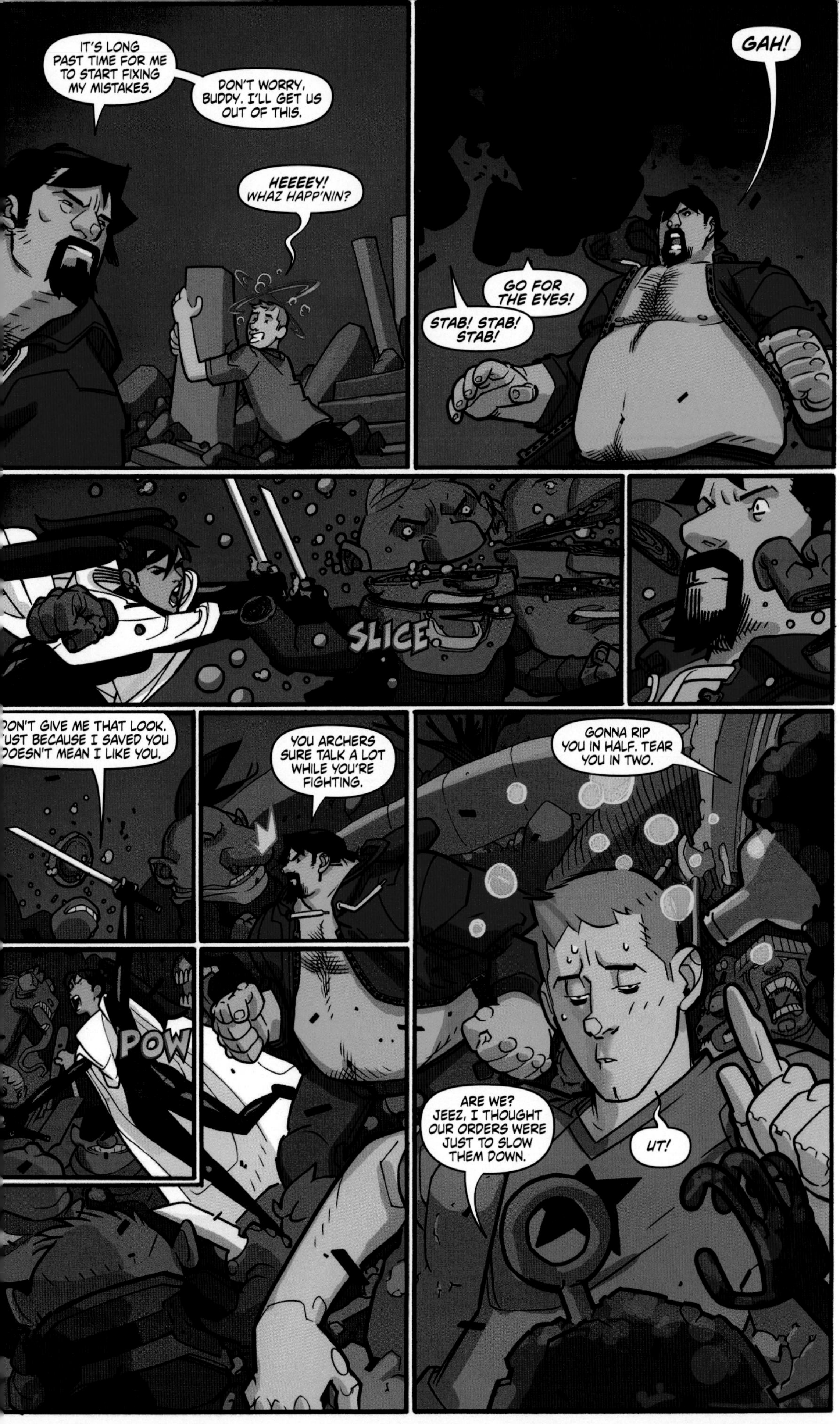

IT'S LONG PAST TIME FOR ME TO START FIXING MY MISTAKES.
DON'T WORRY, BUDDY. I'LL GET US OUT OF THIS.
HEEEEY! WHAZ HAPP'NIN?
GAH!
GO FOR THE EYES!
STAB! STAB! STAB!
SLICE
DON'T GIVE ME THAT LOOK. JUST BECAUSE I SAVED YOU DOESN'T MEAN I LIKE YOU.
YOU ARCHERS SURE TALK A LOT WHILE YOU'RE FIGHTING.
GONNA RIP YOU IN HALF. TEAR YOU IN TWO.
POW
ARE WE? JEEZ, I THOUGHT OUR ORDERS WERE JUST TO SLOW THEM DOWN.
UT!

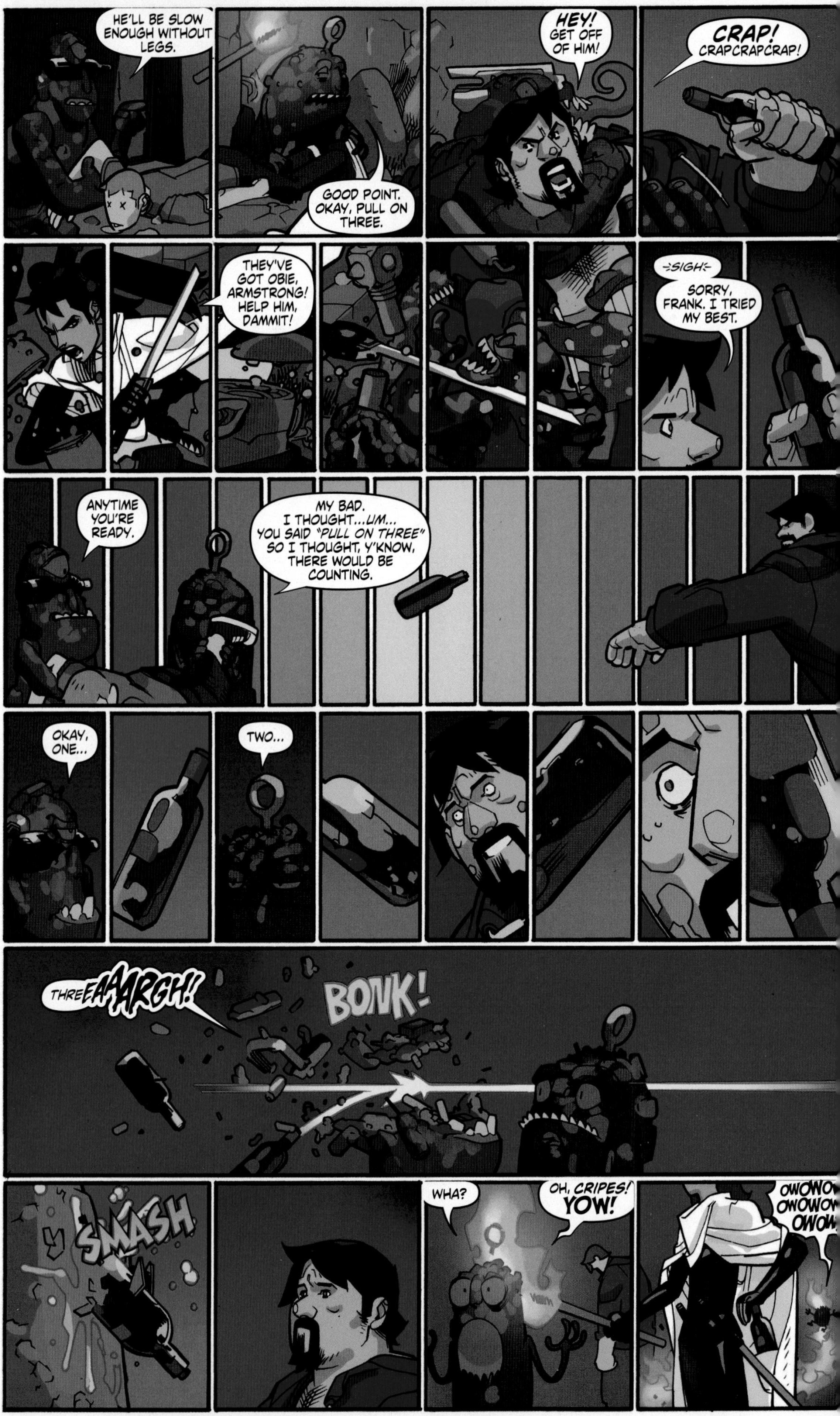
HE'LL BE SLOW ENOUGH WITHOUT LEGS.
GOOD POINT. OKAY, PULL ON THREE.
HEY! GET OFF OF HIM!
CRAP! CRAPCRAPCRAP!
THEY'VE GOT OBIE, ARMSTRONG! HELP HIM, DAMMIT!
SIGH
SORRY, FRANK. I TRIED MY BEST.
ANYTIME YOU'RE READY.
MY BAD. I THOUGHT...UM... YOU SAID "PULL ON THREE" SO I THOUGHT, Y'KNOW, THERE WOULD BE COUNTING.
OKAY, ONE...
TWO...
THREEAAAARGH!
BONK!
SMASH
WHA?
OH, CRIPES! YOW!
OWOWOW OWOWOW OWOW

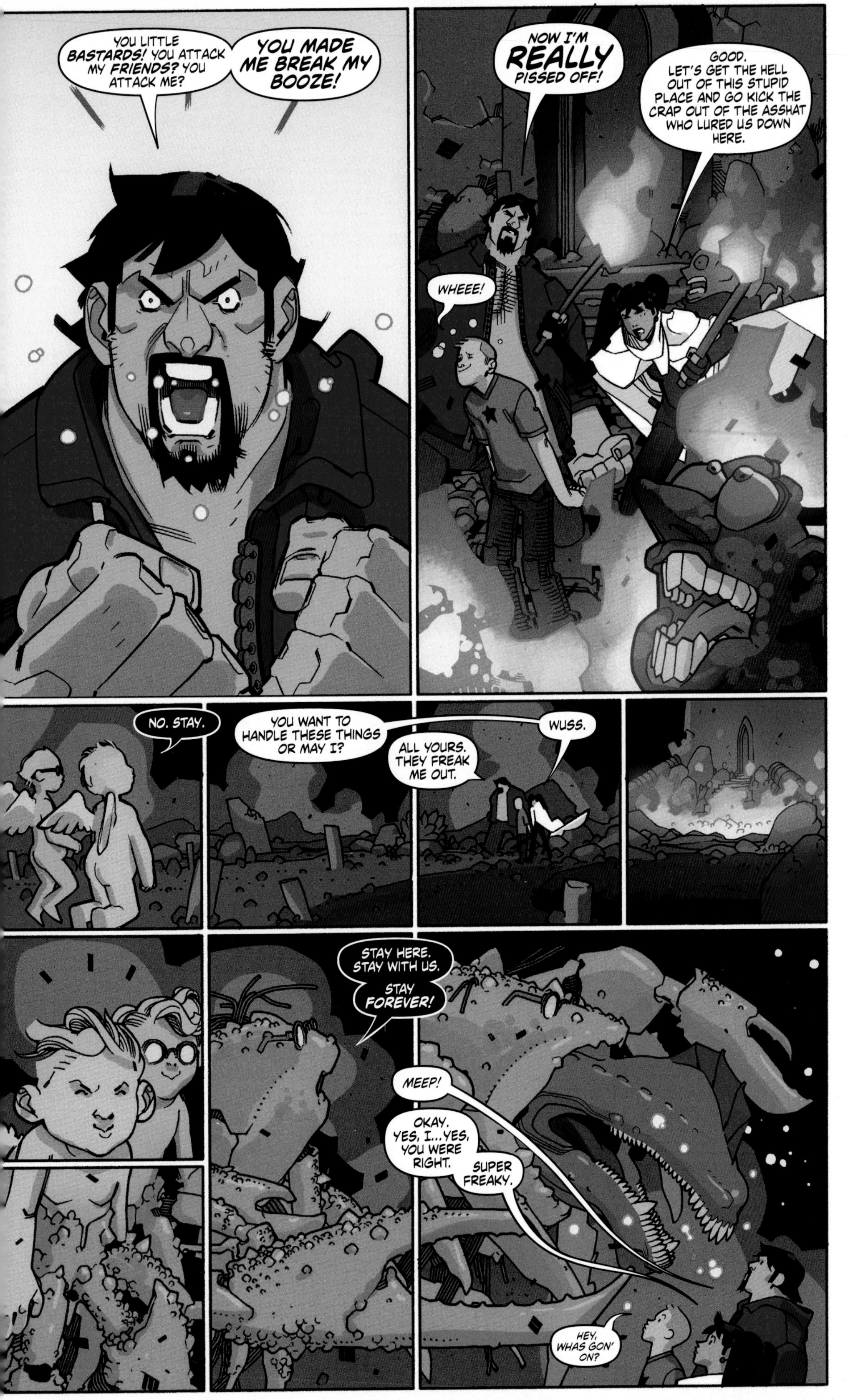
YOU LITTLE BASTARDS! YOU ATTACK MY FRIENDS? YOU ATTACK ME?
YOU MADE ME BREAK MY BOOZE!
NOW I'M REALLY PISSED OFF!
GOOD. LET'S GET THE HELL OUT OF THIS STUPID PLACE AND GO KICK THE CRAP OUT OF THE ASSHAT WHO LURED US DOWN HERE.
WHEEE!
NO. STAY.
YOU WANT TO HANDLE THESE THINGS OR MAY I?
WUSS.
ALL YOURS. THEY FREAK ME OUT.
STAY HERE. STAY WITH US.
STAY FOREVER!
MEEP!
OKAY. YES, I...YES, YOU WERE RIGHT.
SUPER FREAKY.
HEY, WHAS GON' ON?

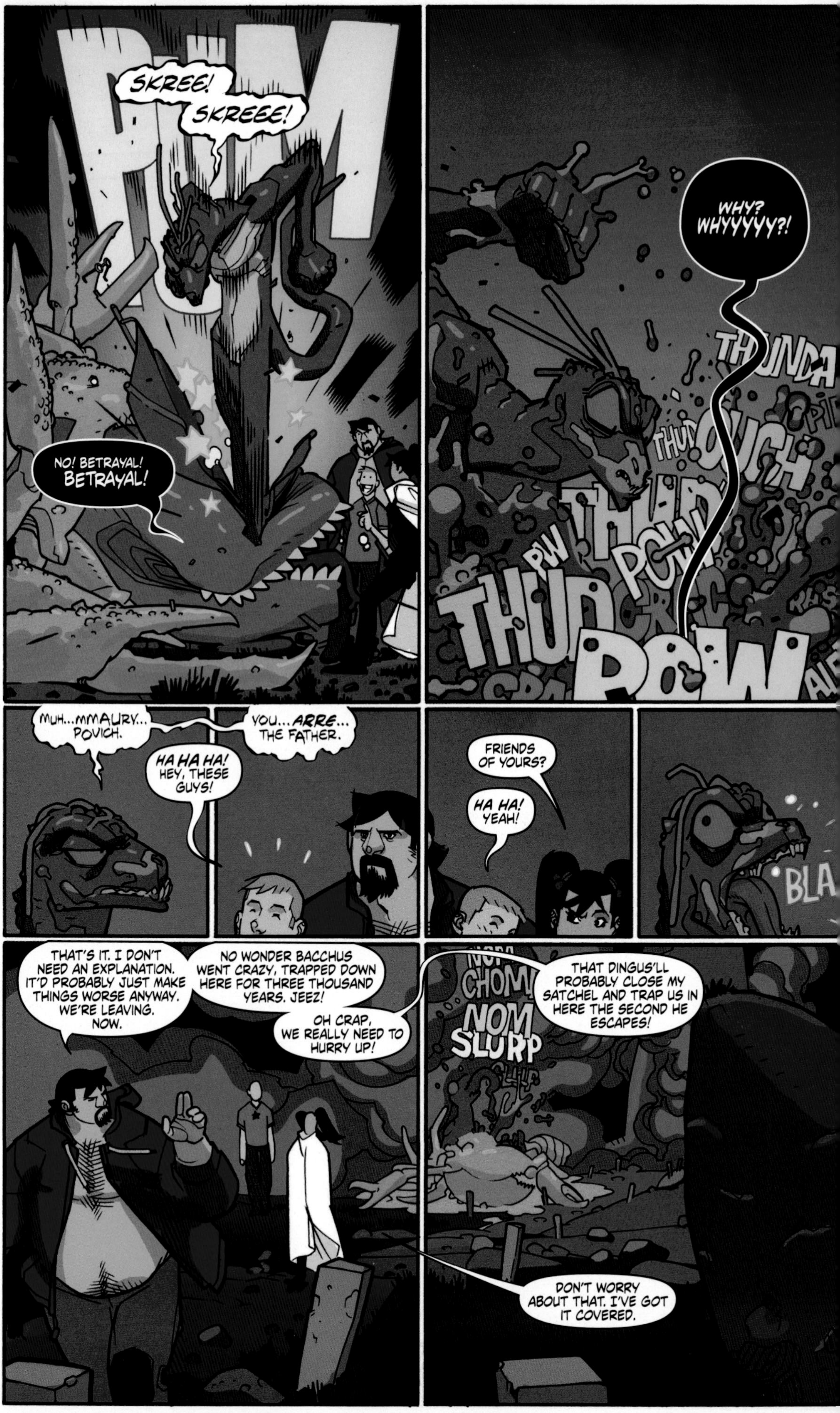
POW
SKREE!
SKREEE!
NO! BETRAYAL! BETRAYAL!
WHY? WHYYYYY?!
THUNDA
OUCH
THUD
POW
PW
THUD
POW
MUH...MMAURY... POVICH.
YOU...ARRE... THE FATHER.
HA HA HA! HEY, THESE GUYS!
FRIENDS OF YOURS?
HA HA! YEAH!
BLA
THAT'S IT. I DON'T NEED AN EXPLANATION. IT'D PROBABLY JUST MAKE THINGS WORSE ANYWAY. WE'RE LEAVING. NOW.
NO WONDER BACCHUS WENT CRAZY, TRAPPED DOWN HERE FOR THREE THOUSAND YEARS. JEEZ!
OH CRAP, WE REALLY NEED TO HURRY UP!
THAT DINGUS'LL PROBABLY CLOSE MY SATCHEL AND TRAP US IN HERE THE SECOND HE ESCAPES!
NOM
SLURP
DON'T WORRY ABOUT THAT. I'VE GOT IT COVERED.

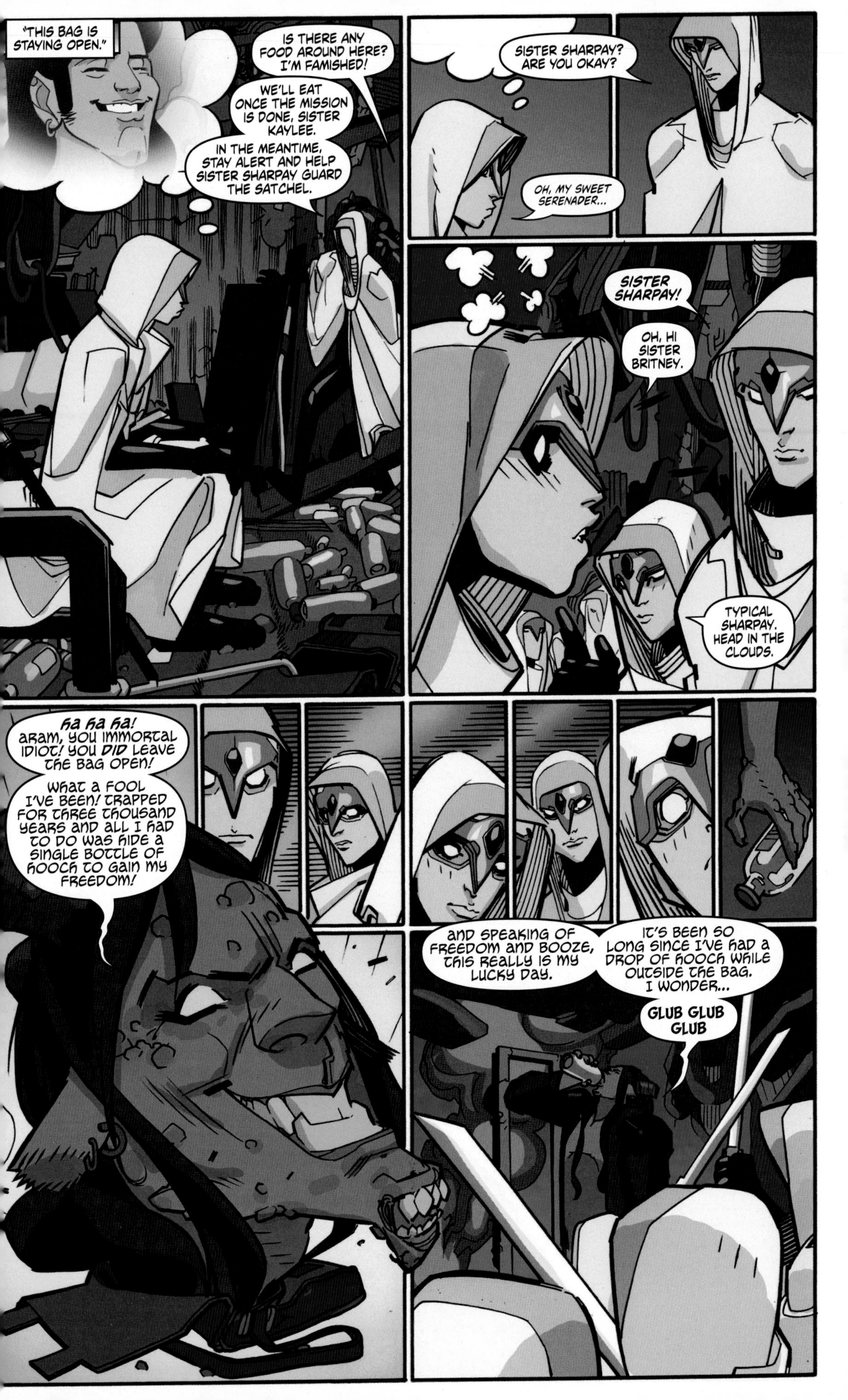
"THIS BAG IS STAYING OPEN."
IS THERE ANY FOOD AROUND HERE? I'M FAMISHED!
WE'LL EAT ONCE THE MISSION IS DONE, SISTER KAYLEE.
IN THE MEANTIME, STAY ALERT AND HELP SISTER SHARPAY GUARD THE SATCHEL.
SISTER SHARPAY? ARE YOU OKAY?
OH, MY SWEET SERENADER...
SISTER SHARPAY!
OH, HI SISTER BRITNEY.
TYPICAL SHARPAY. HEAD IN THE CLOUDS.
HA HA HA! ARAM, YOU IMMORTAL IDIOT! YOU DID LEAVE THE BAG OPEN!
WHAT A FOOL I'VE BEEN! TRAPPED FOR THREE THOUSAND YEARS AND ALL I HAD TO DO WAS HIDE A SINGLE BOTTLE OF HOOCH TO GAIN MY FREEDOM!
AND SPEAKING OF FREEDOM AND BOOZE, THIS REALLY IS MY LUCKY DAY.
IT'S BEEN SO LONG SINCE I'VE HAD A DROP OF HOOCH WHILE OUTSIDE THE BAG. I WONDER...
GLUB GLUB GLUB

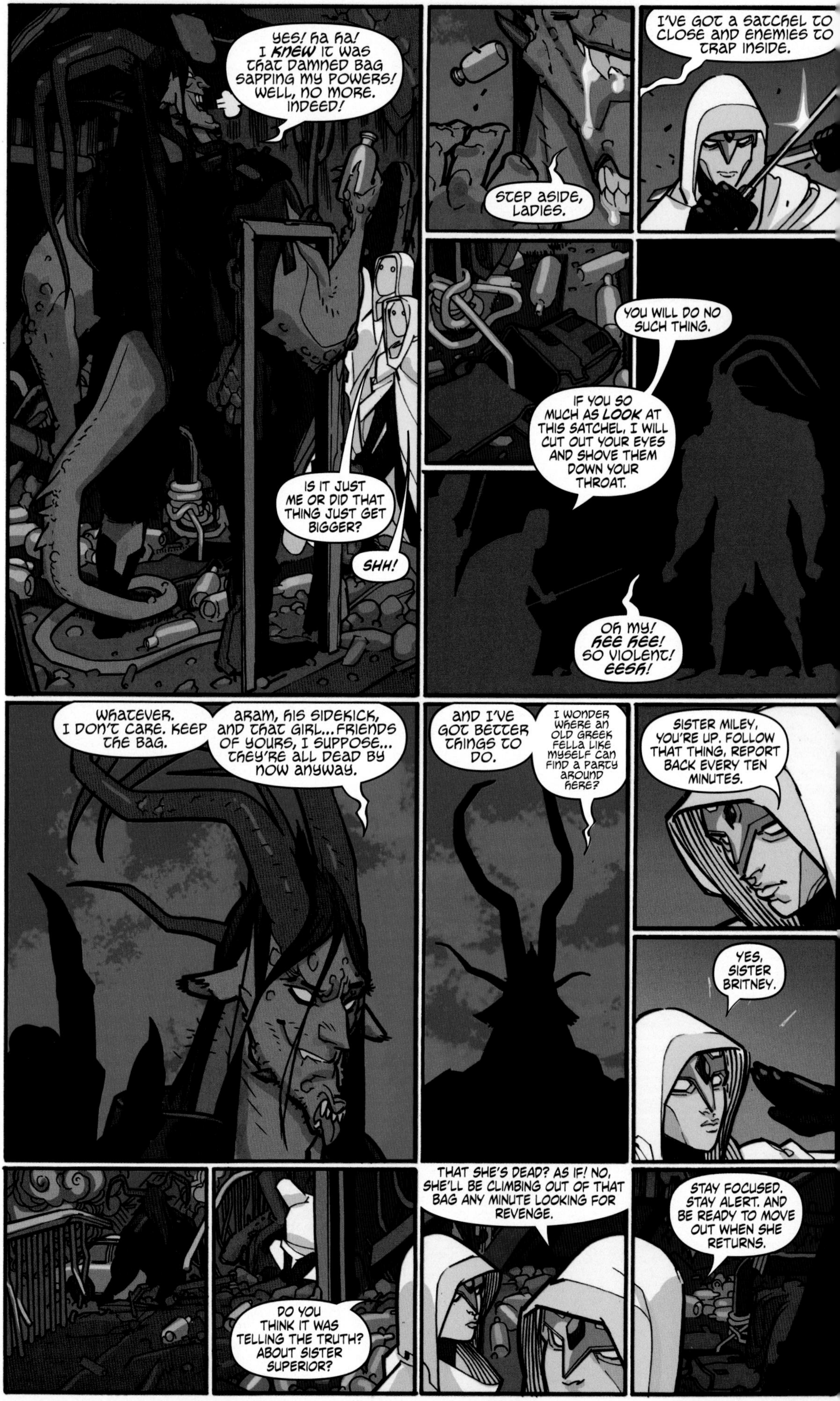
YES! HA HA! I KNEW IT WAS THAT DAMNED BAG SAPPING MY POWERS! WELL, NO MORE. INDEED!
IS IT JUST ME OR DID THAT THING JUST GET BIGGER?
SHH!
STEP ASIDE, LADIES.
I'VE GOT A SATCHEL TO CLOSE AND ENEMIES TO TRAP INSIDE.
YOU WILL DO NO SUCH THING.
IF YOU SO MUCH AS LOOK AT THIS SATCHEL, I WILL CUT OUT YOUR EYES AND SHOVE THEM DOWN YOUR THROAT.
OH MY! HEE HEE! SO VIOLENT! EESH!
WHATEVER. I DON'T CARE. KEEP THE BAG.
ARAM, HIS SIDEKICK, AND THAT GIRL... FRIENDS OF YOURS, I SUPPOSE... THEY'RE ALL DEAD BY NOW ANYWAY.
AND I'VE GOT BETTER THINGS TO DO.
I WONDER WHERE AN OLD GREEK FELLA LIKE MYSELF CAN FIND A PARTY AROUND HERE?
SISTER MILEY, YOU'RE UP. FOLLOW THAT THING. REPORT BACK EVERY TEN MINUTES.
YES, SISTER BRITNEY.
DO YOU THINK IT WAS TELLING THE TRUTH? ABOUT SISTER SUPERIOR?
THAT SHE'S DEAD? AS IF! NO, SHE'LL BE CLIMBING OUT OF THAT BAG ANY MINUTE LOOKING FOR REVENGE.
STAY FOCUSED. STAY ALERT. AND BE READY TO MOVE OUT WHEN SHE RETURNS.

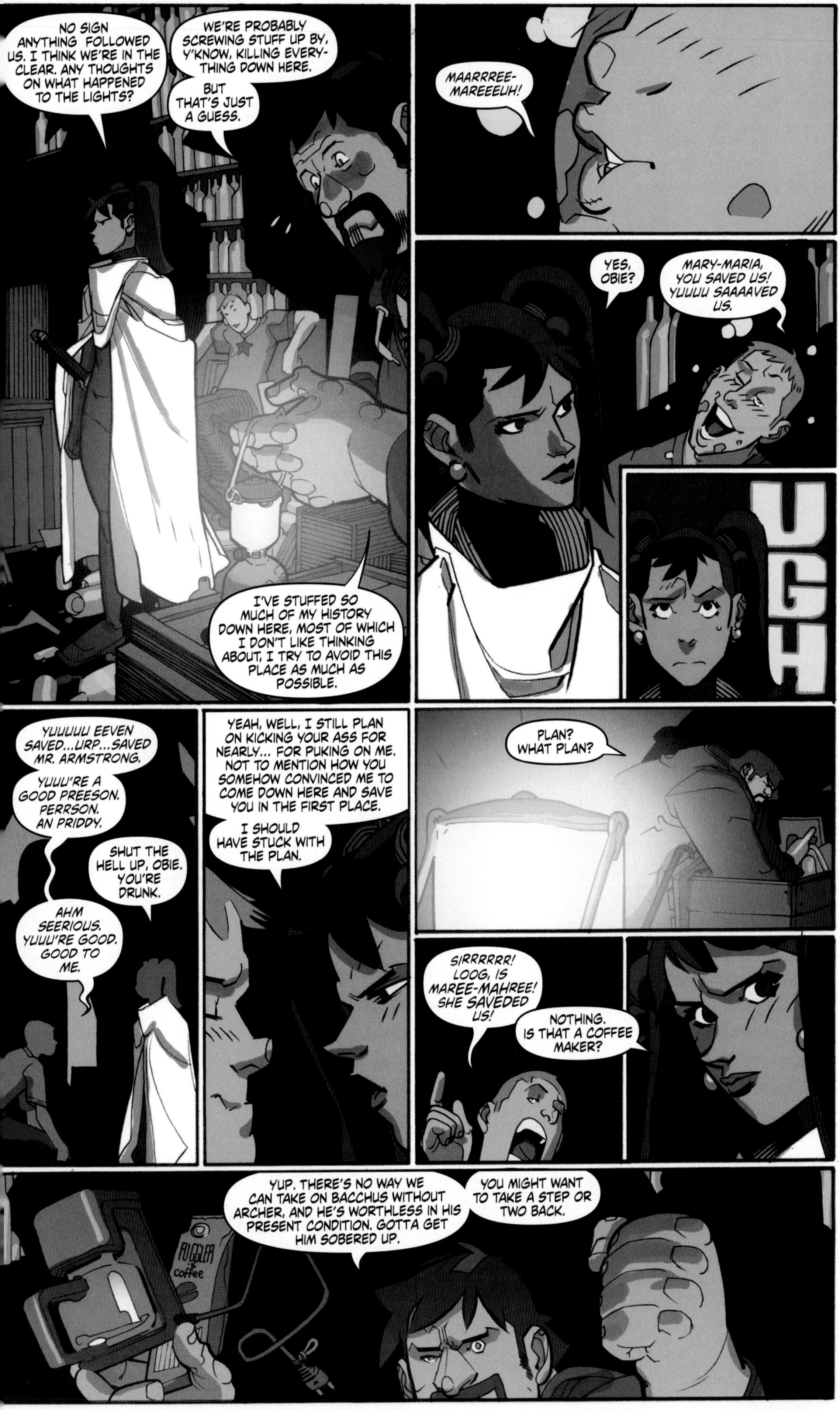
NO SIGN ANYTHING FOLLOWED US. I THINK WE'RE IN THE CLEAR. ANY THOUGHTS ON WHAT HAPPENED TO THE LIGHTS?
WE'RE PROBABLY SCREWING STUFF UP BY, Y'KNOW, KILLING EVERY-THING DOWN HERE.
BUT THAT'S JUST A GUESS.
I'VE STUFFED SO MUCH OF MY HISTORY DOWN HERE, MOST OF WHICH I DON'T LIKE THINKING ABOUT, I TRY TO AVOID THIS PLACE AS MUCH AS POSSIBLE.
MAARRREE-MAREEEUH!
YES, OBIE?
MARY-MARIA, YOU SAVED US! YUUUU SAAAAVED US.
UGH
YUUUUU EEVEN SAVED...URP...SAVED MR. ARMSTRONG.
YUUU'RE A GOOD PREESON. PERRSON. AN PRIDDY.
SHUT THE HELL UP, OBIE. YOU'RE DRUNK.
AHM SEERIOUS. YUUU'RE GOOD. GOOD TO ME.
YEAH, WELL, I STILL PLAN ON KICKING YOUR ASS FOR NEARLY... FOR PUKING ON ME. NOT TO MENTION HOW YOU SOMEHOW CONVINCED ME TO COME DOWN HERE AND SAVE YOU IN THE FIRST PLACE.
I SHOULD HAVE STUCK WITH THE PLAN.
PLAN? WHAT PLAN?
SIRRRRRR! LOOG, IS MAREE-MAHREE! SHE SAVEDED US!
NOTHING. IS THAT A COFFEE MAKER?
YUP. THERE'S NO WAY WE CAN TAKE ON BACCHUS WITHOUT ARCHER, AND HE'S WORTHLESS IN HIS PRESENT CONDITION. GOTTA GET HIM SOBERED UP.
YOU MIGHT WANT TO TAKE A STEP OR TWO BACK.
FUGGLER coffee

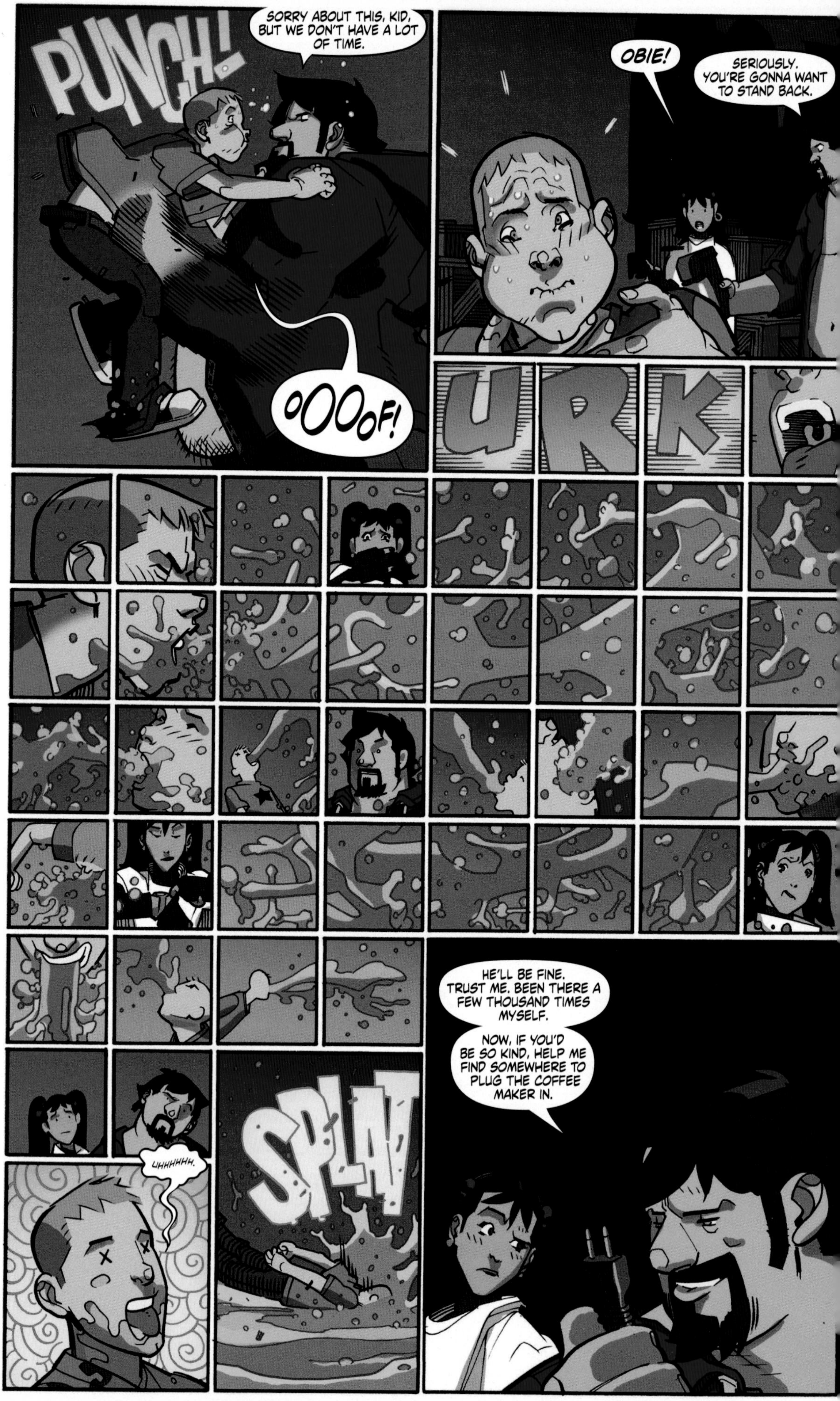

PUNCH!
SORRY ABOUT THIS, KID, BUT WE DON'T HAVE A LOT OF TIME.
OOOOF!
OBIE!
SERIOUSLY. YOU'RE GONNA WANT TO STAND BACK.
URK
UHHHHHH.
SPLAT
HE'LL BE FINE. TRUST ME. BEEN THERE A FEW THOUSAND TIMES MYSELF.
NOW, IF YOU'D BE SO KIND, HELP ME FIND SOMEWHERE TO PLUG THE COFFEE MAKER IN.

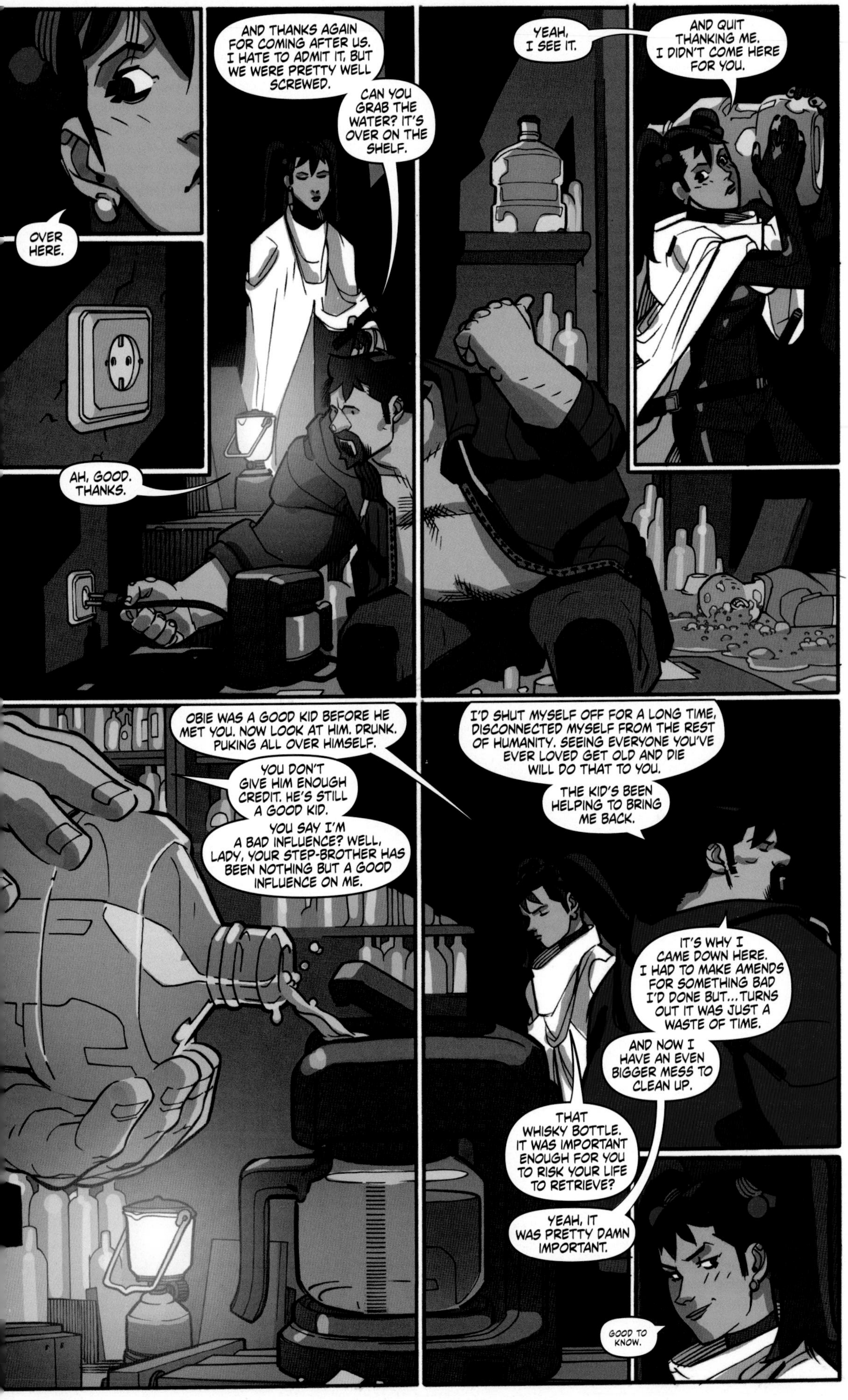

OVER HERE.
AND THANKS AGAIN FOR COMING AFTER US. I HATE TO ADMIT IT, BUT WE WERE PRETTY WELL SCREWED.
CAN YOU GRAB THE WATER? IT'S OVER ON THE SHELF.
YEAH, I SEE IT.
AND QUIT THANKING ME. I DIDN'T COME HERE FOR YOU.
AH, GOOD. THANKS.
OBIE WAS A GOOD KID BEFORE HE MET YOU. NOW LOOK AT HIM. DRUNK. PUKING ALL OVER HIMSELF.
YOU DON'T GIVE HIM ENOUGH CREDIT. HE'S STILL A GOOD KID.
YOU SAY I'M A BAD INFLUENCE? WELL, LADY, YOUR STEP-BROTHER HAS BEEN NOTHING BUT A GOOD INFLUENCE ON ME.
I'D SHUT MYSELF OFF FOR A LONG TIME, DISCONNECTED MYSELF FROM THE REST OF HUMANITY. SEEING EVERYONE YOU'VE EVER LOVED GET OLD AND DIE WILL DO THAT TO YOU.
THE KID'S BEEN HELPING TO BRING ME BACK.
IT'S WHY I CAME DOWN HERE. I HAD TO MAKE AMENDS FOR SOMETHING BAD I'D DONE BUT...TURNS OUT IT WAS JUST A WASTE OF TIME.
AND NOW I HAVE AN EVEN BIGGER MESS TO CLEAN UP.
THAT WHISKY BOTTLE. IT WAS IMPORTANT ENOUGH FOR YOU TO RISK YOUR LIFE TO RETRIEVE?
YEAH, IT WAS PRETTY DAMN IMPORTANT.
GOOD TO KNOW.

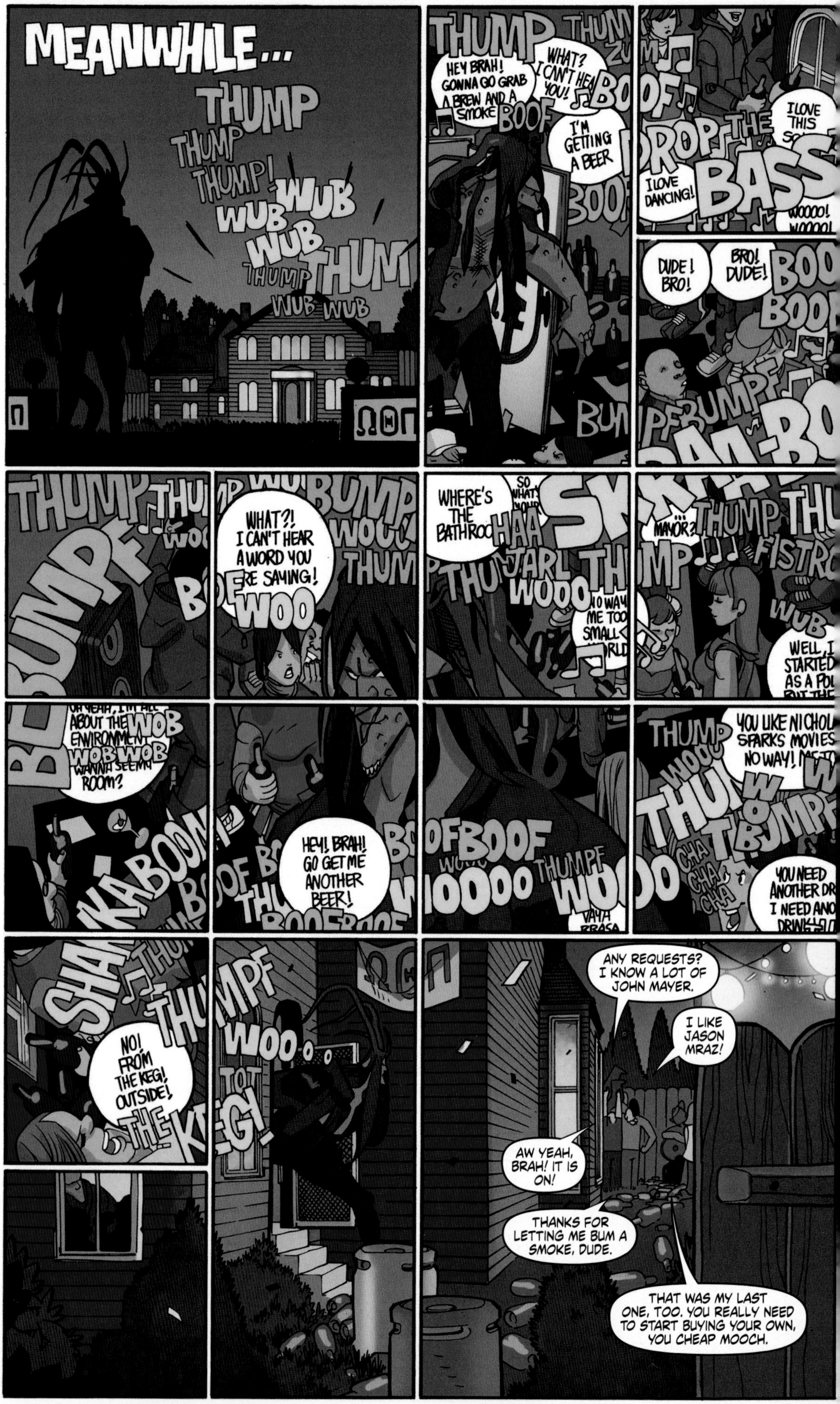
MEANWHILE...
THUMP
THUMP
THUMP!
WUB WUB
WUB
THUMP
WUB WUB
HEY BRAH! GONNA GO GRAB A BREW AND A SMOKE
WHAT? I CAN'T HEA YOU!
BOOF
I'M GETTING A BEER
DROP THE BASS
I LOVE THIS
I LOVE DANCING!
WOOOO! WOOOO!
DUDE! BRO!
BRO! DUDE!
BUMPF BUMPF
THUMP
BUMPF
WHAT?! I CAN'T HEAR A WORD YOU RE SAYING!
WOO
WHERE'S THE BATHROO
HAA
WOOO
NO WAY! ME TOO SMALL
THUMP
FISTRO
WUB
WELL, I STARTED AS A POL
ABOUT THE WOB ENVIRONMEN
WOB WOB
ROOM?
KABOOM
HEY! BRAH! GO GET ME ANOTHER BEER!
BOOFBOOF
WOOOO
THUMPF
WOO
THUMP
YOU LIKE NICHOL SPARKS MOVIES NO WAY!
THU
BUMPF
CHA CHA CHA
YOU NEED ANOTHER DR
I NEED ANO
THUMPF
NO! FROM THE KEG! OUTSIDE!
THE KEG!
THUMPF
WOO
ANY REQUESTS? I KNOW A LOT OF JOHN MAYER.
I LIKE JASON MRAZ!
AW YEAH, BRAH! IT IS ON!
THANKS FOR LETTING ME BUM A SMOKE, DUDE.
THAT WAS MY LAST ONE, TOO. YOU REALLY NEED TO START BUYING YOUR OWN, YOU CHEAP MOOCH.

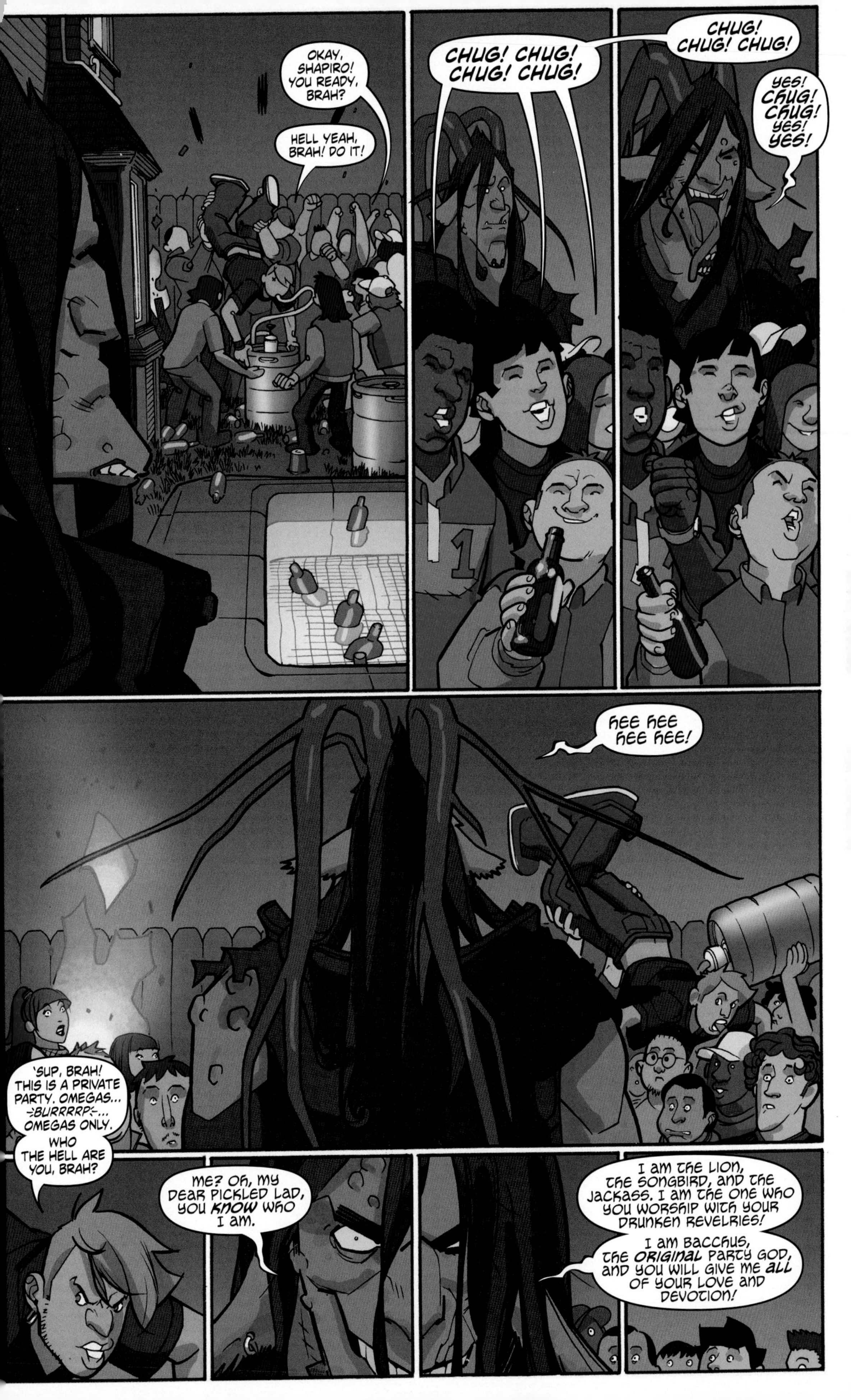
OKAY, SHAPIRO! YOU READY, BRAH?
HELL YEAH, BRAH! DO IT!
CHUG! CHUG! CHUG! CHUG!
CHUG! CHUG! CHUG!
YES! CHUG! CHUG! YES! YES!
HEE HEE HEE HEE!
'SUP, BRAH! THIS IS A PRIVATE PARTY. OMEGAS... -BURRRRP-... OMEGAS ONLY.
WHO THE HELL ARE YOU, BRAH?
ME? OH, MY DEAR PICKLED LAD, YOU KNOW WHO I AM.
I AM THE LION, THE SONGBIRD, AND THE JACKASS. I AM THE ONE WHO YOU WORSHIP WITH YOUR DRUNKEN REVELRIES!
I AM BACCHUS, THE ORIGINAL PARTY GOD, AND YOU WILL GIVE ME ALL OF YOUR LOVE AND DEVOTION!

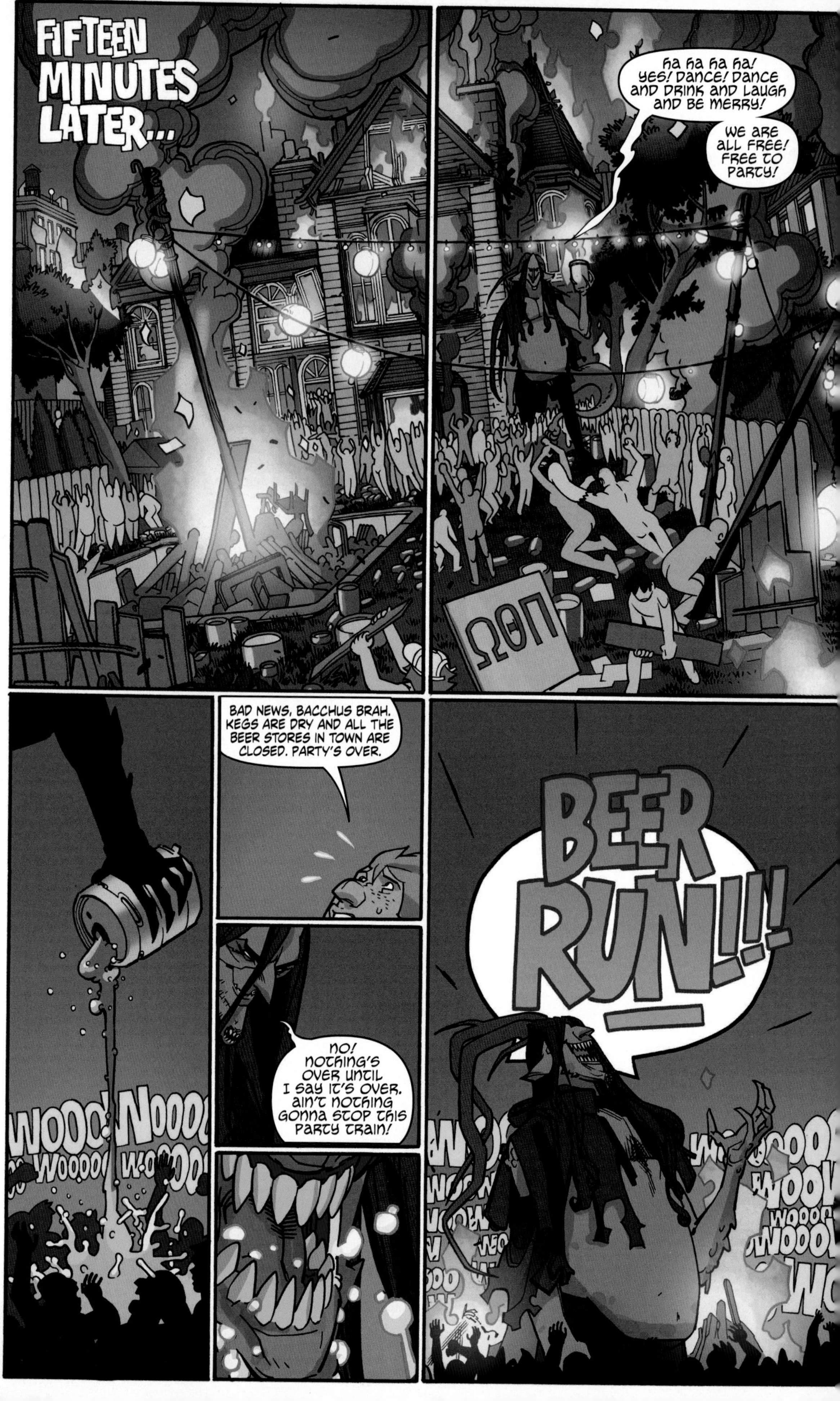
FIFTEEN MINUTES LATER...
HA HA HA HA! YES! DANCE! DANCE AND DRINK AND LAUGH AND BE MERRY!
WE ARE ALL FREE! FREE TO PARTY!
ΩΘΠ
BAD NEWS, BACCHUS BRAH. KEGS ARE DRY AND ALL THE BEER STORES IN TOWN ARE CLOSED. PARTY'S OVER.
NO! NOTHING'S OVER UNTIL I SAY IT'S OVER. AIN'T NOTHING GONNA STOP THIS PARTY TRAIN!
BEER RUN!!!!
WOOO! WOOO!

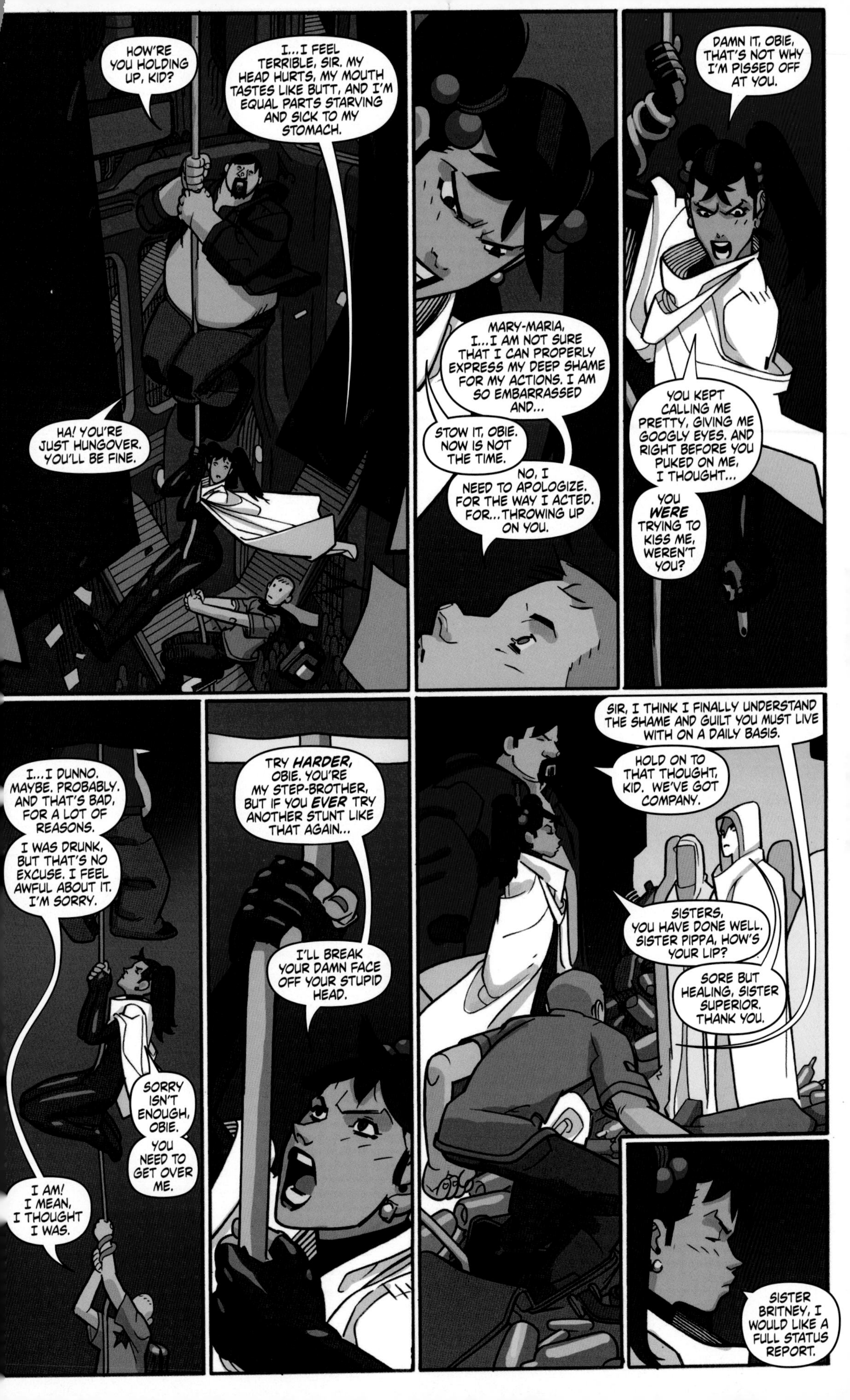
HOW'RE YOU HOLDING UP, KID?
I...I FEEL TERRIBLE, SIR. MY HEAD HURTS, MY MOUTH TASTES LIKE BUTT, AND I'M EQUAL PARTS STARVING AND SICK TO MY STOMACH.
HA! YOU'RE JUST HUNGOVER. YOU'LL BE FINE.
MARY-MARIA, I...I AM NOT SURE THAT I CAN PROPERLY EXPRESS MY DEEP SHAME FOR MY ACTIONS. I AM SO EMBARRASSED AND...
STOW IT, OBIE. NOW IS NOT THE TIME.
NO, I NEED TO APOLOGIZE. FOR THE WAY I ACTED. FOR...THROWING UP ON YOU.
DAMN IT, OBIE, THAT'S NOT WHY I'M PISSED OFF AT YOU.
YOU KEPT CALLING ME PRETTY, GIVING ME GOOGLY EYES. AND RIGHT BEFORE YOU PUKED ON ME, I THOUGHT...
YOU ***WERE*** TRYING TO KISS ME, WEREN'T YOU?
I...I DUNNO. MAYBE. PROBABLY. AND THAT'S BAD, FOR A LOT OF REASONS.
I WAS DRUNK, BUT THAT'S NO EXCUSE. I FEEL AWFUL ABOUT IT. I'M SORRY.
SORRY ISN'T ENOUGH, OBIE.
YOU NEED TO GET OVER ME.
I AM! I MEAN, I THOUGHT I WAS.
TRY ***HARDER,*** OBIE. YOU'RE MY STEP-BROTHER, BUT IF YOU ***EVER*** TRY ANOTHER STUNT LIKE THAT AGAIN...
I'LL BREAK YOUR DAMN FACE OFF YOUR STUPID HEAD.
SIR, I THINK I FINALLY UNDERSTAND THE SHAME AND GUILT YOU MUST LIVE WITH ON A DAILY BASIS.
HOLD ON TO THAT THOUGHT, KID. WE'VE GOT COMPANY.
SISTERS, YOU HAVE DONE WELL. SISTER PIPPA, HOW'S YOUR LIP?
SORE BUT HEALING, SISTER SUPERIOR. THANK YOU.
SISTER BRITNEY, I WOULD LIKE A FULL STATUS REPORT.

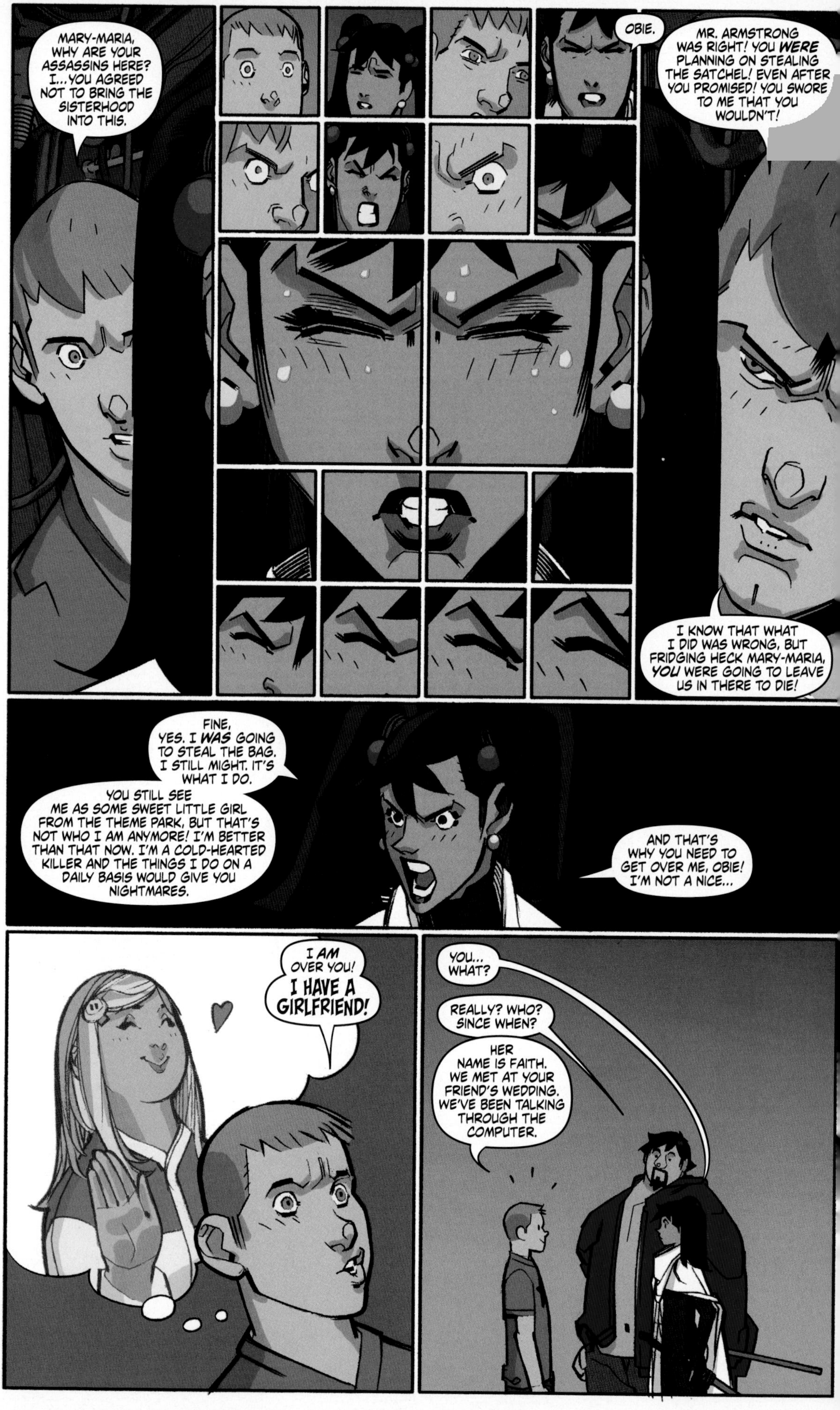

MARY-MARIA, WHY ARE YOUR ASSASSINS HERE? I...YOU AGREED NOT TO BRING THE SISTERHOOD INTO THIS.
OBIE.
MR. ARMSTRONG WAS RIGHT! YOU WERE PLANNING ON STEALING THE SATCHEL! EVEN AFTER YOU PROMISED! YOU SWORE TO ME THAT YOU WOULDN'T!
I KNOW THAT WHAT I DID WAS WRONG, BUT FRIDGING HECK MARY-MARIA, YOU WERE GOING TO LEAVE US IN THERE TO DIE!
FINE, YES. I WAS GOING TO STEAL THE BAG. I STILL MIGHT. IT'S WHAT I DO.
YOU STILL SEE ME AS SOME SWEET LITTLE GIRL FROM THE THEME PARK, BUT THAT'S NOT WHO I AM ANYMORE! I'M BETTER THAN THAT NOW. I'M A COLD-HEARTED KILLER AND THE THINGS I DO ON A DAILY BASIS WOULD GIVE YOU NIGHTMARES.
AND THAT'S WHY YOU NEED TO GET OVER ME, OBIE! I'M NOT A NICE...
I AM OVER YOU! I HAVE A GIRLFRIEND!
YOU... WHAT?
REALLY? WHO? SINCE WHEN?
HER NAME IS FAITH. WE MET AT YOUR FRIEND'S WEDDING. WE'VE BEEN TALKING THROUGH THE COMPUTER.

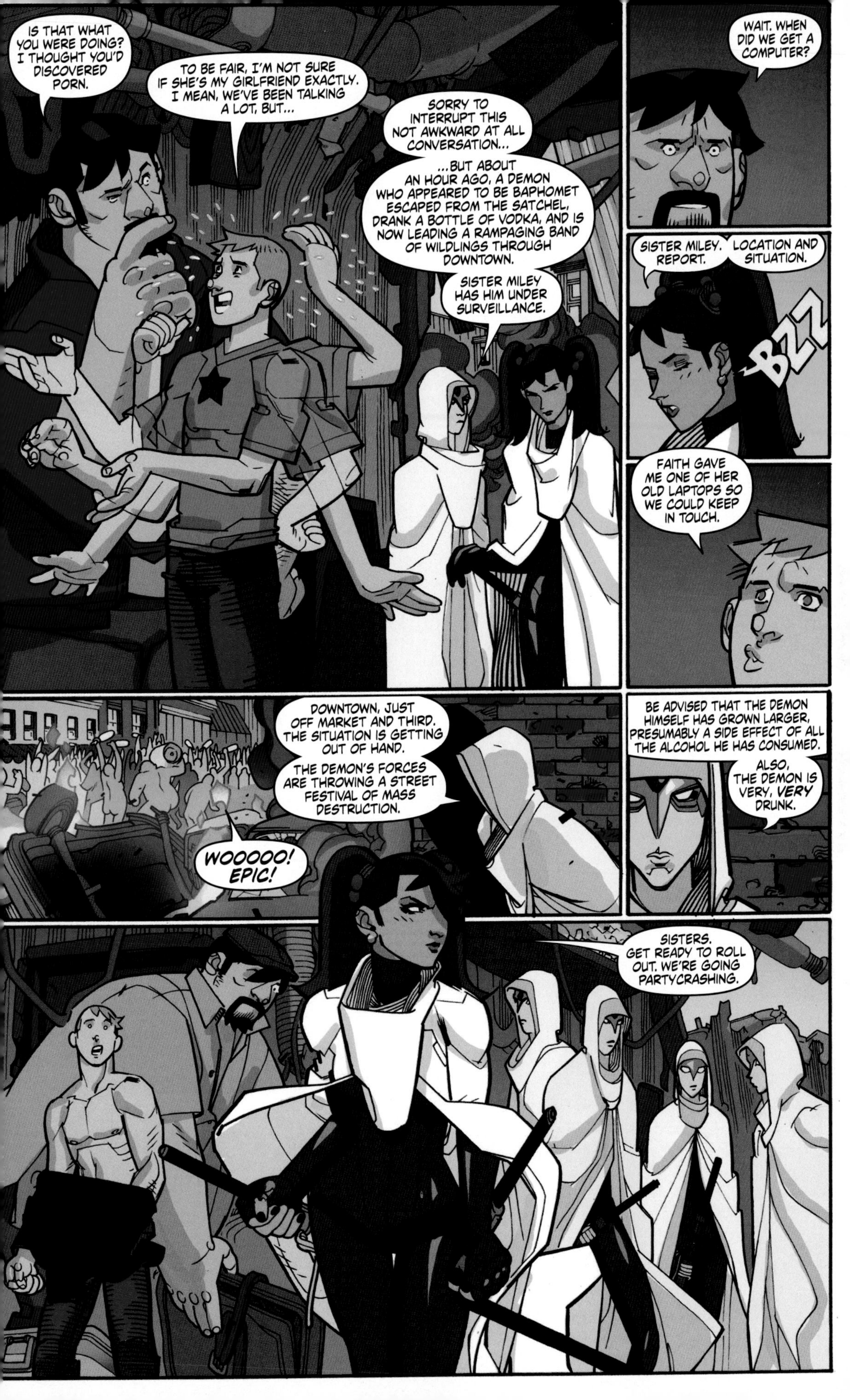
IS THAT WHAT YOU WERE DOING? I THOUGHT YOU'D DISCOVERED PORN.
TO BE FAIR, I'M NOT SURE IF SHE'S MY GIRLFRIEND EXACTLY. I MEAN, WE'VE BEEN TALKING A LOT, BUT...
SORRY TO INTERRUPT THIS NOT AWKWARD AT ALL CONVERSATION...
...BUT ABOUT AN HOUR AGO, A DEMON WHO APPEARED TO BE BAPHOMET ESCAPED FROM THE SATCHEL, DRANK A BOTTLE OF VODKA, AND IS NOW LEADING A RAMPAGING BAND OF WILDLINGS THROUGH DOWNTOWN.
SISTER MILEY HAS HIM UNDER SURVEILLANCE.
WAIT. WHEN DID WE GET A COMPUTER?
SISTER MILEY. REPORT.
LOCATION AND SITUATION.
BZZ
FAITH GAVE ME ONE OF HER OLD LAPTOPS SO WE COULD KEEP IN TOUCH.
DOWNTOWN, JUST OFF MARKET AND THIRD. THE SITUATION IS GETTING OUT OF HAND.
THE DEMON'S FORCES ARE THROWING A STREET FESTIVAL OF MASS DESTRUCTION.
WOOOOO! EPIC!
BE ADVISED THAT THE DEMON HIMSELF HAS GROWN LARGER, PRESUMABLY A SIDE EFFECT OF ALL THE ALCOHOL HE HAS CONSUMED.
ALSO, THE DEMON IS VERY, VERY DRUNK.
SISTERS. GET READY TO ROLL OUT. WE'RE GOING PARTYCRASHING.

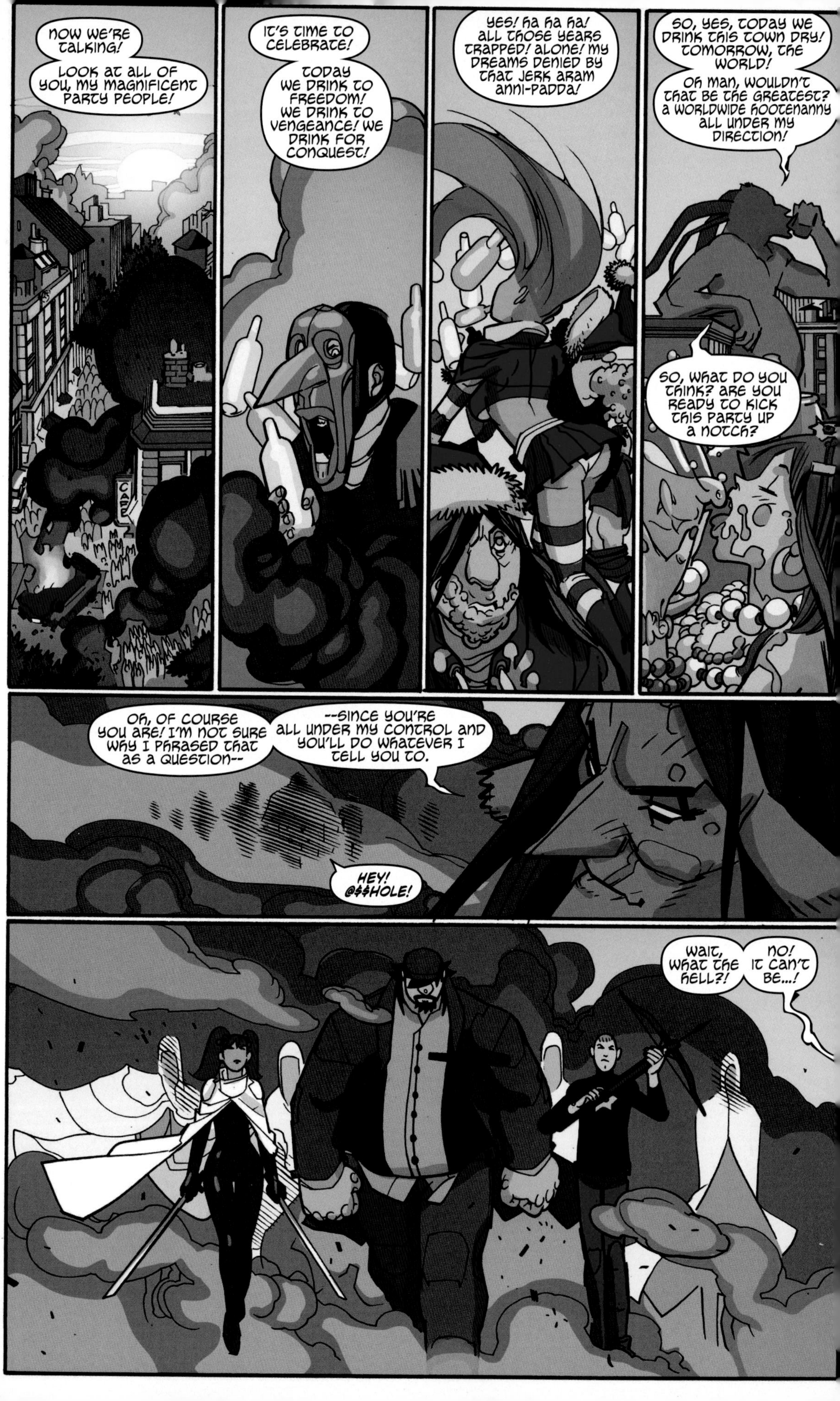
NOW WE'RE TALKING!
LOOK AT ALL OF YOU, MY MAGNIFICENT PARTY PEOPLE!
IT'S TIME TO CELEBRATE!
TODAY WE DRINK TO FREEDOM! WE DRINK TO VENGEANCE! WE DRINK FOR CONQUEST!
YES! HA HA HA! ALL THOSE YEARS TRAPPED! ALONE! MY DREAMS DENIED BY THAT JERK ARAM ANNI-PADDA!
SO, YES, TODAY WE DRINK THIS TOWN DRY! TOMORROW, THE WORLD!
OH MAN, WOULDN'T THAT BE THE GREATEST? A WORLDWIDE HOOTENANNY ALL UNDER MY DIRECTION!
SO, WHAT DO YOU THINK? ARE YOU READY TO KICK THIS PARTY UP A NOTCH?
CAFE
OH, OF COURSE YOU ARE! I'M NOT SURE WHY I PHRASED THAT AS A QUESTION--
--SINCE YOU'RE ALL UNDER MY CONTROL AND YOU'LL DO WHATEVER I TELL YOU TO.
HEY! @$$HOLE!
WAIT, WHAT THE HELL?!
NO! IT CAN'T BE...!

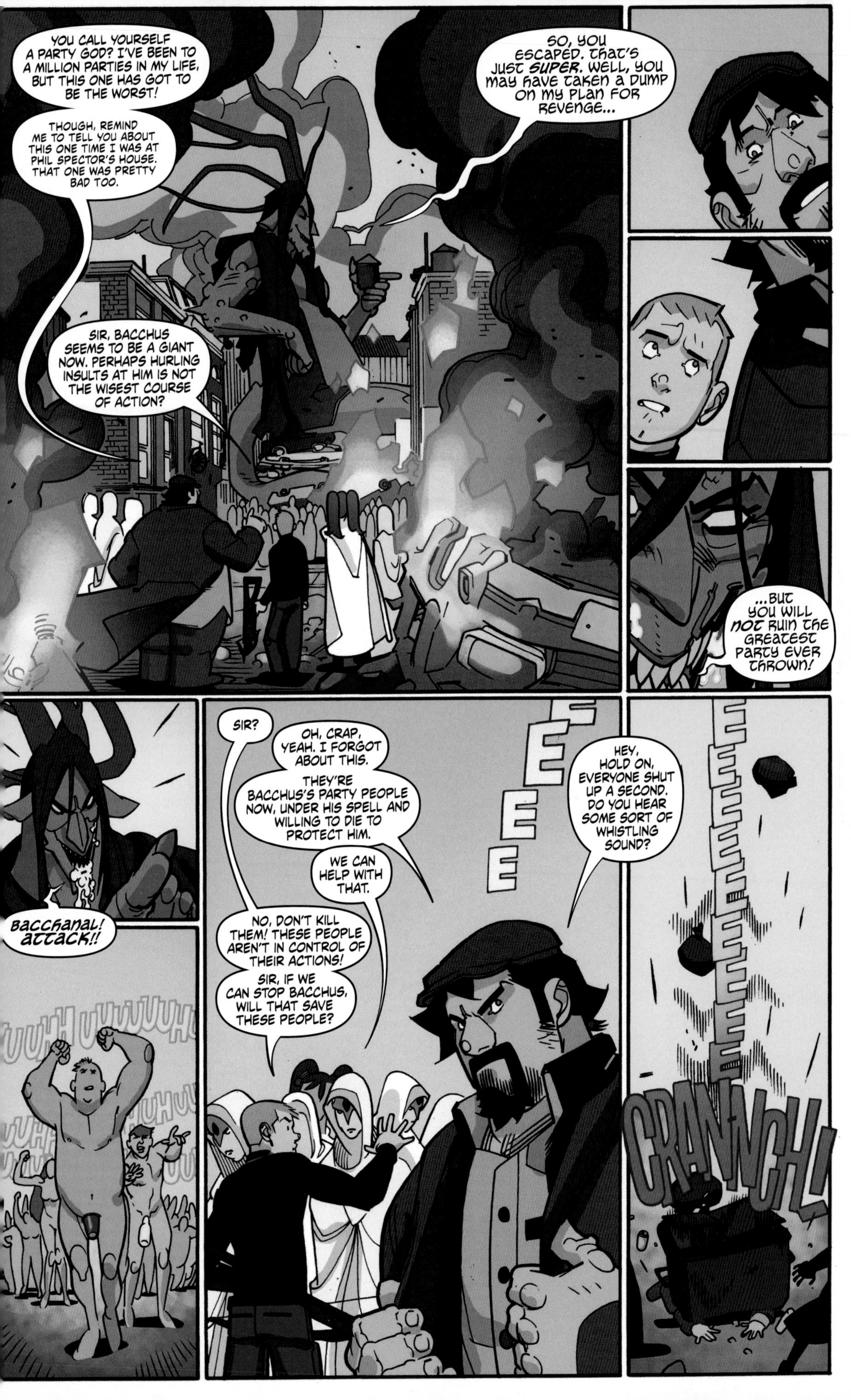
YOU CALL YOURSELF A PARTY GOD? I'VE BEEN TO A MILLION PARTIES IN MY LIFE, BUT THIS ONE HAS GOT TO BE THE WORST!
THOUGH, REMIND ME TO TELL YOU ABOUT THIS ONE TIME I WAS AT PHIL SPECTOR'S HOUSE. THAT ONE WAS PRETTY BAD TOO.
SO, YOU ESCAPED. THAT'S JUST SUPER. WELL, YOU MAY HAVE TAKEN A DUMP ON MY PLAN FOR REVENGE...
SIR, BACCHUS SEEMS TO BE A GIANT NOW. PERHAPS HURLING INSULTS AT HIM IS NOT THE WISEST COURSE OF ACTION?
...BUT YOU WILL NOT RUIN THE GREATEST PARTY EVER THROWN!
BACCHANAL! ATTACK!!
UUHH UUUUUUH
SIR?
OH, CRAP, YEAH. I FORGOT ABOUT THIS.
THEY'RE BACCHUS'S PARTY PEOPLE NOW, UNDER HIS SPELL AND WILLING TO DIE TO PROTECT HIM.
WE CAN HELP WITH THAT.
NO, DON'T KILL THEM! THESE PEOPLE AREN'T IN CONTROL OF THEIR ACTIONS!
SIR, IF WE CAN STOP BACCHUS, WILL THAT SAVE THESE PEOPLE?
EEEEE
HEY, HOLD ON, EVERYONE SHUT UP A SECOND. DO YOU HEAR SOME SORT OF WHISTLING SOUND?
EEEEEEEEEEEEEEEE
CRANNCH!

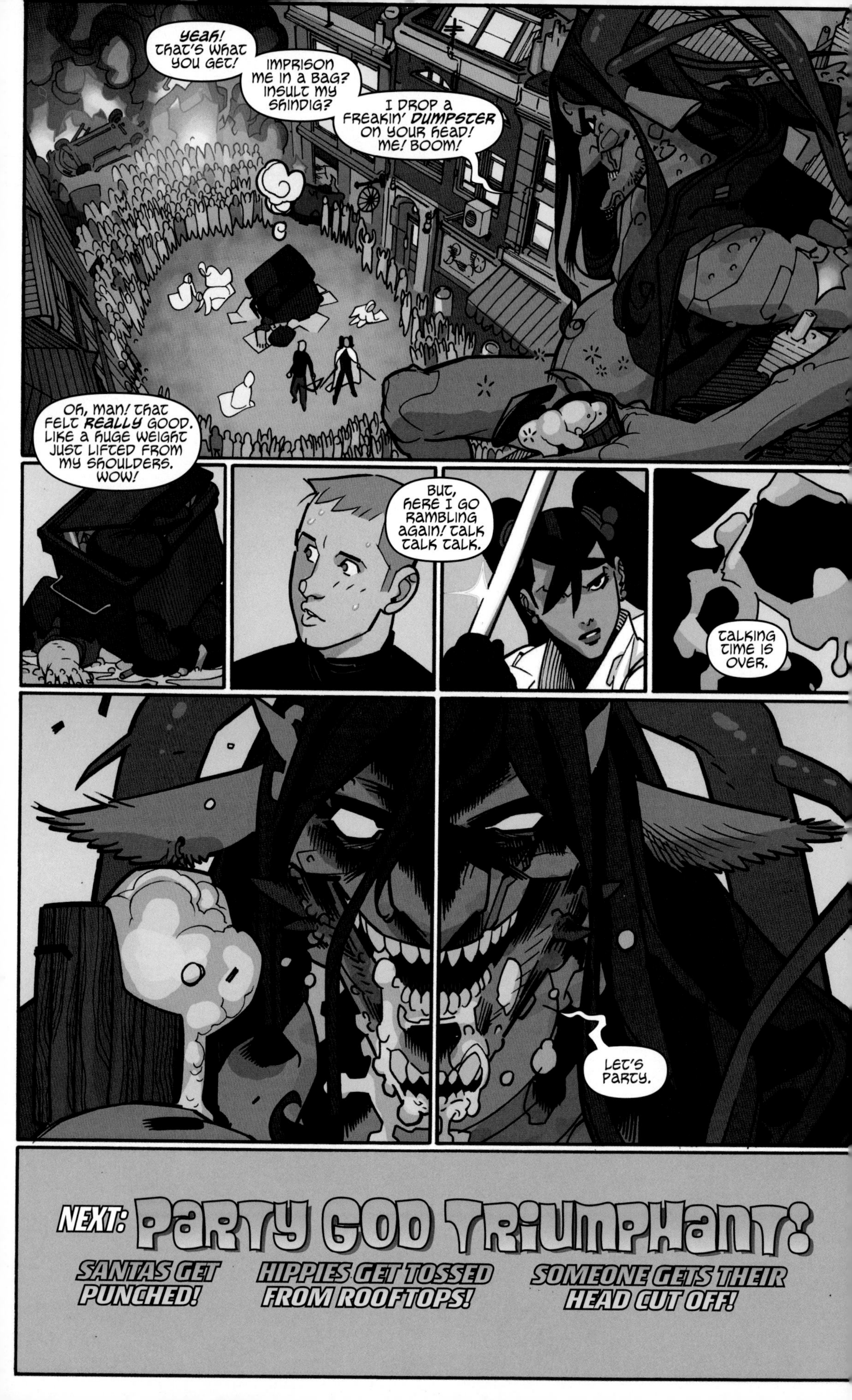
YEAH! THAT'S WHAT YOU GET!
IMPRISON ME IN A BAG? INSULT MY SHINDIG?
I DROP A FREAKIN' DUMPSTER ON YOUR HEAD! ME! BOOM!
OH, MAN! THAT FELT REALLY GOOD. LIKE A HUGE WEIGHT JUST LIFTED FROM MY SHOULDERS. WOW!
BUT, HERE I GO RAMBLING AGAIN! TALK TALK TALK.
TALKING TIME IS OVER.
LET'S PARTY.

NEXT: PARTY GOD TRIUMPHANT!

SANTAS GET PUNCHED! HIPPIES GET TOSSED FROM ROOFTOPS! SOMEONE GETS THEIR HEAD CUT OFF!

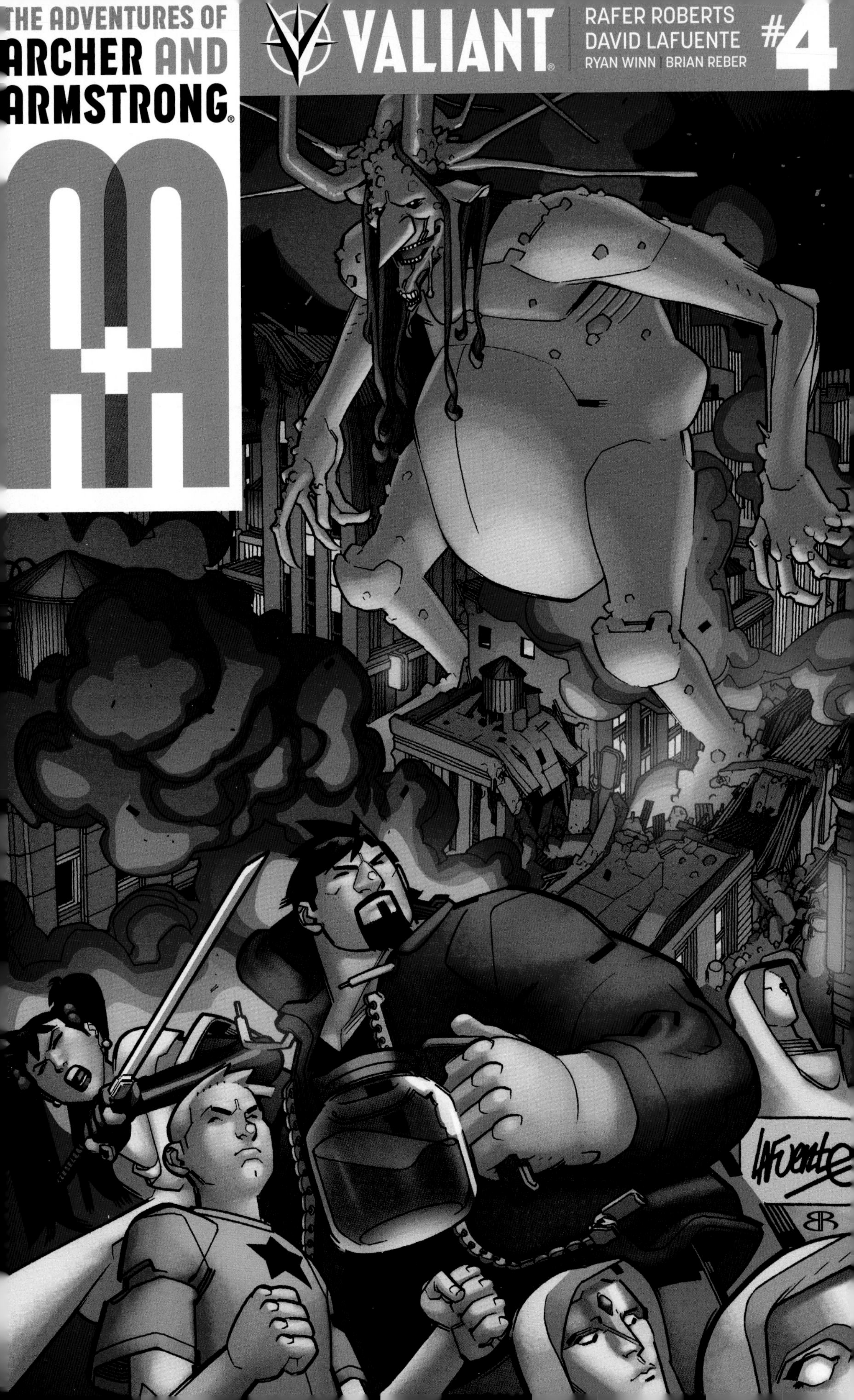
THE ADVENTURES OF
ARCHER AND
ARMSTRONG
VALIANT
RAFER ROBERTS
DAVID LAFUENTE
RYAN WINN | BRIAN REBER
#4
LAFUENTE
BR

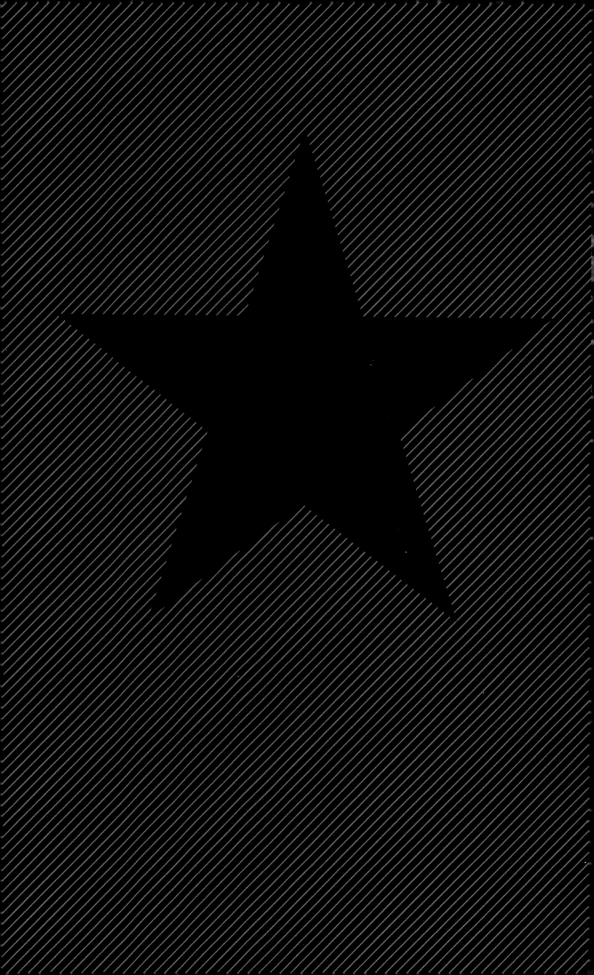

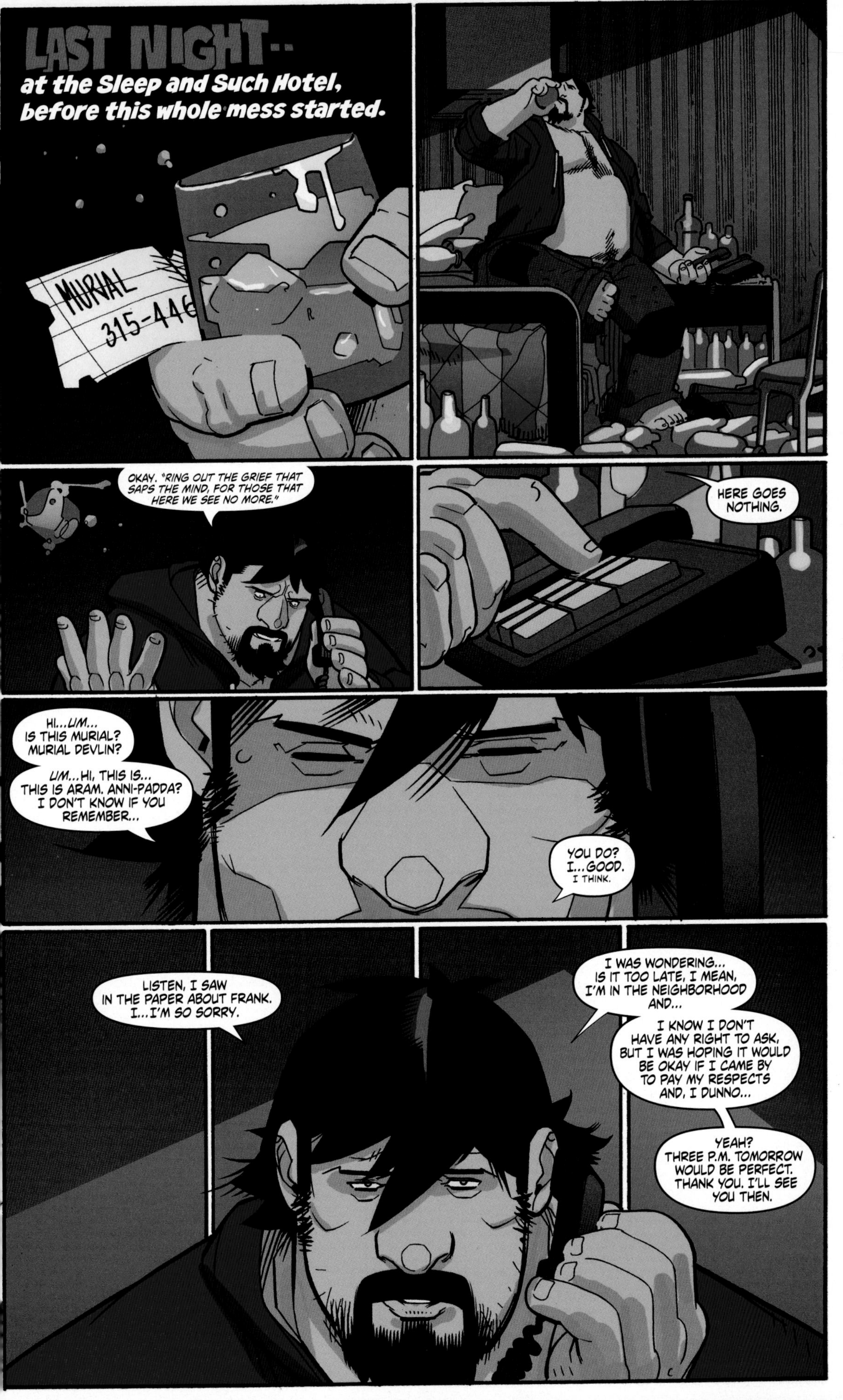
LAST NIGHT..
at the Sleep and Such Hotel, before this whole mess started.
MURIAL
315-446
OKAY. "RING OUT THE GRIEF THAT SAPS THE MIND, FOR THOSE THAT HERE WE SEE NO MORE."
HERE GOES NOTHING.
HI...UM... IS THIS MURIAL? MURIAL DEVLIN?
UM...HI, THIS IS... THIS IS ARAM. ANNI-PADDA? I DON'T KNOW IF YOU REMEMBER...
YOU DO? I...GOOD. I THINK.
LISTEN, I SAW IN THE PAPER ABOUT FRANK. I...I'M SO SORRY.
I WAS WONDERING... IS IT TOO LATE, I MEAN, I'M IN THE NEIGHBORHOOD AND...
I KNOW I DON'T HAVE ANY RIGHT TO ASK, BUT I WAS HOPING IT WOULD BE OKAY IF I CAME BY TO PAY MY RESPECTS AND, I DUNNO...
YEAH? THREE P.M. TOMORROW WOULD BE PERFECT. THANK YOU. I'LL SEE YOU THEN.

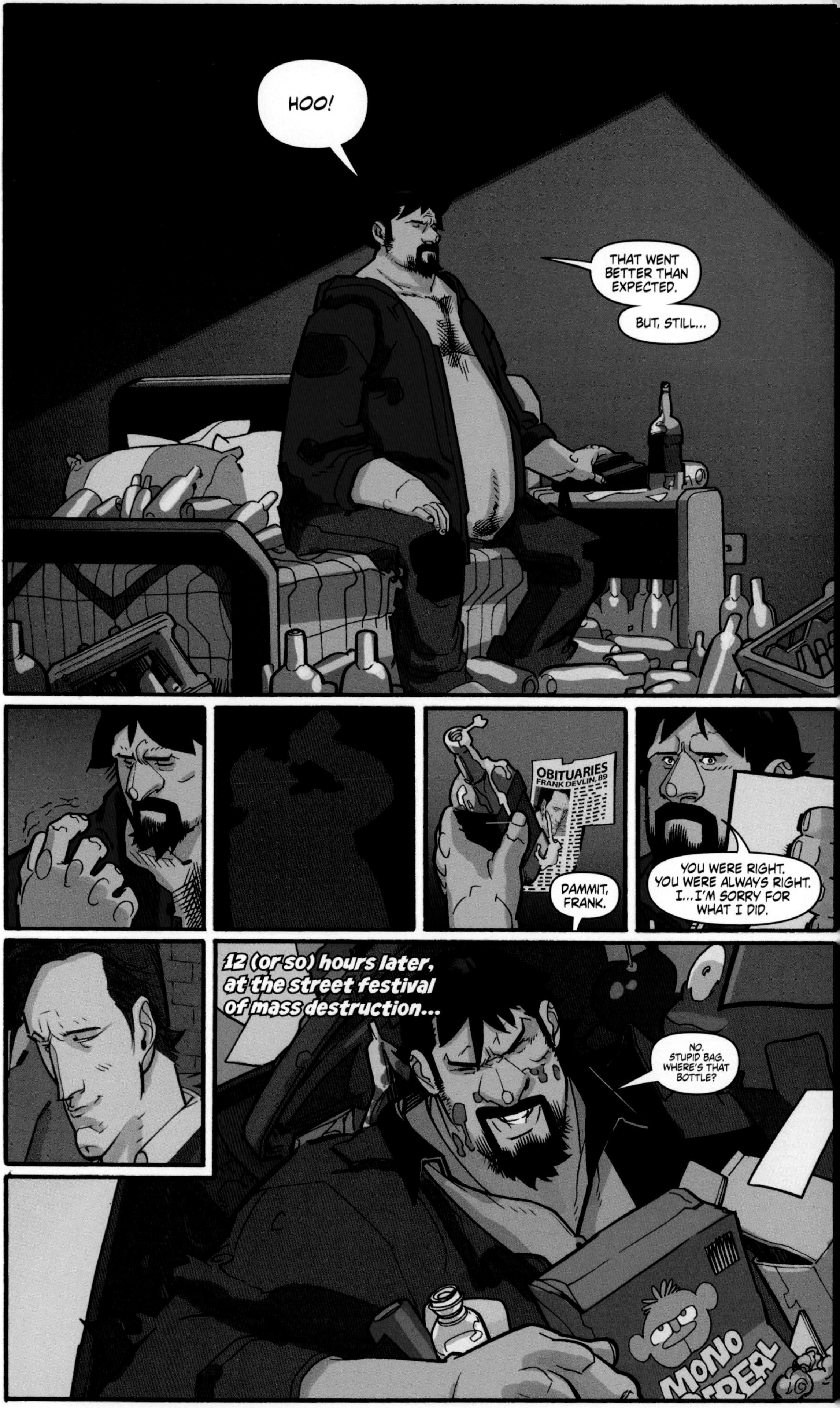
HOO!
THAT WENT BETTER THAN EXPECTED.
BUT, STILL...
OBITUARIES
FRANK DEVLIN, 89
DAMMIT, FRANK.
YOU WERE RIGHT. YOU WERE ALWAYS RIGHT. I...I'M SORRY FOR WHAT I DID.
12 (or so) hours later, at the street festival of mass destruction...
NO. STUPID BAG. WHERE'S THAT BOTTLE?
MONO CEREAL

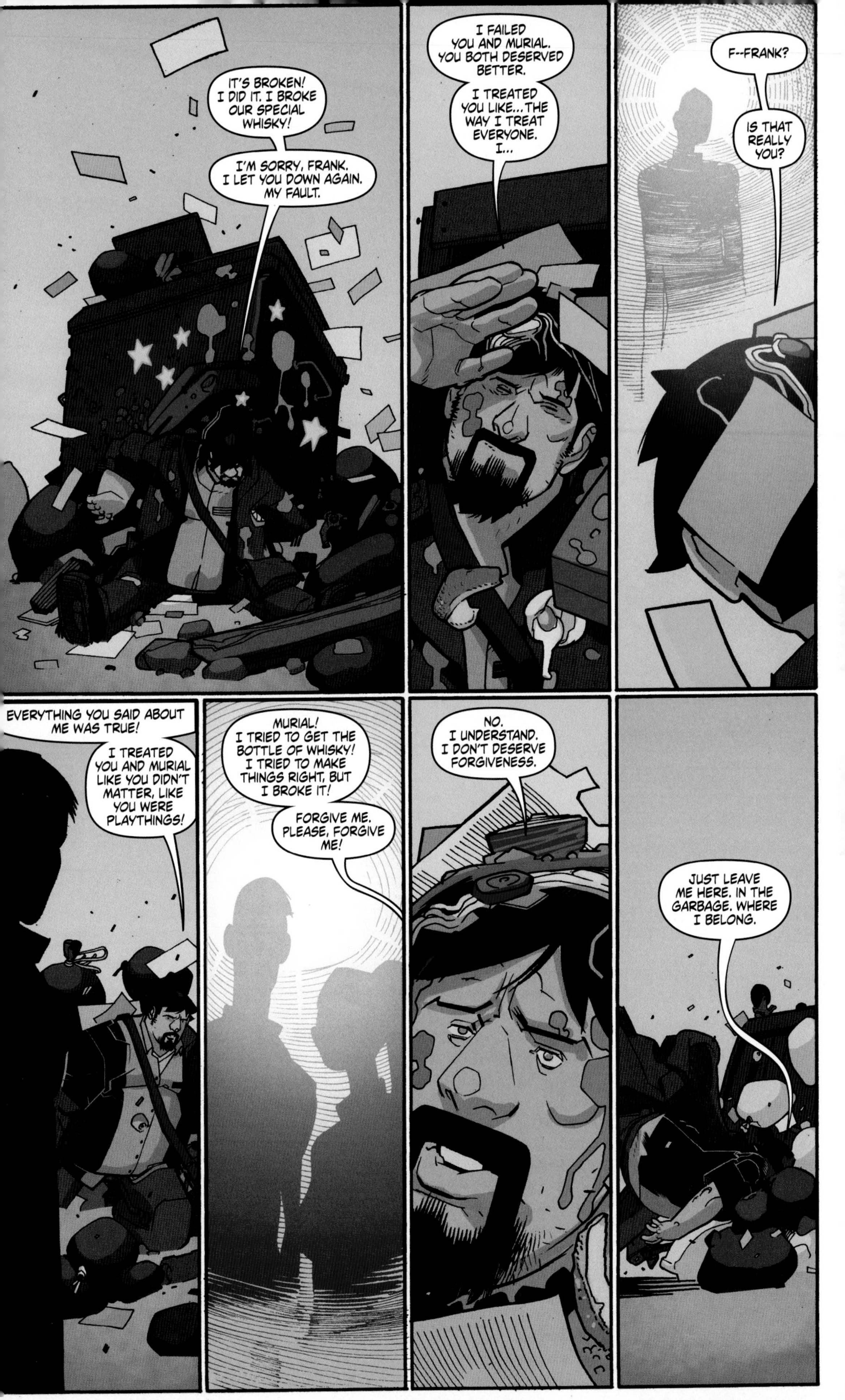
IT'S BROKEN! I DID IT. I BROKE OUR SPECIAL WHISKY!
I'M SORRY, FRANK. I LET YOU DOWN AGAIN. MY FAULT.
I FAILED YOU AND MURIAL. YOU BOTH DESERVED BETTER.
I TREATED YOU LIKE...THE WAY I TREAT EVERYONE. I...
F--FRANK?
IS THAT REALLY YOU?
EVERYTHING YOU SAID ABOUT ME WAS TRUE!
I TREATED YOU AND MURIAL LIKE YOU DIDN'T MATTER, LIKE YOU WERE PLAYTHINGS!
MURIAL! I TRIED TO GET THE BOTTLE OF WHISKY! I TRIED TO MAKE THINGS RIGHT, BUT I BROKE IT!
FORGIVE ME. PLEASE, FORGIVE ME!
NO. I UNDERSTAND. I DON'T DESERVE FORGIVENESS.
JUST LEAVE ME HERE. IN THE GARBAGE. WHERE I BELONG.

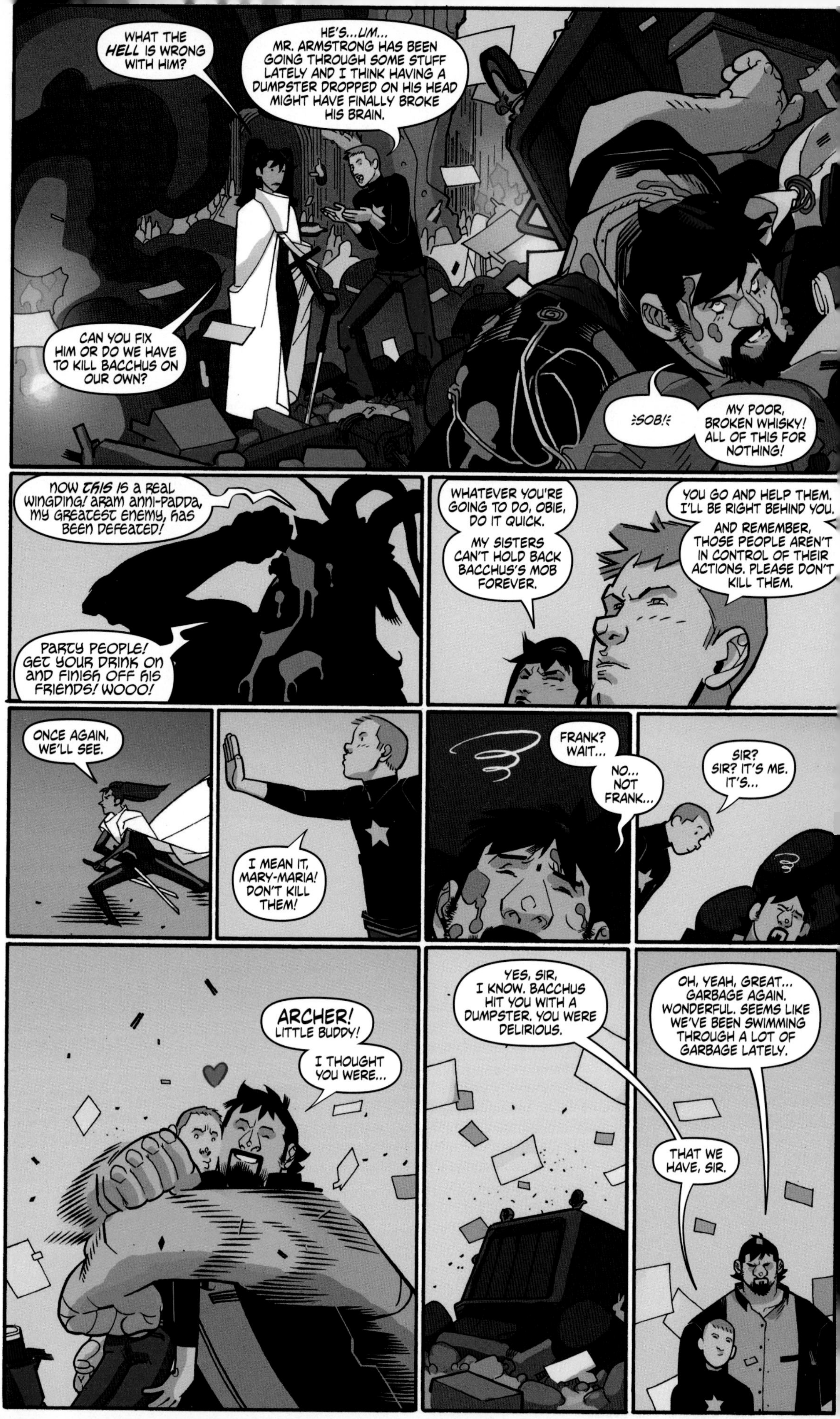
WHAT THE HELL IS WRONG WITH HIM?
HE'S...UM... MR. ARMSTRONG HAS BEEN GOING THROUGH SOME STUFF LATELY AND I THINK HAVING A DUMPSTER DROPPED ON HIS HEAD MIGHT HAVE FINALLY BROKE HIS BRAIN.
CAN YOU FIX HIM OR DO WE HAVE TO KILL BACCHUS ON OUR OWN?
SOB!
MY POOR, BROKEN WHISKY! ALL OF THIS FOR NOTHING!
NOW THIS IS A REAL WINGDING! ARAM ANNI-PADDA, MY GREATEST ENEMY, HAS BEEN DEFEATED!
PARTY PEOPLE! GET YOUR DRINK ON AND FINISH OFF HIS FRIENDS! WOOO!
WHATEVER YOU'RE GOING TO DO, OBIE, DO IT QUICK.
MY SISTERS CAN'T HOLD BACK BACCHUS'S MOB FOREVER.
YOU GO AND HELP THEM. I'LL BE RIGHT BEHIND YOU.
AND REMEMBER, THOSE PEOPLE AREN'T IN CONTROL OF THEIR ACTIONS. PLEASE DON'T KILL THEM.
ONCE AGAIN, WE'LL SEE.
I MEAN IT, MARY-MARIA! DON'T KILL THEM!
FRANK? WAIT...
NO... NOT FRANK...
SIR? SIR? IT'S ME. IT'S...
ARCHER! LITTLE BUDDY!
I THOUGHT YOU WERE...
YES, SIR, I KNOW. BACCHUS HIT YOU WITH A DUMPSTER. YOU WERE DELIRIOUS.
OH, YEAH, GREAT... GARBAGE AGAIN. WONDERFUL. SEEMS LIKE WE'VE BEEN SWIMMING THROUGH A LOT OF GARBAGE LATELY.
THAT WE HAVE, SIR.

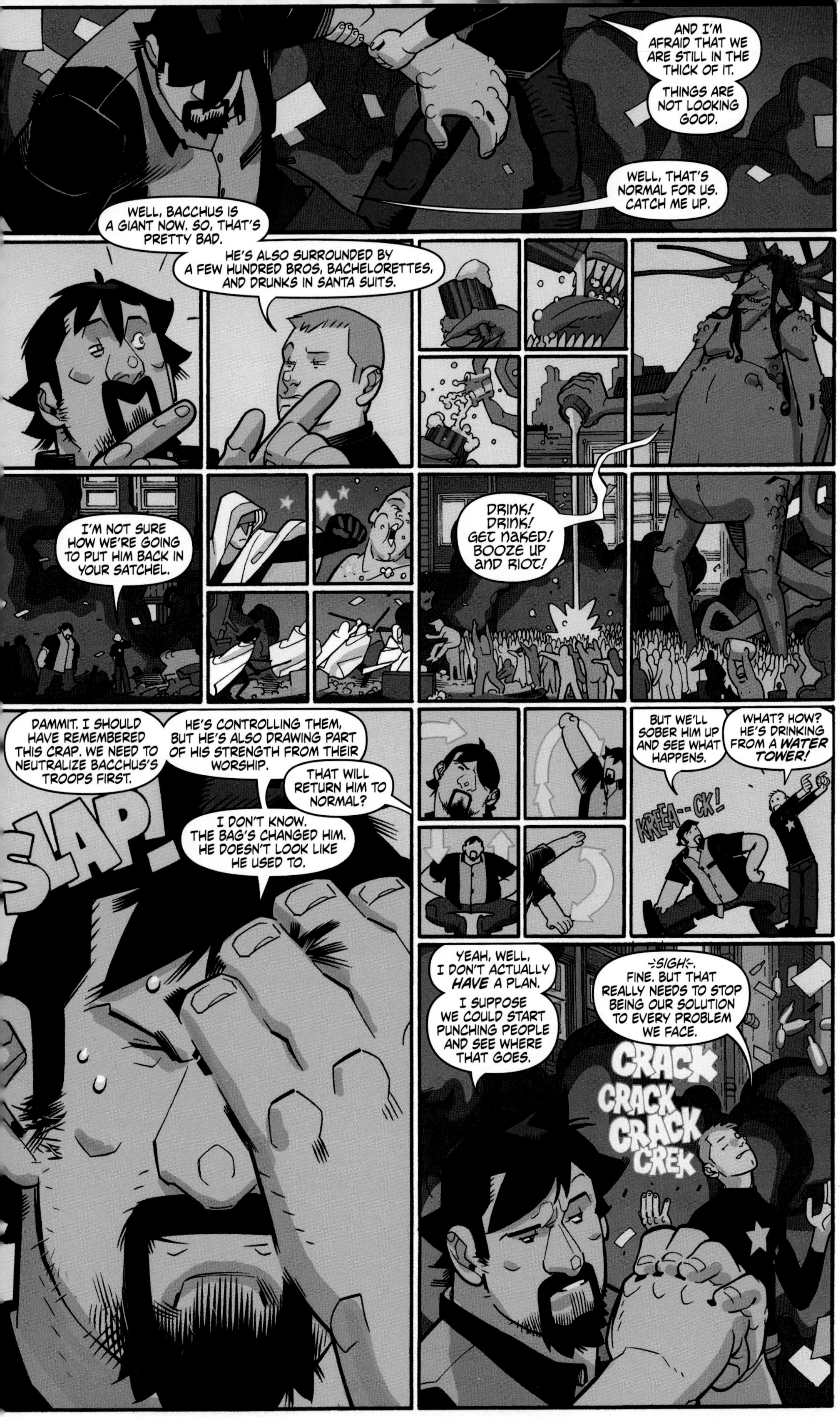
AND I'M AFRAID THAT WE ARE STILL IN THE THICK OF IT.
THINGS ARE NOT LOOKING GOOD.
WELL, THAT'S NORMAL FOR US. CATCH ME UP.
WELL, BACCHUS IS A GIANT NOW. SO, THAT'S PRETTY BAD.
HE'S ALSO SURROUNDED BY A FEW HUNDRED BROS, BACHELORETTES, AND DRUNKS IN SANTA SUITS.
I'M NOT SURE HOW WE'RE GOING TO PUT HIM BACK IN YOUR SATCHEL.
DRINK! DRINK! GET NAKED! BOOZE UP AND RIOT!
DAMMIT. I SHOULD HAVE REMEMBERED THIS CRAP. WE NEED TO NEUTRALIZE BACCHUS'S TROOPS FIRST.
HE'S CONTROLLING THEM, BUT HE'S ALSO DRAWING PART OF HIS STRENGTH FROM THEIR WORSHIP.
THAT WILL RETURN HIM TO NORMAL?
I DON'T KNOW. THE BAG'S CHANGED HIM. HE DOESN'T LOOK LIKE HE USED TO.
SLAP!
BUT WE'LL SOBER HIM UP AND SEE WHAT HAPPENS.
WHAT? HOW? HE'S DRINKING FROM A WATER TOWER!
KREEA--CK!
YEAH, WELL, I DON'T ACTUALLY HAVE A PLAN.
I SUPPOSE WE COULD START PUNCHING PEOPLE AND SEE WHERE THAT GOES.
=SIGH=. FINE. BUT THAT REALLY NEEDS TO STOP BEING OUR SOLUTION TO EVERY PROBLEM WE FACE.
CRACK
CRACK
CRACK
CREK

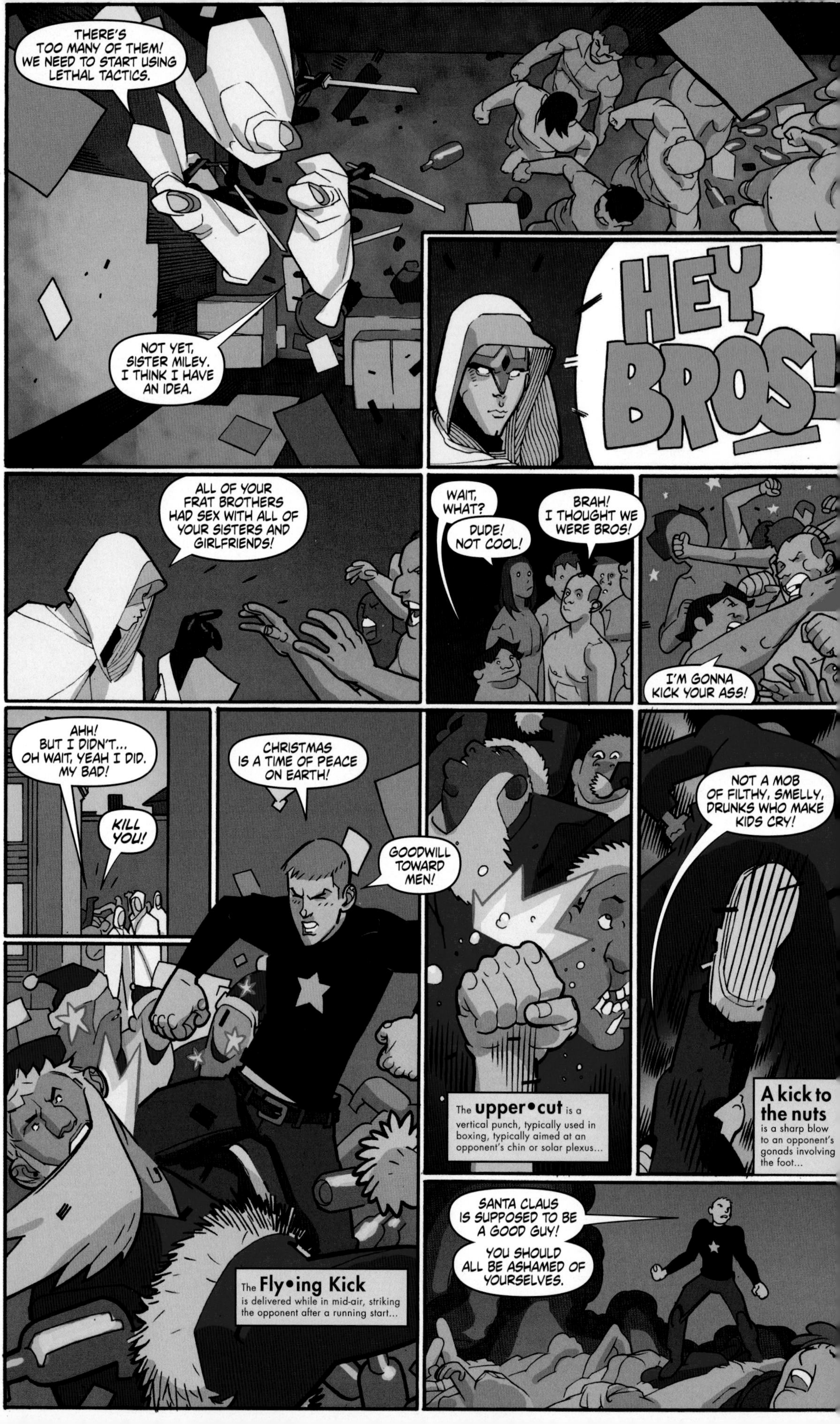
THERE'S TOO MANY OF THEM! WE NEED TO START USING LETHAL TACTICS.
NOT YET, SISTER MILEY. I THINK I HAVE AN IDEA.
HEY, BROS!
ALL OF YOUR FRAT BROTHERS HAD SEX WITH ALL OF YOUR SISTERS AND GIRLFRIENDS!
WAIT, WHAT?
DUDE! NOT COOL!
BRAH! I THOUGHT WE WERE BROS!
I'M GONNA KICK YOUR ASS!
AHH! BUT I DIDN'T... OH WAIT, YEAH I DID. MY BAD!
KILL YOU!
CHRISTMAS IS A TIME OF PEACE ON EARTH!
GOODWILL TOWARD MEN!
NOT A MOB OF FILTHY, SMELLY, DRUNKS WHO MAKE KIDS CRY!
The upper•cut is a vertical punch, typically used in boxing, typically aimed at an opponent's chin or solar plexus...
A kick to the nuts is a sharp blow to an opponent's gonads involving the foot...
The Fly•ing Kick is delivered while in mid-air, striking the opponent after a running start...
SANTA CLAUS IS SUPPOSED TO BE A GOOD GUY!
YOU SHOULD ALL BE ASHAMED OF YOURSELVES.

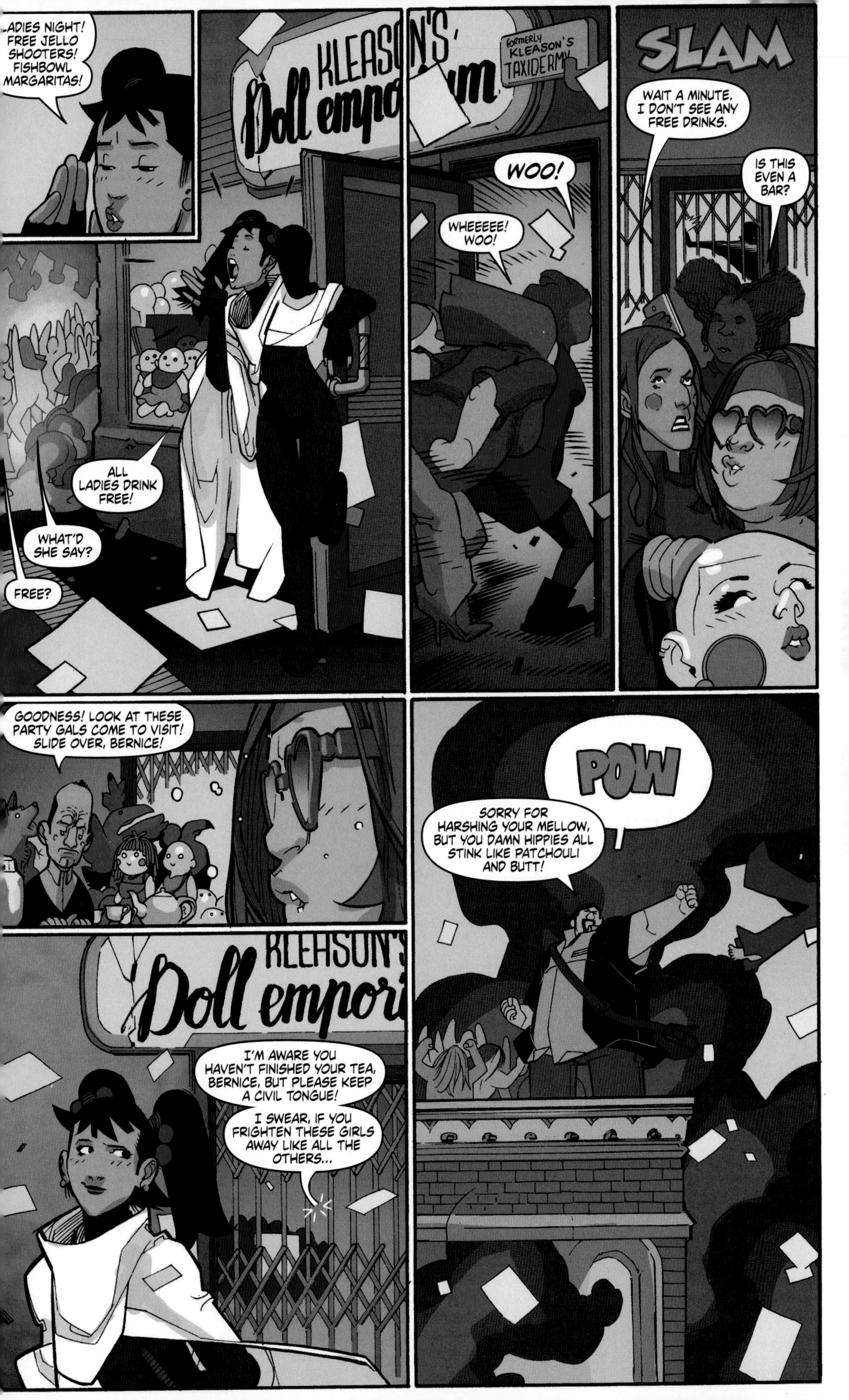
LADIES NIGHT! FREE JELLO SHOOTERS! FISHBOWL MARGARITAS!
KLEASON'S Doll emporium
FORMERLY KLEASON'S TAXIDERMY
ALL LADIES DRINK FREE!
WHAT'D SHE SAY?
FREE?
WOO!
WHEEEEE! WOO!
SLAM
WAIT A MINUTE. I DON'T SEE ANY FREE DRINKS.
IS THIS EVEN A BAR?
GOODNESS! LOOK AT THESE PARTY GALS COME TO VISIT! SLIDE OVER, BERNICE!
KLEASON'S Doll empori
I'M AWARE YOU HAVEN'T FINISHED YOUR TEA, BERNICE, BUT PLEASE KEEP A CIVIL TONGUE!
I SWEAR, IF YOU FRIGHTEN THESE GIRLS AWAY LIKE ALL THE OTHERS...
POW
SORRY FOR HARSHING YOUR MELLOW, BUT YOU DAMN HIPPIES ALL STINK LIKE PATCHOULI AND BUTT!

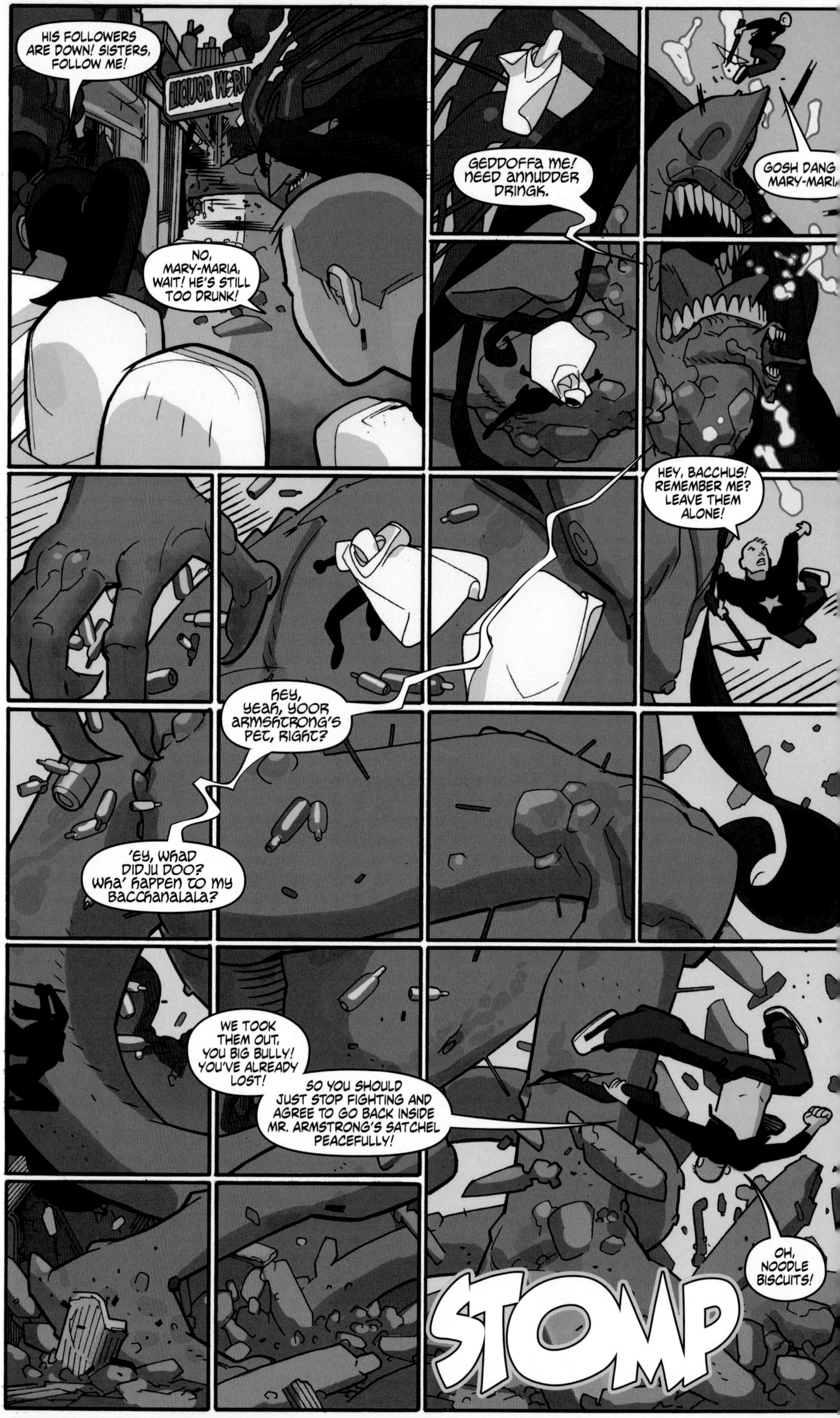
HIS FOLLOWERS ARE DOWN! SISTERS, FOLLOW ME!
LIQUOR WORLD
NO, MARY-MARIA, WAIT! HE'S STILL TOO DRUNK!
GEDDOFFA ME! NEED ANNUDDER DRINGK.
GOSH DANG MARY-MARIA
HEY, BACCHUS! REMEMBER ME? LEAVE THEM ALONE!
HEY, YEAH, YOOR ARMSHTRONG'S PET, RIGHT?
'EY, WHAD DIDJU DOO? WHA' HAPPEN TO MY BACCHANALALA?
WE TOOK THEM OUT, YOU BIG BULLY! YOU'VE ALREADY LOST!
SO YOU SHOULD JUST STOP FIGHTING AND AGREE TO GO BACK INSIDE MR. ARMSTRONG'S SATCHEL PEACEFULLY!
OH, NOODLE BISCUITS!
STOMP

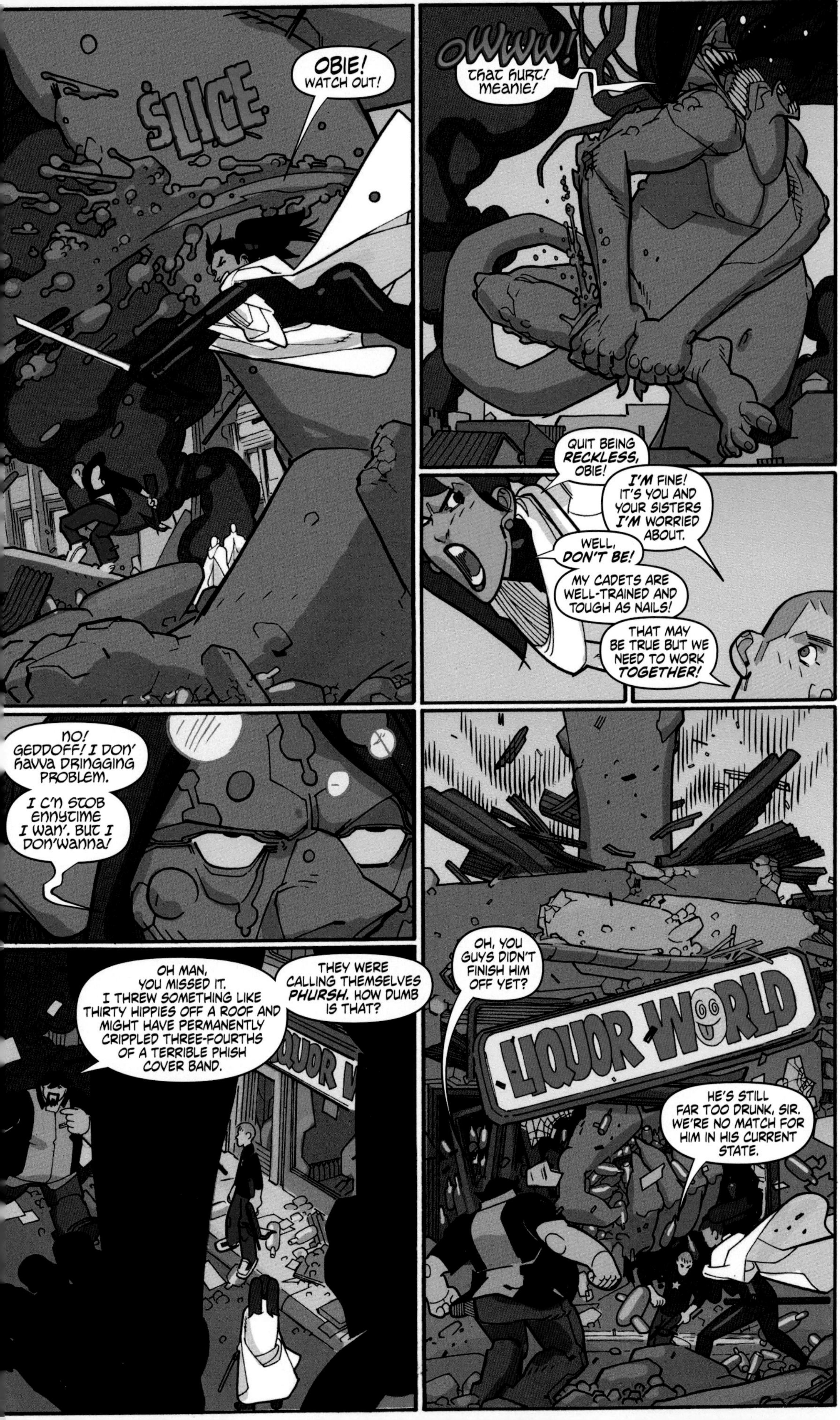
SLICE
OBIE! WATCH OUT!
OWWW!
THAT HURT! MEANIE!
QUIT BEING RECKLESS, OBIE!
I'M FINE! IT'S YOU AND YOUR SISTERS I'M WORRIED ABOUT.
WELL, DON'T BE!
MY CADETS ARE WELL-TRAINED AND TOUGH AS NAILS!
THAT MAY BE TRUE BUT WE NEED TO WORK TOGETHER!
NO! GEDDOFF! I DON' HAVVA DRINGGING PROBLEM.
I C'N STOB ENNYTIME I WAN'. BUT I DON'WANNA!
OH MAN, YOU MISSED IT. I THREW SOMETHING LIKE THIRTY HIPPIES OFF A ROOF AND MIGHT HAVE PERMANENTLY CRIPPLED THREE-FOURTHS OF A TERRIBLE PHISH COVER BAND.
THEY WERE CALLING THEMSELVES PHURSH. HOW DUMB IS THAT?
OH, YOU GUYS DIDN'T FINISH HIM OFF YET?
LIQUOR WORLD
HE'S STILL FAR TOO DRUNK, SIR. WE'RE NO MATCH FOR HIM IN HIS CURRENT STATE.

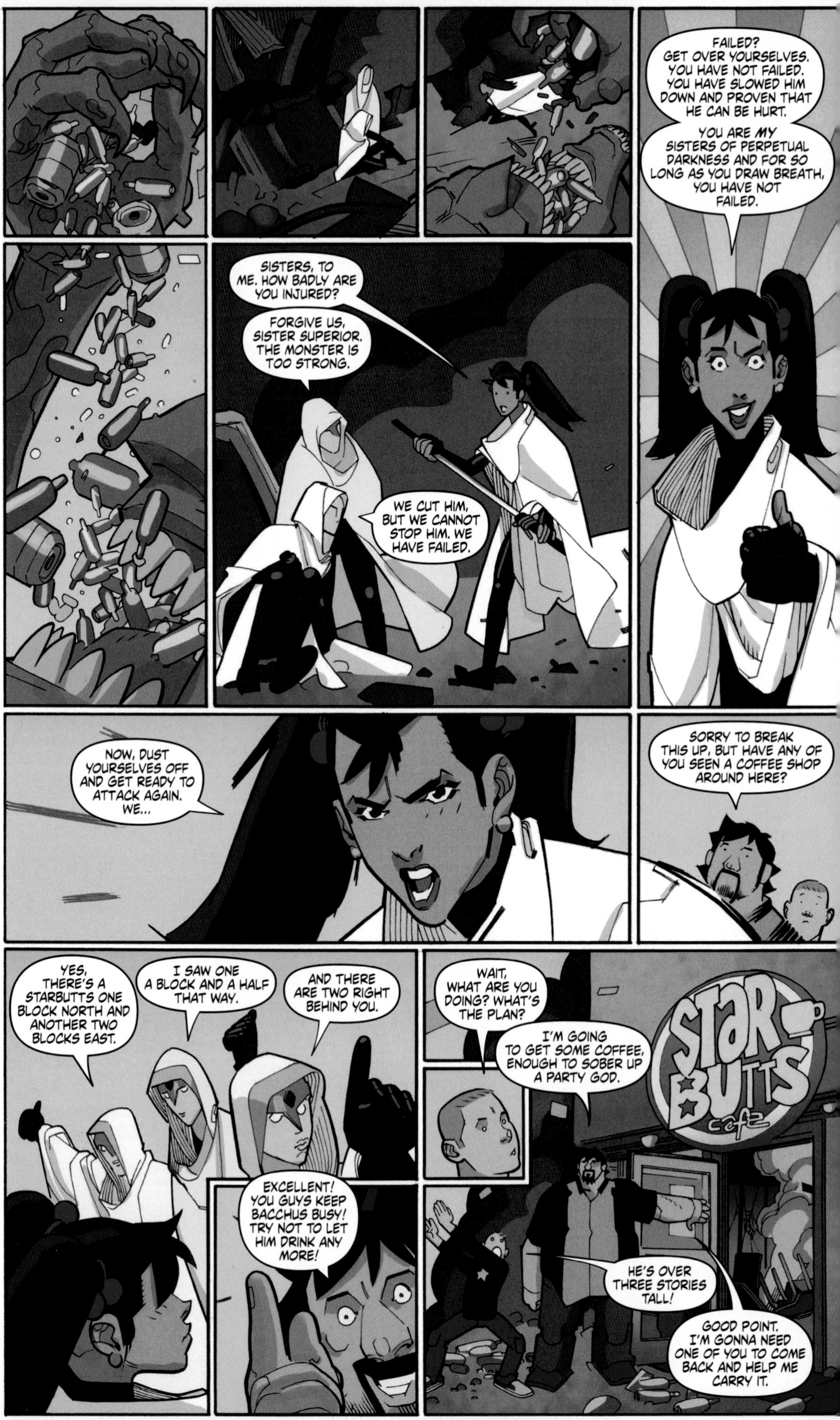
FAILED? GET OVER YOURSELVES. YOU HAVE NOT FAILED. YOU HAVE SLOWED HIM DOWN AND PROVEN THAT HE CAN BE HURT.
YOU ARE MY SISTERS OF PERPETUAL DARKNESS AND FOR SO LONG AS YOU DRAW BREATH, YOU HAVE NOT FAILED.
SISTERS, TO ME. HOW BADLY ARE YOU INJURED?
FORGIVE US, SISTER SUPERIOR. THE MONSTER IS TOO STRONG.
WE CUT HIM, BUT WE CANNOT STOP HIM. WE HAVE FAILED.
NOW, DUST YOURSELVES OFF AND GET READY TO ATTACK AGAIN. WE...
SORRY TO BREAK THIS UP, BUT HAVE ANY OF YOU SEEN A COFFEE SHOP AROUND HERE?
YES, THERE'S A STARBUTTS ONE BLOCK NORTH AND ANOTHER TWO BLOCKS EAST.
I SAW ONE A BLOCK AND A HALF THAT WAY.
AND THERE ARE TWO RIGHT BEHIND YOU.
EXCELLENT! YOU GUYS KEEP BACCHUS BUSY! TRY NOT TO LET HIM DRINK ANY MORE!
WAIT, WHAT ARE YOU DOING? WHAT'S THE PLAN?
I'M GOING TO GET SOME COFFEE, ENOUGH TO SOBER UP A PARTY GOD.
STAR-BUTTS cafe
HE'S OVER THREE STORIES TALL!
GOOD POINT. I'M GONNA NEED ONE OF YOU TO COME BACK AND HELP ME CARRY IT.

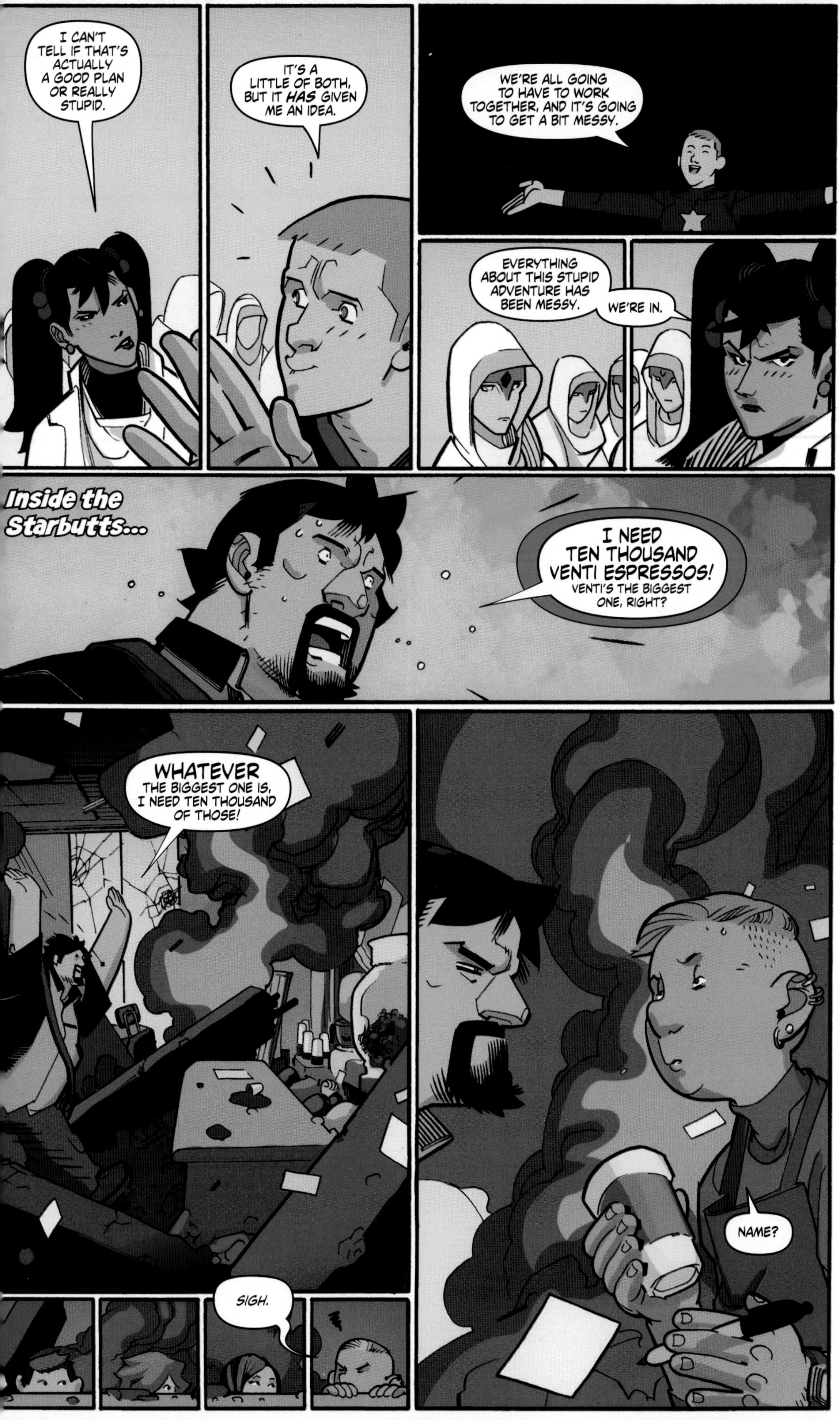
I CAN'T TELL IF THAT'S ACTUALLY A GOOD PLAN OR REALLY STUPID.
IT'S A LITTLE OF BOTH, BUT IT HAS GIVEN ME AN IDEA.
WE'RE ALL GOING TO HAVE TO WORK TOGETHER, AND IT'S GOING TO GET A BIT MESSY.
EVERYTHING ABOUT THIS STUPID ADVENTURE HAS BEEN MESSY.
WE'RE IN.
Inside the Starbutts...
I NEED TEN THOUSAND VENTI ESPRESSOS! VENTI'S THE BIGGEST ONE, RIGHT?
WHATEVER THE BIGGEST ONE IS, I NEED TEN THOUSAND OF THOSE!
NAME?
SIGH.

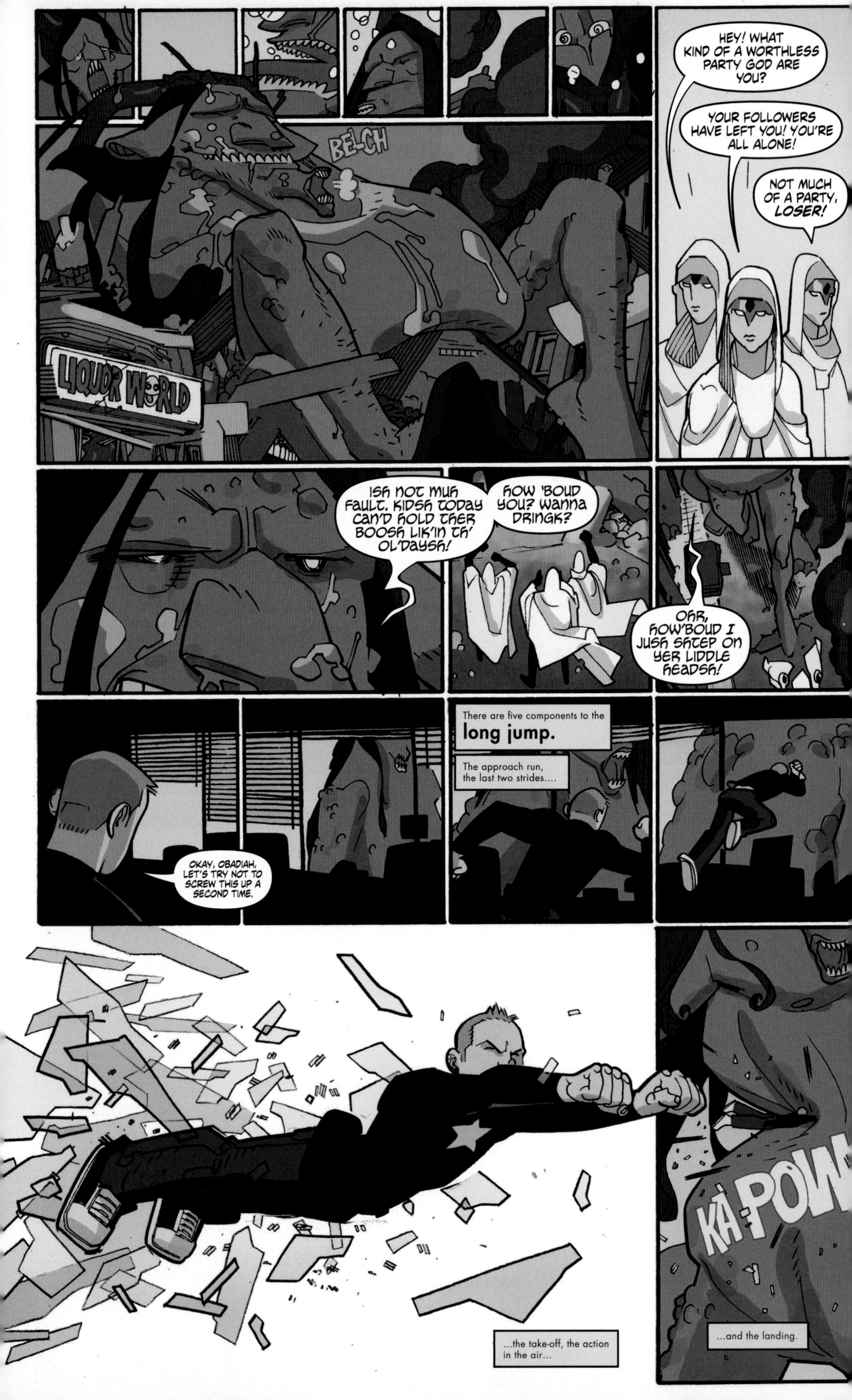
BELCH
LIQUOR WORLD
HEY! WHAT KIND OF A WORTHLESS PARTY GOD ARE YOU?
YOUR FOLLOWERS HAVE LEFT YOU! YOU'RE ALL ALONE!
NOT MUCH OF A PARTY, LOSER!
ISH NOT MUH FAULT. KIDSH TODAY CAN'D HOLD THER BOOSH LIK'IN TH' OL'DAYSH!
HOW 'BOUD YOU? WANNA DRINGK?
OHR, HOW'BOUD I JUSH SHTEP ON YER LIDDLE HEADSH!
OKAY, OBADIAH, LET'S TRY NOT TO SCREW THIS UP A SECOND TIME.
There are five components to the long jump.
The approach run, the last two strides....
KA-POW
...the take-off, the action in the air...
...and the landing.

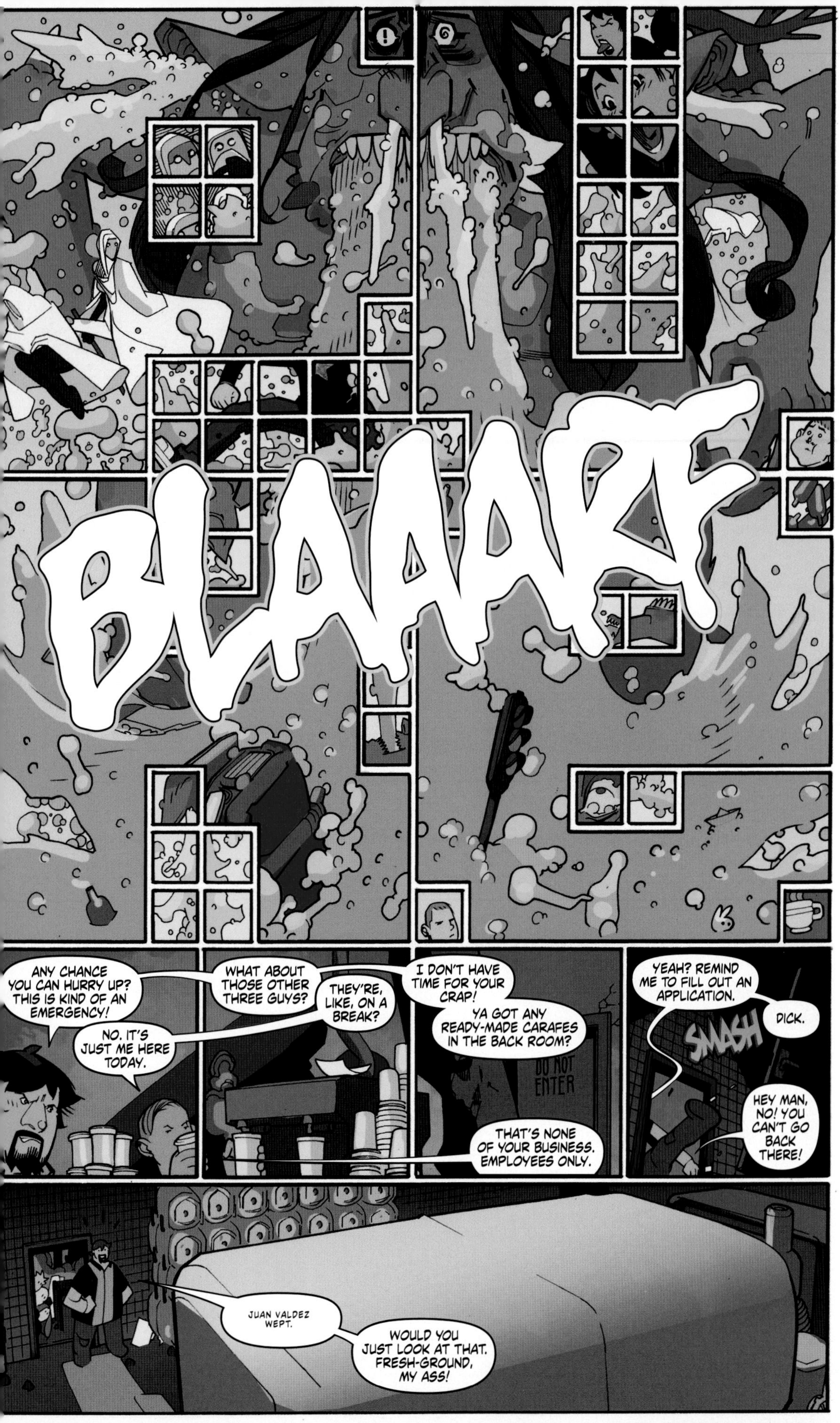
BLAAARF
ANY CHANCE YOU CAN HURRY UP? THIS IS KIND OF AN EMERGENCY!
NO. IT'S JUST ME HERE TODAY.
WHAT ABOUT THOSE OTHER THREE GUYS?
THEY'RE, LIKE, ON A BREAK?
I DON'T HAVE TIME FOR YOUR CRAP!
YA GOT ANY READY-MADE CARAFES IN THE BACK ROOM?
DO NOT ENTER
THAT'S NONE OF YOUR BUSINESS. EMPLOYEES ONLY.
YEAH? REMIND ME TO FILL OUT AN APPLICATION.
SMASH
DICK.
HEY MAN, NO! YOU CAN'T GO BACK THERE!
JUAN VALDEZ WEPT.
WOULD YOU JUST LOOK AT THAT. FRESH-GROUND, MY ASS!

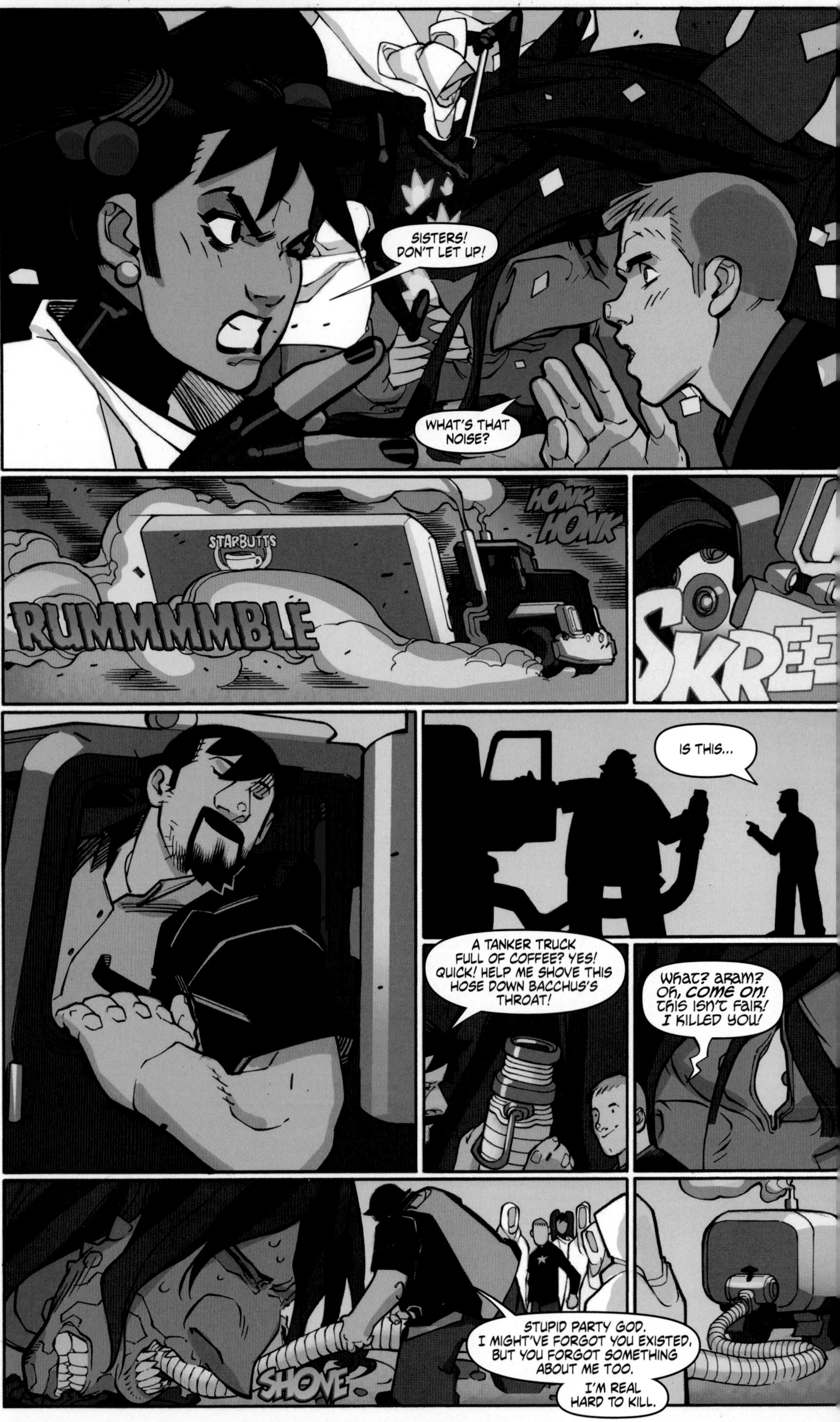

SISTERS! DON'T LET UP!
WHAT'S THAT NOISE?
HONK HONK
STARBUTTS
RUMMMMMBLE
SKREE
IS THIS...
A TANKER TRUCK FULL OF COFFEE? YES! QUICK! HELP ME SHOVE THIS HOSE DOWN BACCHUS'S THROAT!
WHAT? ARAM? OH, COME ON! THIS ISN'T FAIR! I KILLED YOU!
SHOVE
STUPID PARTY GOD. I MIGHT'VE FORGOT YOU EXISTED, BUT YOU FORGOT SOMETHING ABOUT ME TOO.
I'M REAL HARD TO KILL.

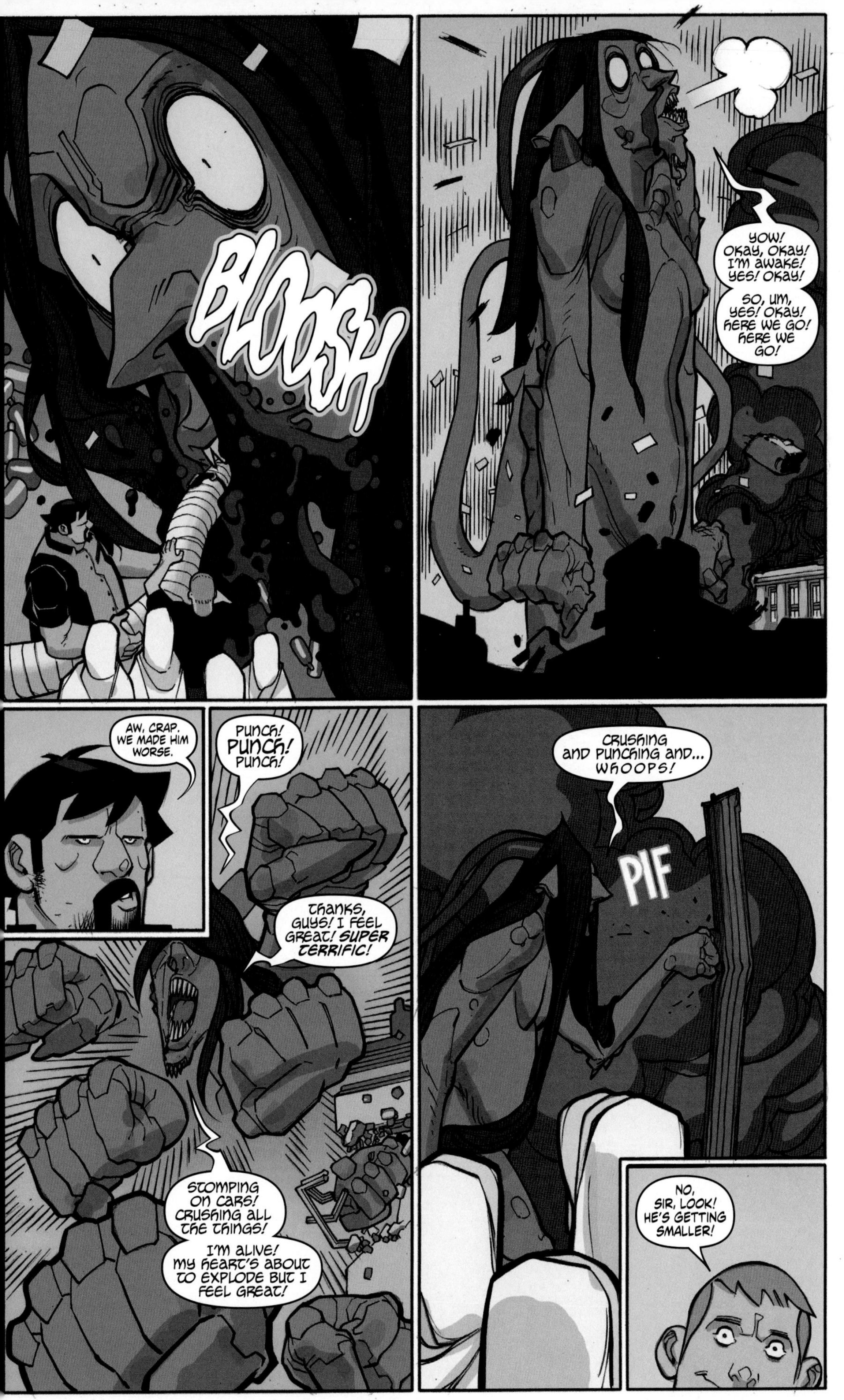
BLOOSH
YOW! OKAY, OKAY! I'M AWAKE! YES! OKAY!
SO, UM, YES! OKAY! HERE WE GO! HERE WE GO!
AW, CRAP. WE MADE HIM WORSE.
PUNCH! PUNCH! PUNCH!
THANKS, GUYS! I FEEL GREAT! SUPER TERRIFIC!
STOMPING ON CARS! CRUSHING ALL THE THINGS!
I'M ALIVE! MY HEART'S ABOUT TO EXPLODE BUT I FEEL GREAT!
CRUSHING AND PUNCHING AND... WHOOPS!
PIF
NO, SIR, LOOK! HE'S GETTING SMALLER!

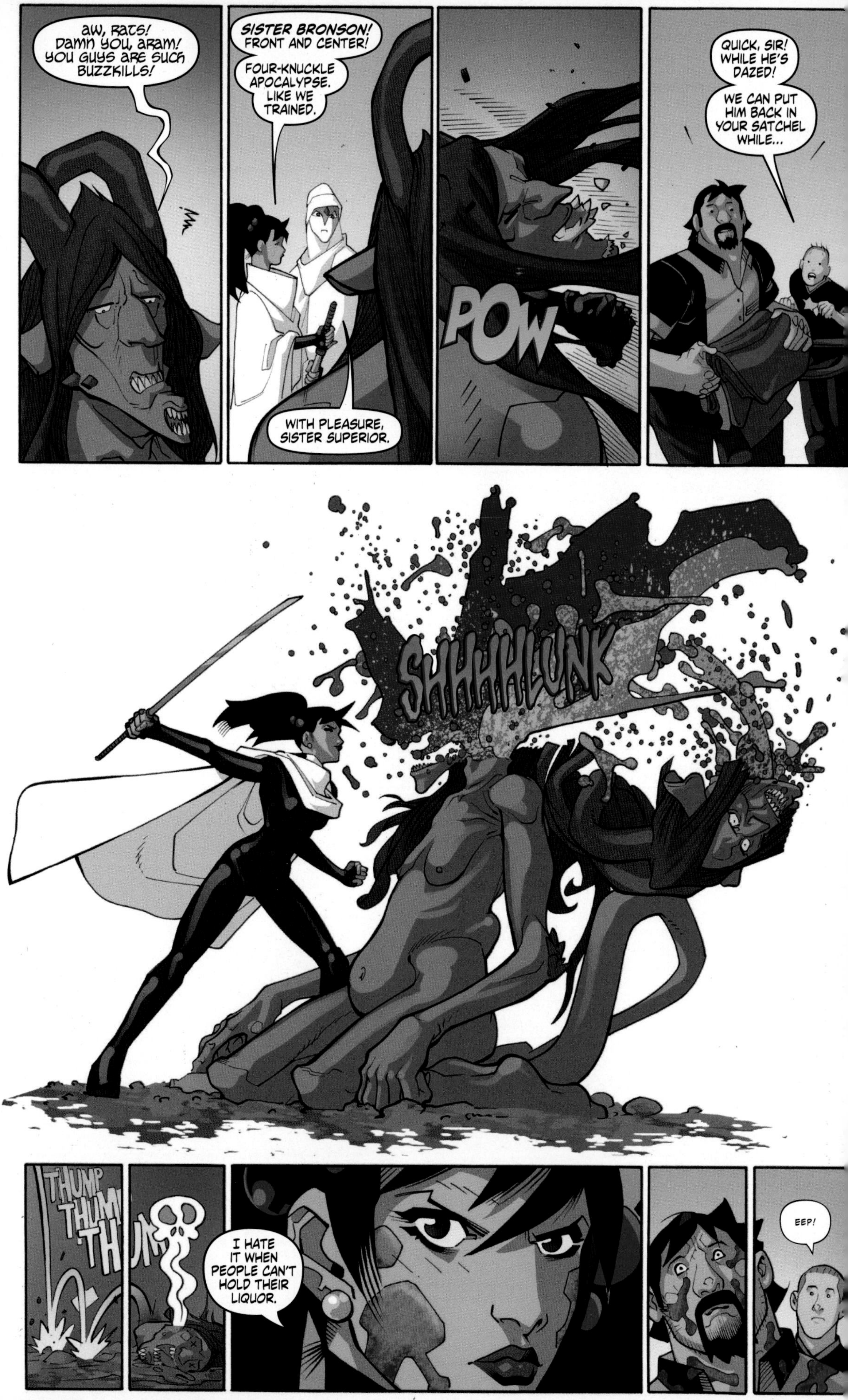

AW, RATS! DAMN YOU, ARAM! YOU GUYS ARE SUCH BUZZKILLS!
SISTER BRONSON! FRONT AND CENTER!
FOUR-KNUCKLE APOCALYPSE. LIKE WE TRAINED.
WITH PLEASURE, SISTER SUPERIOR.
POW
QUICK, SIR! WHILE HE'S DAZED!
WE CAN PUT HIM BACK IN YOUR SATCHEL WHILE...
SHHHHLUNK
THUMP THUMP TH
I HATE IT WHEN PEOPLE CAN'T HOLD THEIR LIQUOR.
EEP!

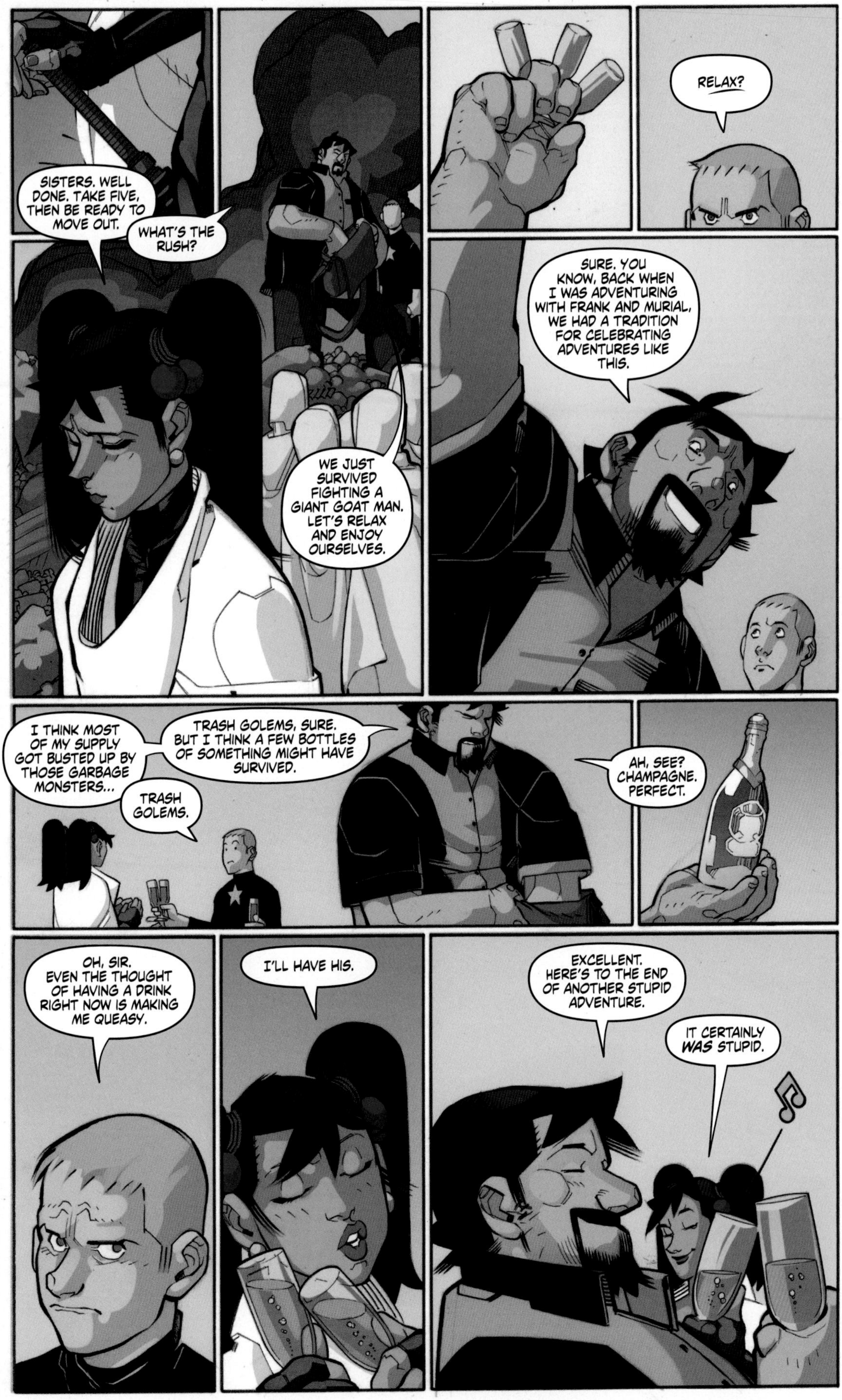
SISTERS. WELL DONE. TAKE FIVE, THEN BE READY TO MOVE OUT.
WHAT'S THE RUSH?
WE JUST SURVIVED FIGHTING A GIANT GOAT MAN. LET'S RELAX AND ENJOY OURSELVES.
RELAX?
SURE. YOU KNOW, BACK WHEN I WAS ADVENTURING WITH FRANK AND MURIAL, WE HAD A TRADITION FOR CELEBRATING ADVENTURES LIKE THIS.
I THINK MOST OF MY SUPPLY GOT BUSTED UP BY THOSE GARBAGE MONSTERS...
TRASH GOLEMS.
TRASH GOLEMS, SURE. BUT I THINK A FEW BOTTLES OF SOMETHING MIGHT HAVE SURVIVED.
AH, SEE? CHAMPAGNE. PERFECT.
OH, SIR. EVEN THE THOUGHT OF HAVING A DRINK RIGHT NOW IS MAKING ME QUEASY.
I'LL HAVE HIS.
EXCELLENT. HERE'S TO THE END OF ANOTHER STUPID ADVENTURE.
IT CERTAINLY WAS STUPID.

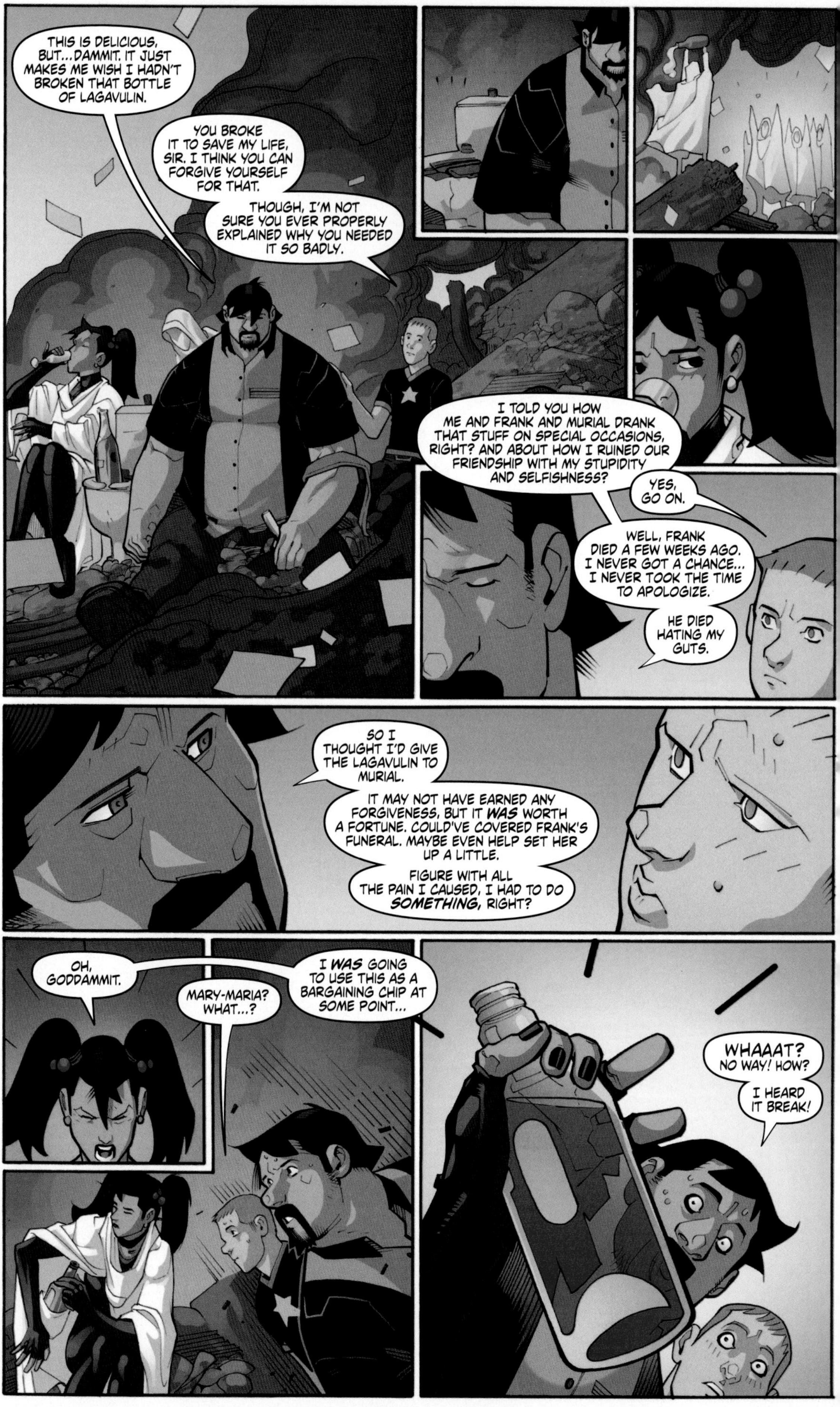

THIS IS DELICIOUS, BUT...DAMMIT. IT JUST MAKES ME WISH I HADN'T BROKEN THAT BOTTLE OF LAGAVULIN.
YOU BROKE IT TO SAVE MY LIFE, SIR. I THINK YOU CAN FORGIVE YOURSELF FOR THAT.
THOUGH, I'M NOT SURE YOU EVER PROPERLY EXPLAINED WHY YOU NEEDED IT SO BADLY.
I TOLD YOU HOW ME AND FRANK AND MURIAL DRANK THAT STUFF ON SPECIAL OCCASIONS, RIGHT? AND ABOUT HOW I RUINED OUR FRIENDSHIP WITH MY STUPIDITY AND SELFISHNESS?
YES, GO ON.
WELL, FRANK DIED A FEW WEEKS AGO. I NEVER GOT A CHANCE... I NEVER TOOK THE TIME TO APOLOGIZE.
HE DIED HATING MY GUTS.
SO I THOUGHT I'D GIVE THE LAGAVULIN TO MURIAL.
IT MAY NOT HAVE EARNED ANY FORGIVENESS, BUT IT WAS WORTH A FORTUNE. COULD'VE COVERED FRANK'S FUNERAL. MAYBE EVEN HELP SET HER UP A LITTLE.
FIGURE WITH ALL THE PAIN I CAUSED, I HAD TO DO SOMETHING, RIGHT?
OH, GODDAMMIT.
MARY-MARIA? WHAT...?
I WAS GOING TO USE THIS AS A BARGAINING CHIP AT SOME POINT...
WHAAAT? NO WAY! HOW?
I HEARD IT BREAK!

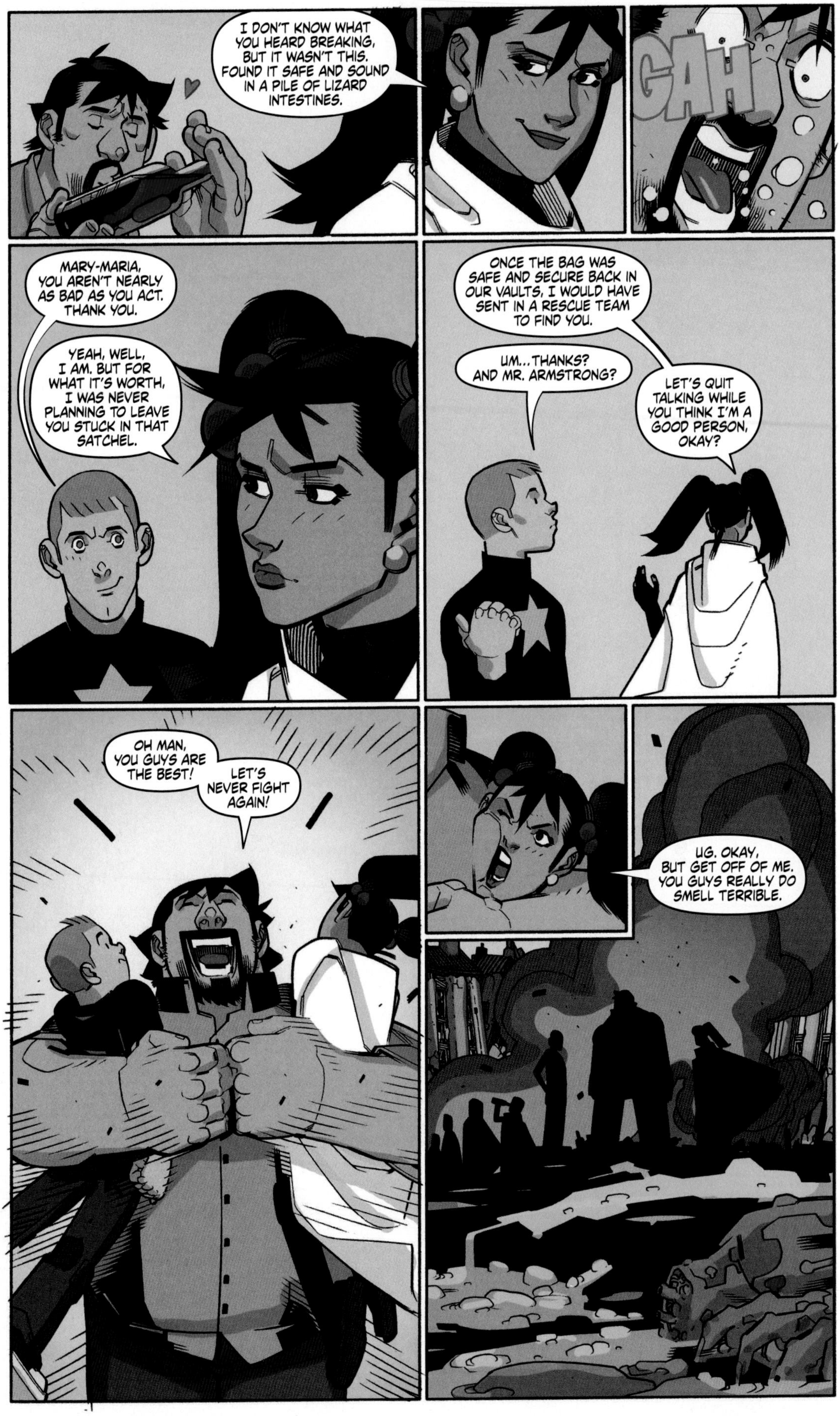
I DON'T KNOW WHAT YOU HEARD BREAKING, BUT IT WASN'T THIS. FOUND IT SAFE AND SOUND IN A PILE OF LIZARD INTESTINES.
GAH!
MARY-MARIA, YOU AREN'T NEARLY AS BAD AS YOU ACT. THANK YOU.
YEAH, WELL, I AM. BUT FOR WHAT IT'S WORTH, I WAS NEVER PLANNING TO LEAVE YOU STUCK IN THAT SATCHEL.
ONCE THE BAG WAS SAFE AND SECURE BACK IN OUR VAULTS, I WOULD HAVE SENT IN A RESCUE TEAM TO FIND YOU.
UM...THANKS? AND MR. ARMSTRONG?
LET'S QUIT TALKING WHILE YOU THINK I'M A GOOD PERSON, OKAY?
OH MAN, YOU GUYS ARE THE BEST!
LET'S NEVER FIGHT AGAIN!
UG. OKAY, BUT GET OFF OF ME. YOU GUYS REALLY DO SMELL TERRIBLE.

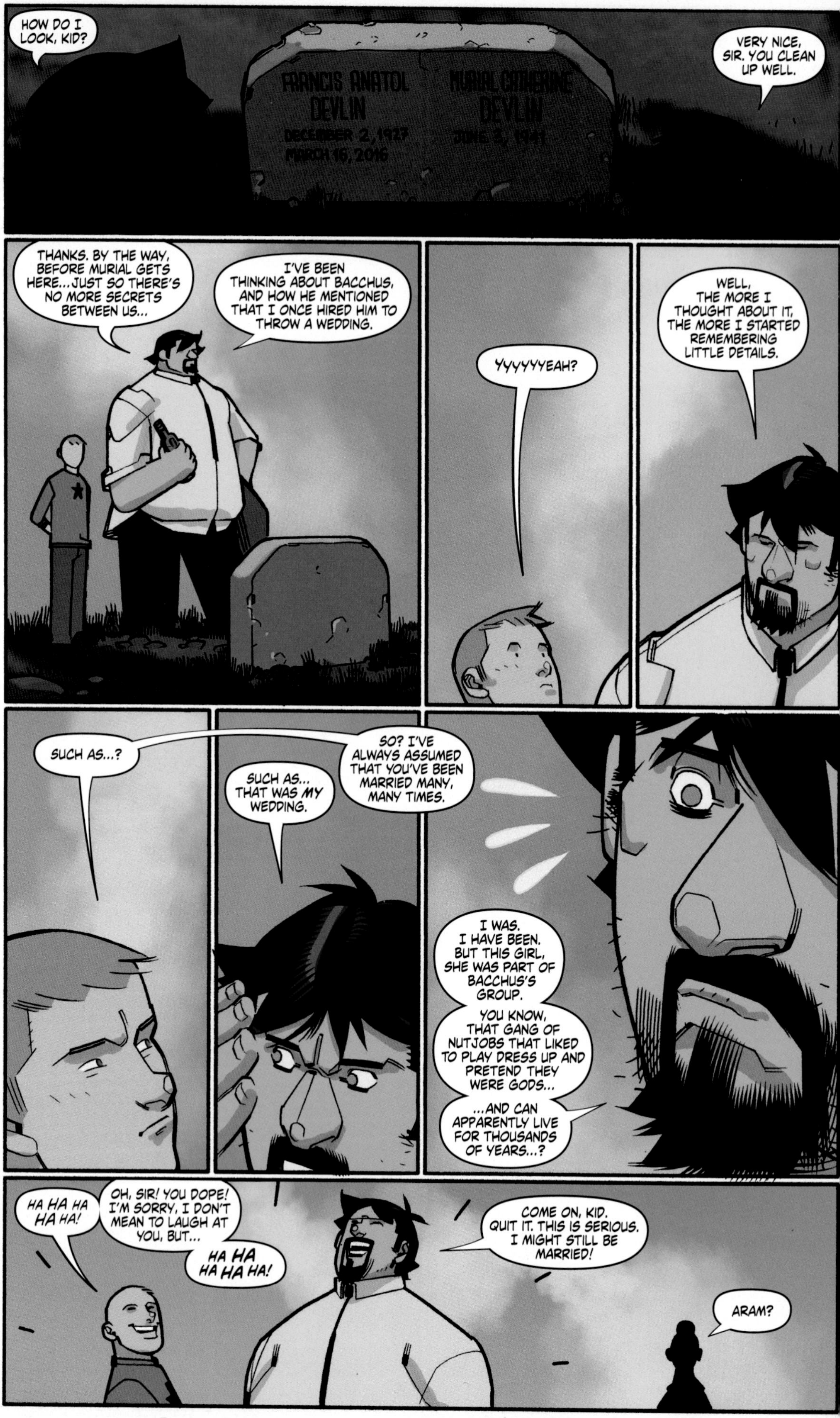
HOW DO I LOOK, KID?
FRANCIS ANATOL DEVLIN
DECEMBER 2, 1927
MARCH 16, 2016
MURIAL CATHERINE DEVLIN
JUNE 3, 1941
VERY NICE, SIR. YOU CLEAN UP WELL.
THANKS. BY THE WAY, BEFORE MURIAL GETS HERE...JUST SO THERE'S NO MORE SECRETS BETWEEN US...
I'VE BEEN THINKING ABOUT BACCHUS, AND HOW HE MENTIONED THAT I ONCE HIRED HIM TO THROW A WEDDING.
YYYYYYEAH?
WELL, THE MORE I THOUGHT ABOUT IT, THE MORE I STARTED REMEMBERING LITTLE DETAILS.
SUCH AS...?
SUCH AS... THAT WAS MY WEDDING.
SO? I'VE ALWAYS ASSUMED THAT YOU'VE BEEN MARRIED MANY, MANY TIMES.
I WAS. I HAVE BEEN. BUT THIS GIRL, SHE WAS PART OF BACCHUS'S GROUP.
YOU KNOW, THAT GANG OF NUTJOBS THAT LIKED TO PLAY DRESS UP AND PRETEND THEY WERE GODS...
...AND CAN APPARENTLY LIVE FOR THOUSANDS OF YEARS...?
HA HA HA HA HA!
OH, SIR! YOU DOPE! I'M SORRY, I DON'T MEAN TO LAUGH AT YOU, BUT...
HA HA HA HA HA!
COME ON, KID. QUIT IT. THIS IS SERIOUS. I MIGHT STILL BE MARRIED!
ARAM?

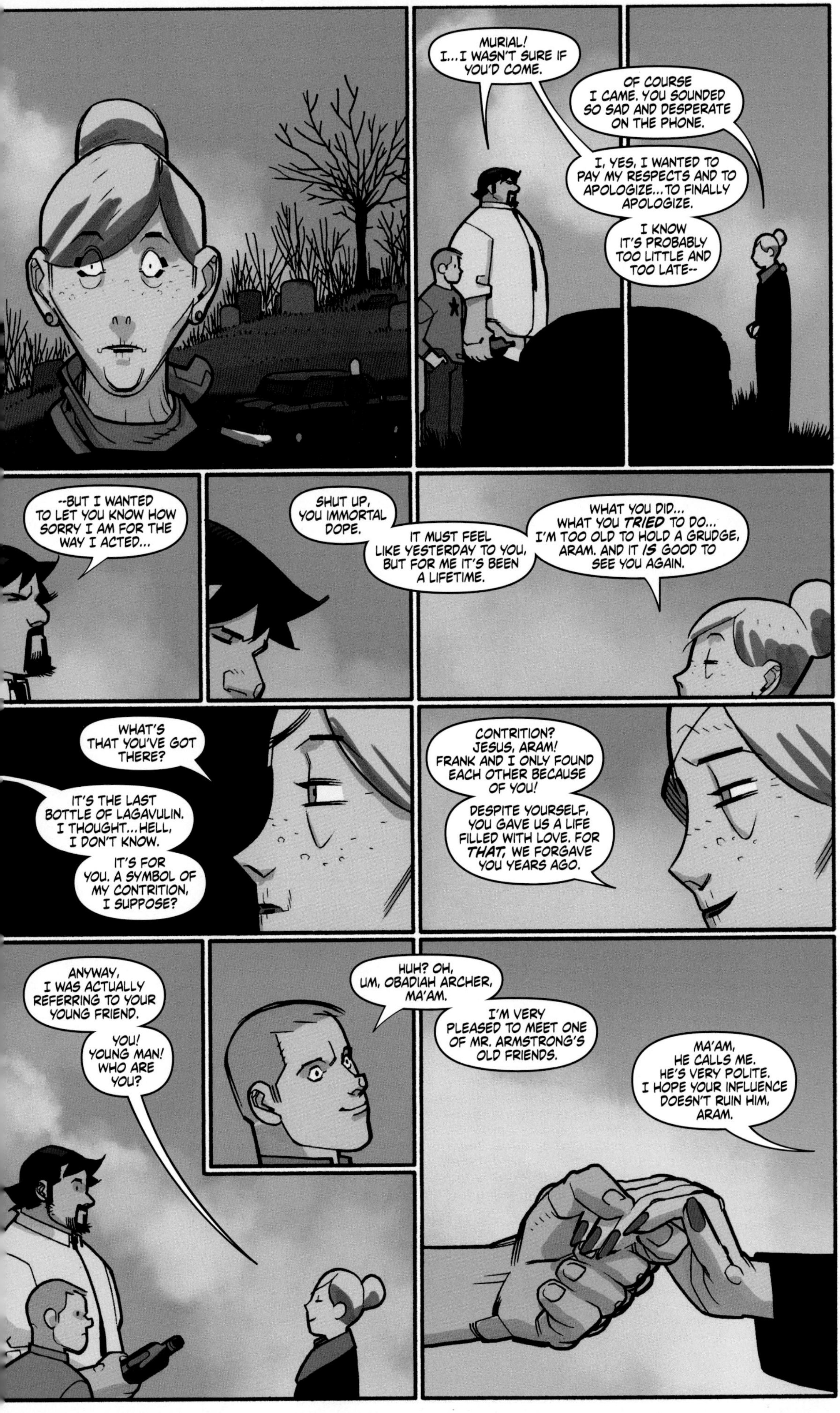
MURIAL! I...I WASN'T SURE IF YOU'D COME.
OF COURSE I CAME. YOU SOUNDED SO SAD AND DESPERATE ON THE PHONE.
I, YES, I WANTED TO PAY MY RESPECTS AND TO APOLOGIZE...TO FINALLY APOLOGIZE.
I KNOW IT'S PROBABLY TOO LITTLE AND TOO LATE--
--BUT I WANTED TO LET YOU KNOW HOW SORRY I AM FOR THE WAY I ACTED...
SHUT UP, YOU IMMORTAL DOPE.
IT MUST FEEL LIKE YESTERDAY TO YOU, BUT FOR ME IT'S BEEN A LIFETIME.
WHAT YOU DID... WHAT YOU *TRIED* TO DO... I'M TOO OLD TO HOLD A GRUDGE, ARAM. AND IT *IS* GOOD TO SEE YOU AGAIN.
WHAT'S THAT YOU'VE GOT THERE?
IT'S THE LAST BOTTLE OF LAGAVULIN. I THOUGHT...HELL, I DON'T KNOW.
IT'S FOR YOU. A SYMBOL OF MY CONTRITION, I SUPPOSE?
CONTRITION? JESUS, ARAM! FRANK AND I ONLY FOUND EACH OTHER BECAUSE OF YOU!
DESPITE YOURSELF, YOU GAVE US A LIFE FILLED WITH LOVE. FOR *THAT,* WE FORGAVE YOU YEARS AGO.
ANYWAY, I WAS ACTUALLY REFERRING TO YOUR YOUNG FRIEND.
YOU! YOUNG MAN! WHO ARE YOU?
HUH? OH, UM, OBADIAH ARCHER, MA'AM.
I'M VERY PLEASED TO MEET ONE OF MR. ARMSTRONG'S OLD FRIENDS.
MA'AM, HE CALLS ME. HE'S VERY POLITE. I HOPE YOUR INFLUENCE DOESN'T RUIN HIM, ARAM.

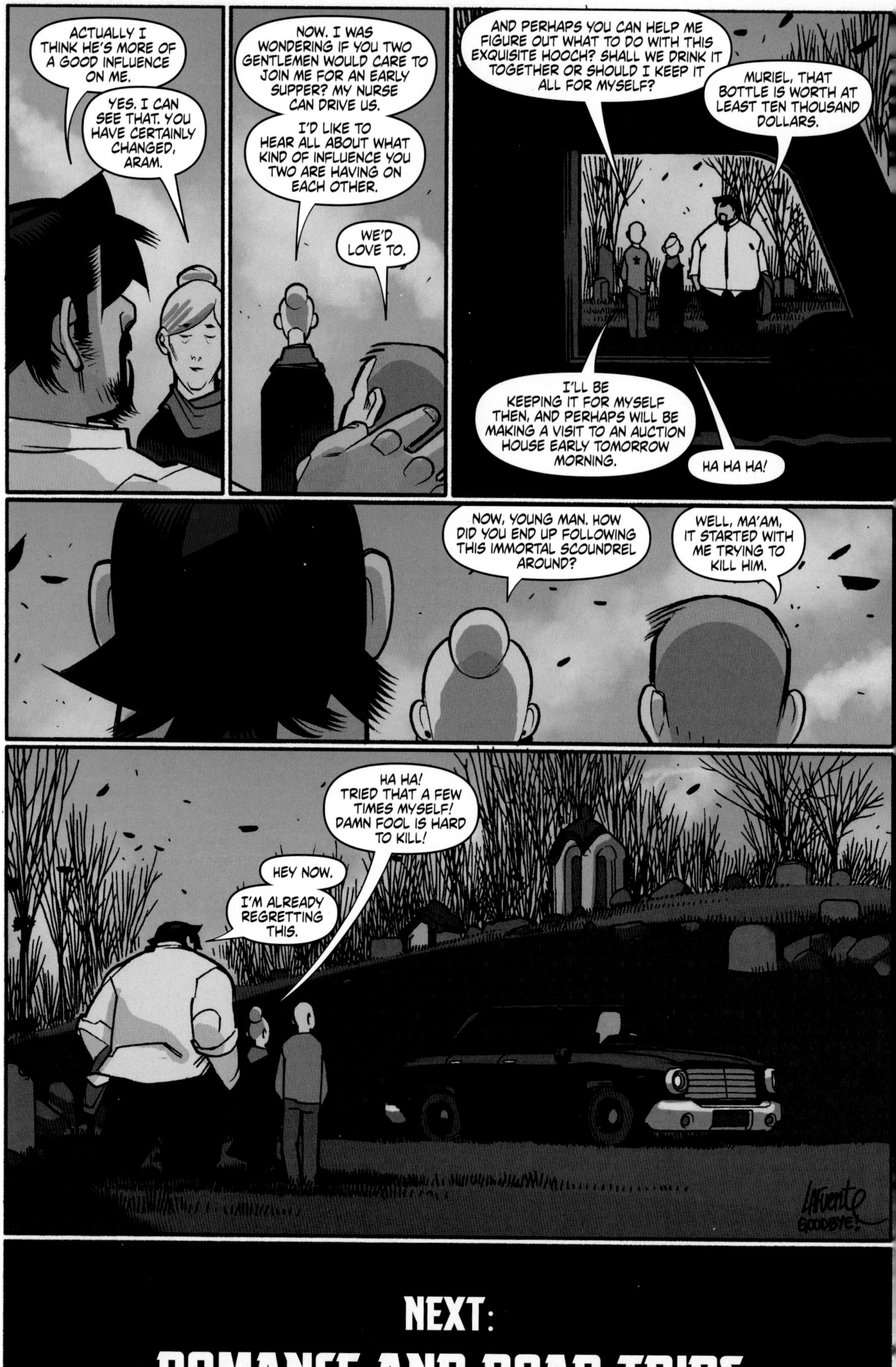
ACTUALLY I THINK HE'S MORE OF A GOOD INFLUENCE ON ME.
YES. I CAN SEE THAT. YOU HAVE CERTAINLY CHANGED, ARAM.
NOW. I WAS WONDERING IF YOU TWO GENTLEMEN WOULD CARE TO JOIN ME FOR AN EARLY SUPPER? MY NURSE CAN DRIVE US.
I'D LIKE TO HEAR ALL ABOUT WHAT KIND OF INFLUENCE YOU TWO ARE HAVING ON EACH OTHER.
WE'D LOVE TO.
AND PERHAPS YOU CAN HELP ME FIGURE OUT WHAT TO DO WITH THIS EXQUISITE HOOCH? SHALL WE DRINK IT TOGETHER OR SHOULD I KEEP IT ALL FOR MYSELF?
MURIEL, THAT BOTTLE IS WORTH AT LEAST TEN THOUSAND DOLLARS.
I'LL BE KEEPING IT FOR MYSELF THEN, AND PERHAPS WILL BE MAKING A VISIT TO AN AUCTION HOUSE EARLY TOMORROW MORNING.
HA HA HA!
NOW, YOUNG MAN. HOW DID YOU END UP FOLLOWING THIS IMMORTAL SCOUNDREL AROUND?
WELL, MA'AM, IT STARTED WITH ME TRYING TO KILL HIM.
HA HA! TRIED THAT A FEW TIMES MYSELF! DAMN FOOL IS HARD TO KILL!
HEY NOW.
I'M ALREADY REGRETTING THIS.

NEXT:

ROMANCE AND ROAD TRIPS

GALLERY

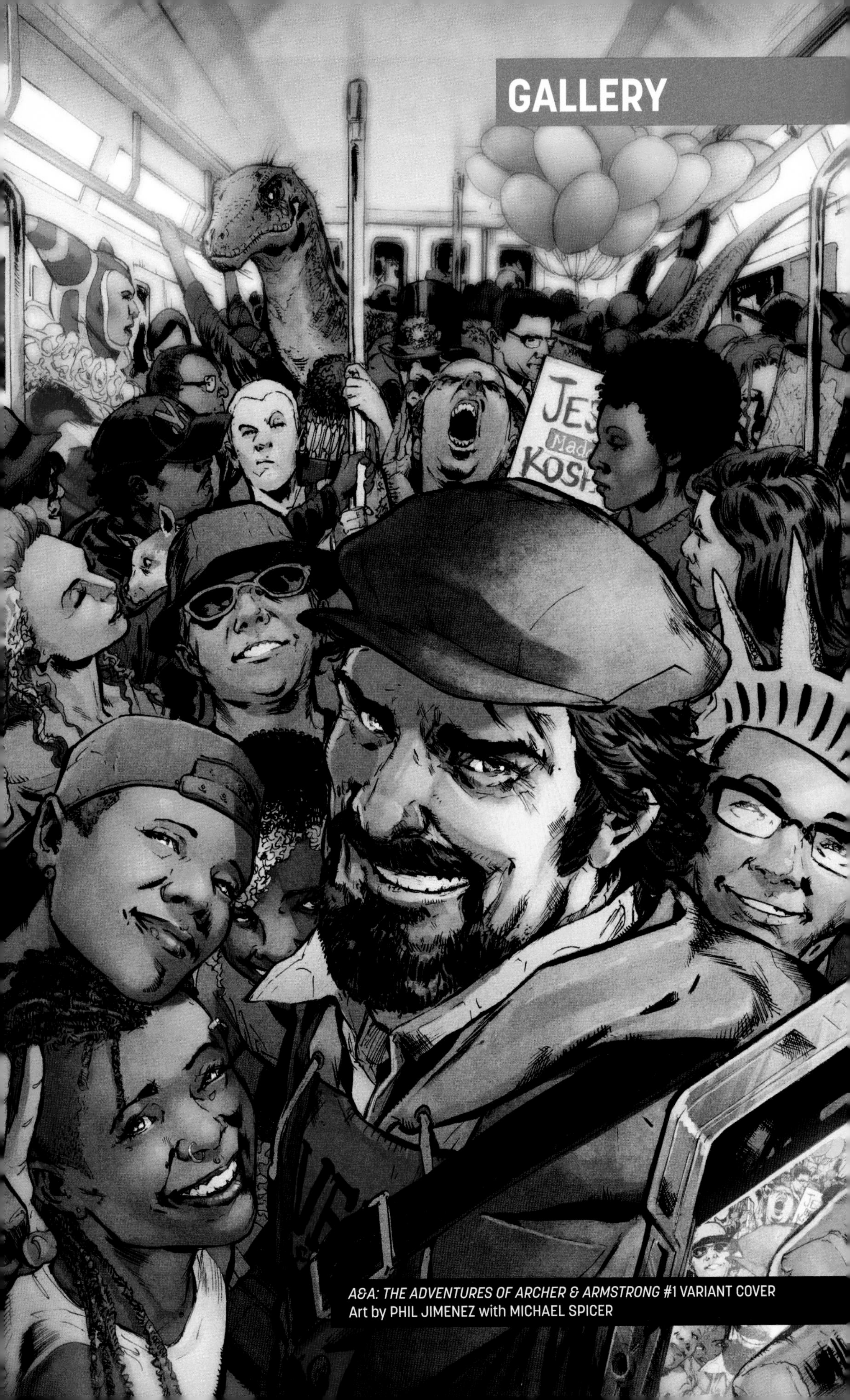

A&A: THE ADVENTURES OF ARCHER & ARMSTRONG #1 VARIANT COVER
Art by PHIL JIMENEZ with MICHAEL SPICER

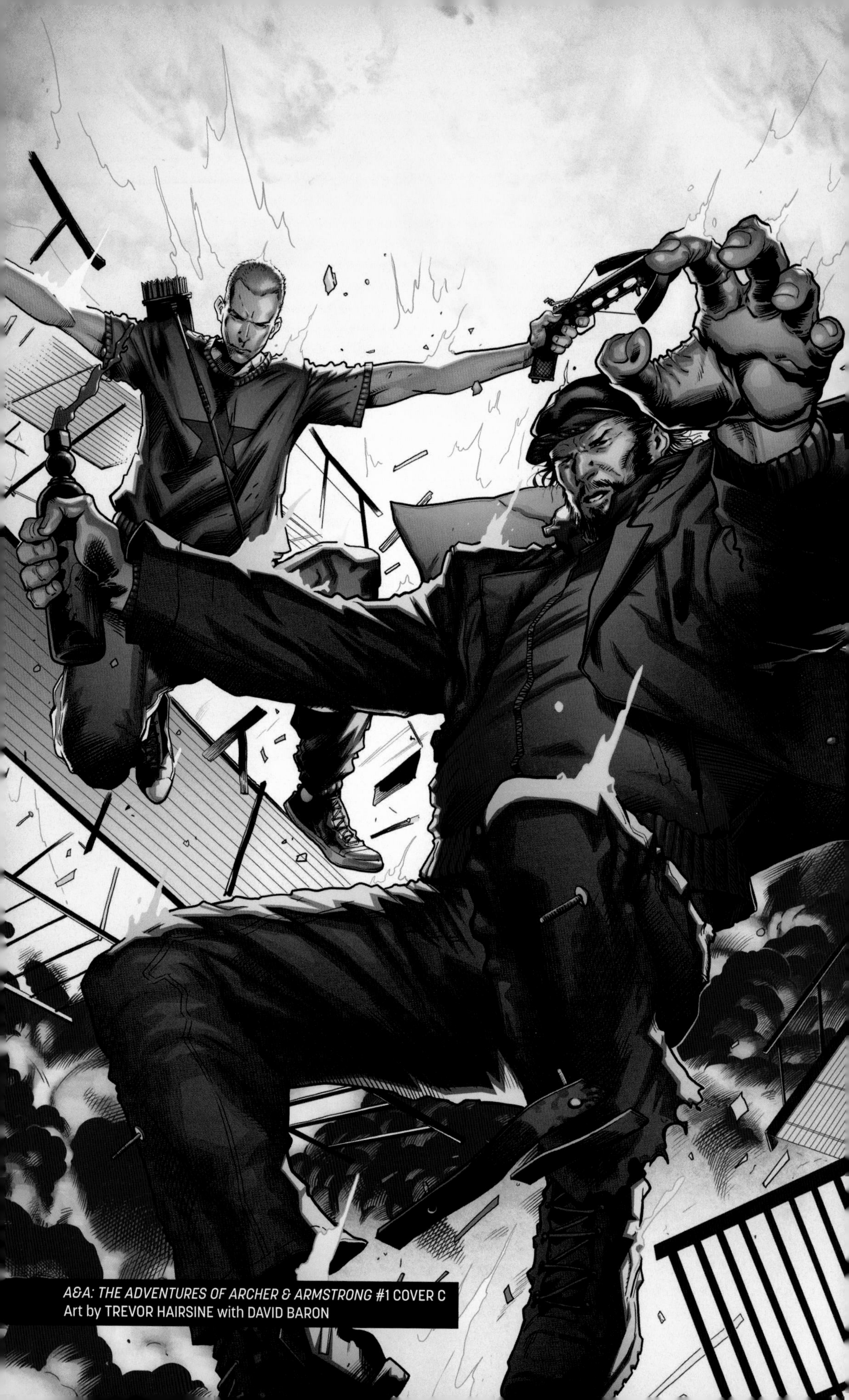

A&A: THE ADVENTURES OF ARCHER & ARMSTRONG #1 COVER C
Art by TREVOR HAIRSINE with DAVID BARON

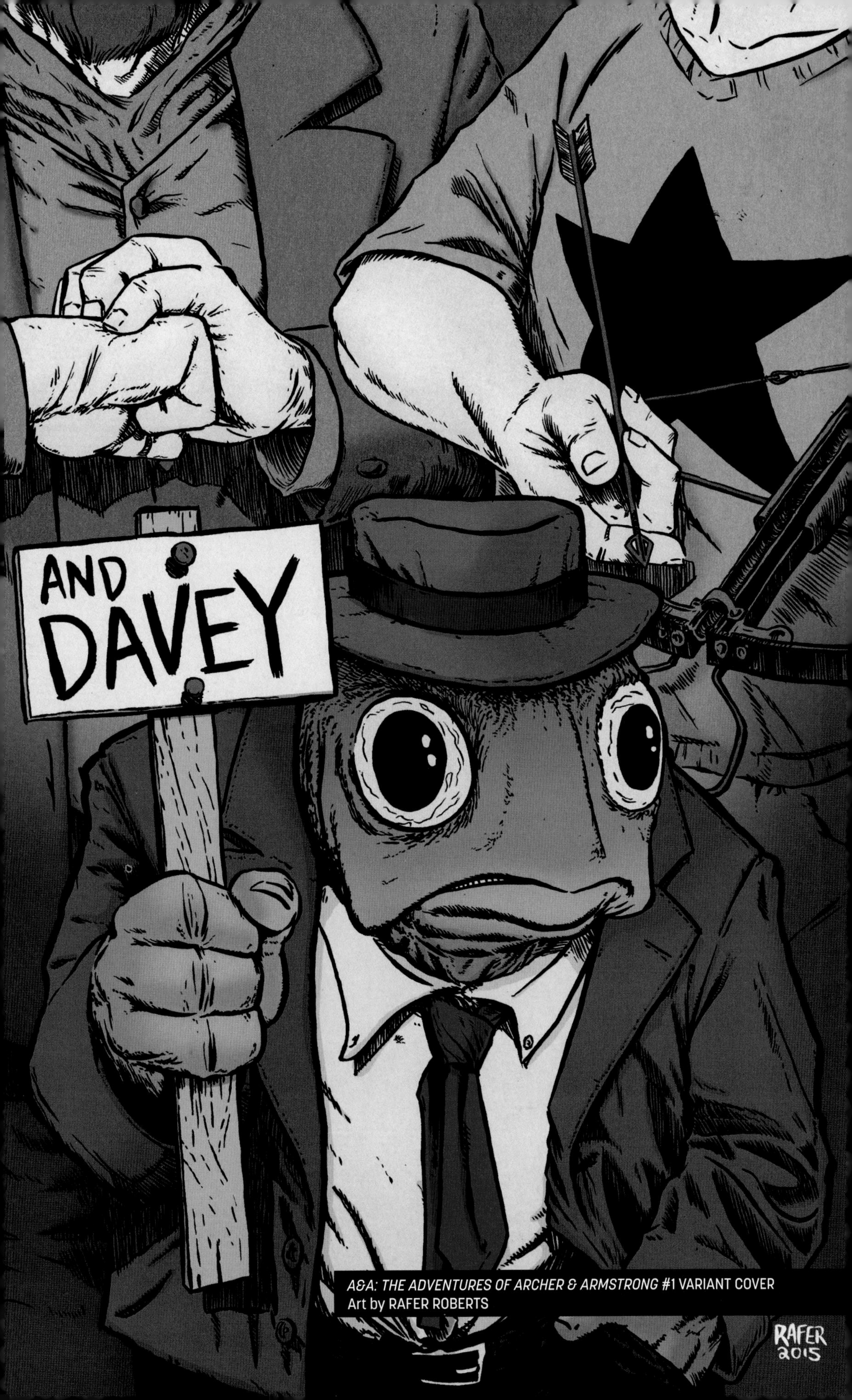
AND DAVEY
RAFER 2015

A&A: THE ADVENTURES OF ARCHER & ARMSTRONG #1 VARIANT COVER
Art by RAFER ROBERTS

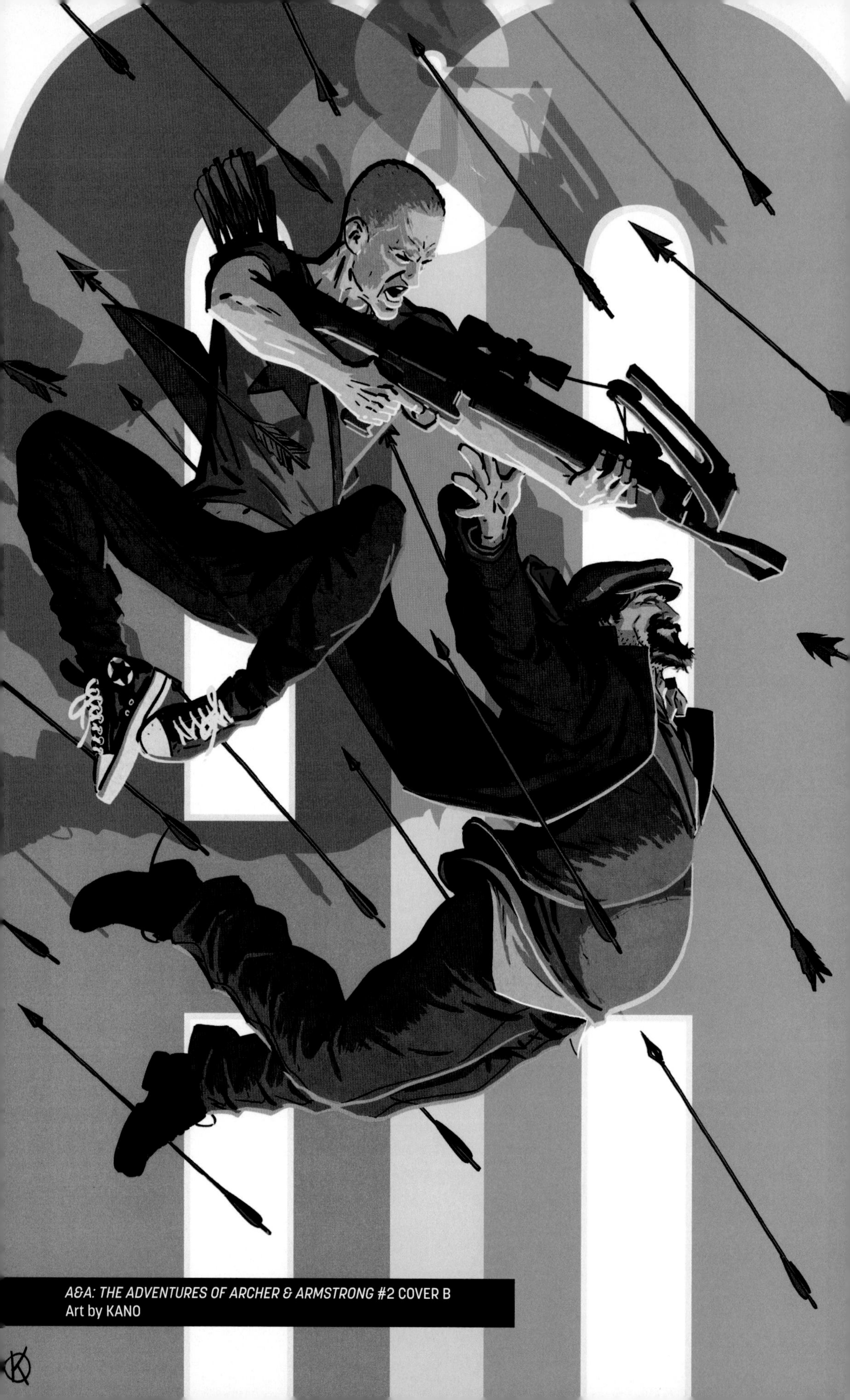

A&A: THE ADVENTURES OF ARCHER & ARMSTRONG #2 COVER B
Art by KANO

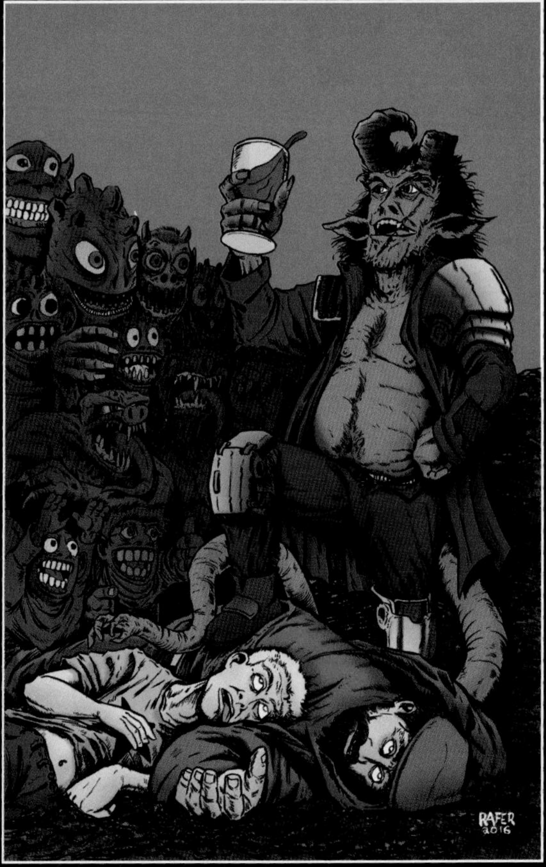
RAFER
2016

A&A: THE ADVENTURES OF ARCHER & ARMSTRONG #3
VARIANT COVER
Art by RAFER ROBERTS

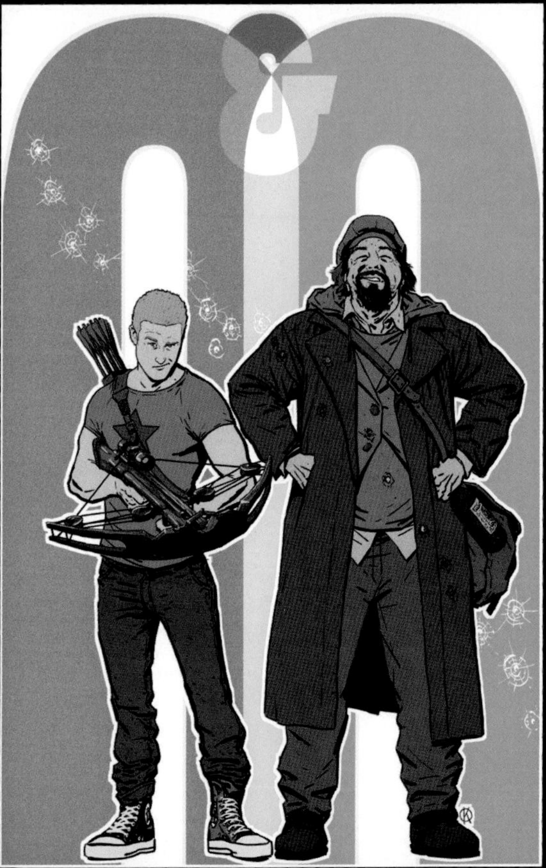

A&A: THE ADVENTURES OF ARCHER & ARMSTRONG #3
COVER B
Art by KANO

A&A: THE ADVENTURES OF ARCHER & ARMSTRONG #3
VARIANT COVER
Art by BEN OLIVER

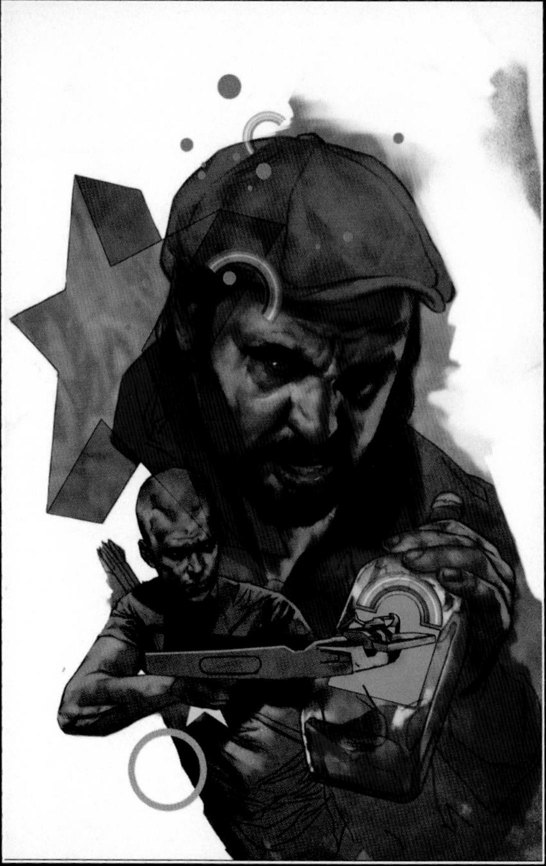

A&A: THE ADVENTURES OF ARCHER & ARMSTRONG #4
VARIANT COVER
Art by THONY SILAS

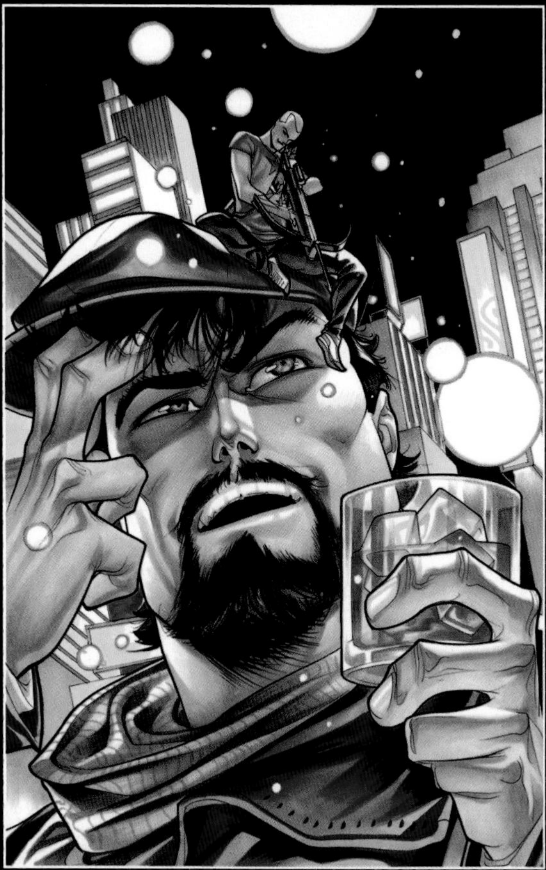

A&A: THE ADVENTURES OF ARCHER & ARMSTRONG #2-4
COVER C
Art by MONICA GALLAGHER

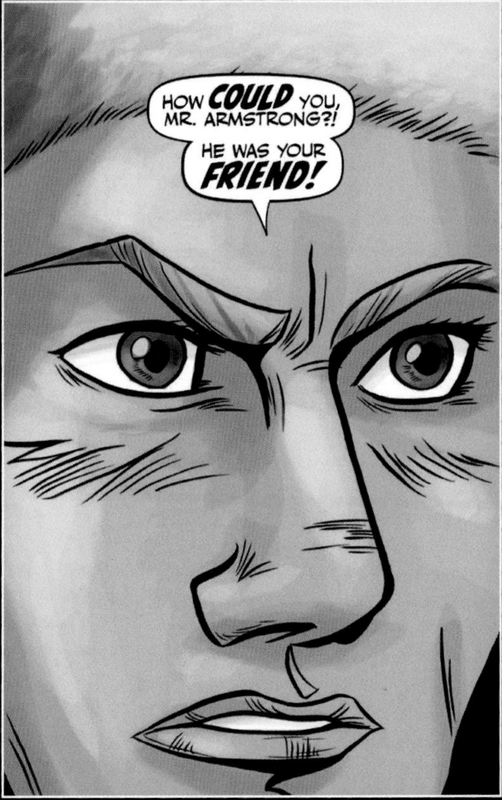
HOW COULD YOU, MR. ARMSTRONG?!
HE WAS YOUR FRIEND!

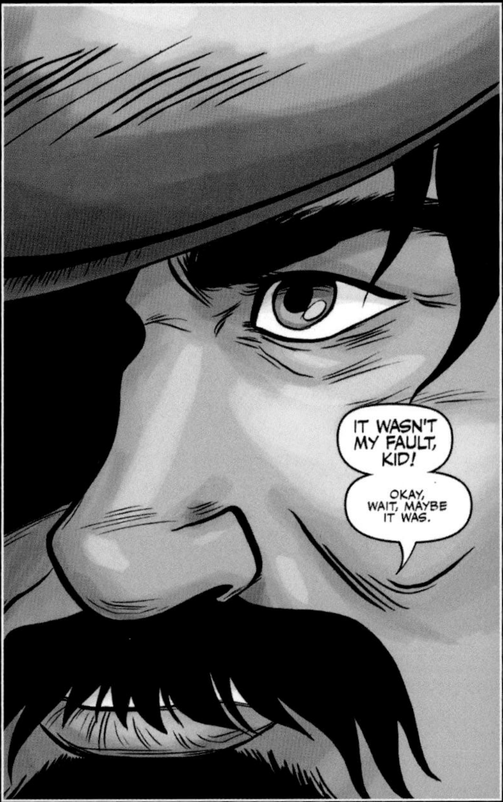
IT WASN'T MY FAULT, KID!
OKAY, WAIT, MAYBE IT WAS.

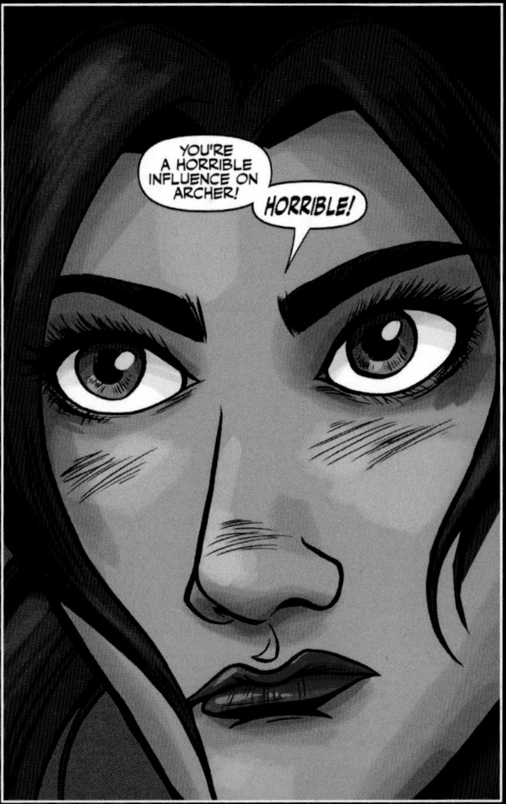
YOU'RE A HORRIBLE INFLUENCE ON ARCHER!
HORRIBLE!

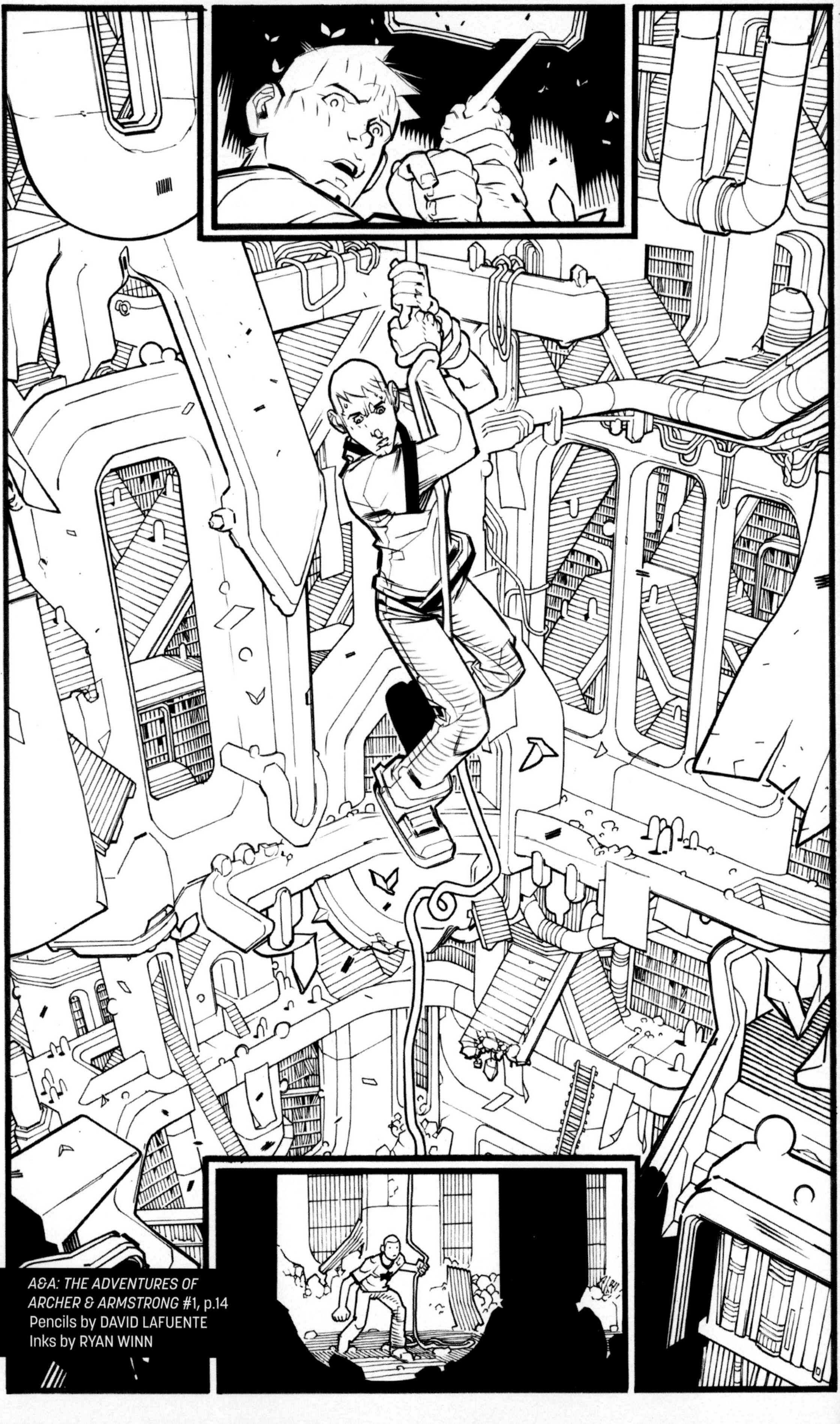

A&A: THE ADVENTURES OF ARCHER & ARMSTRONG #1, p.14
Pencils by DAVID LAFUENTE
Inks by RYAN WINN

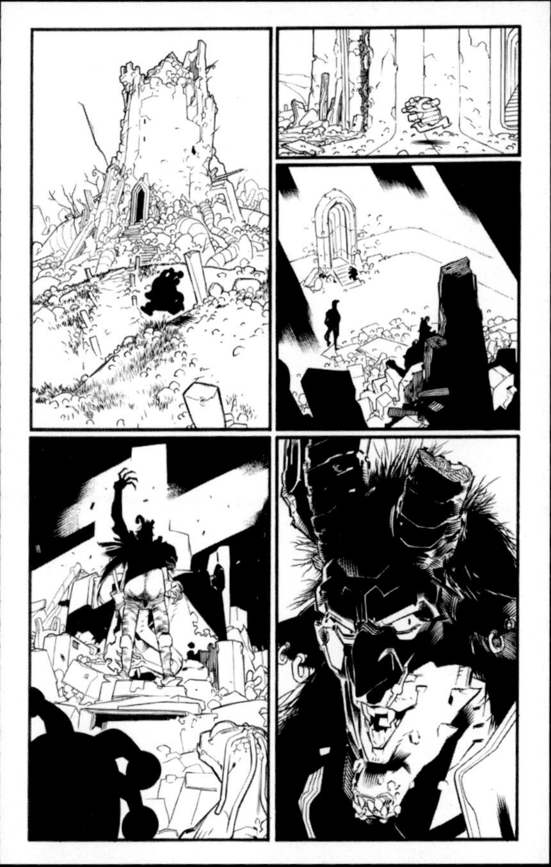

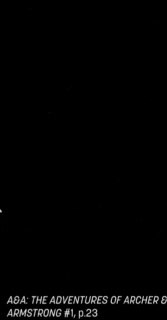

A&A: THE ADVENTURES OF ARCHER & ARMSTRONG #1, p.19
Pencils by DAVID LAFUENTE
Inks by RYAN WINN

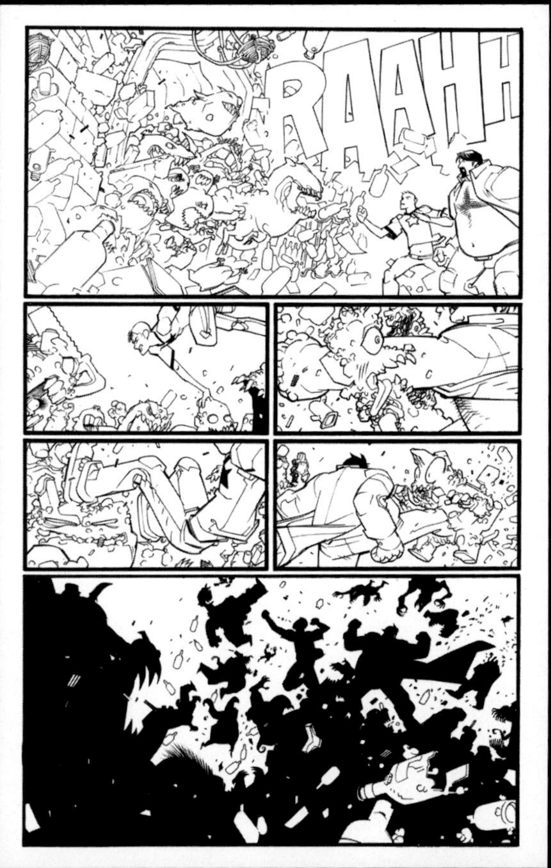
RAAHH

A&A: THE ADVENTURES OF ARCHER & ARMSTRONG #1, p.23
Pencils by DAVID LAFUENTE
Inks by RYAN WINN

A&A: THE ADVENTURES OF ARCHER & ARMSTRONG #2, p.1
Pencils by DAVID LAFUENTE
Inks by RYAN WINN

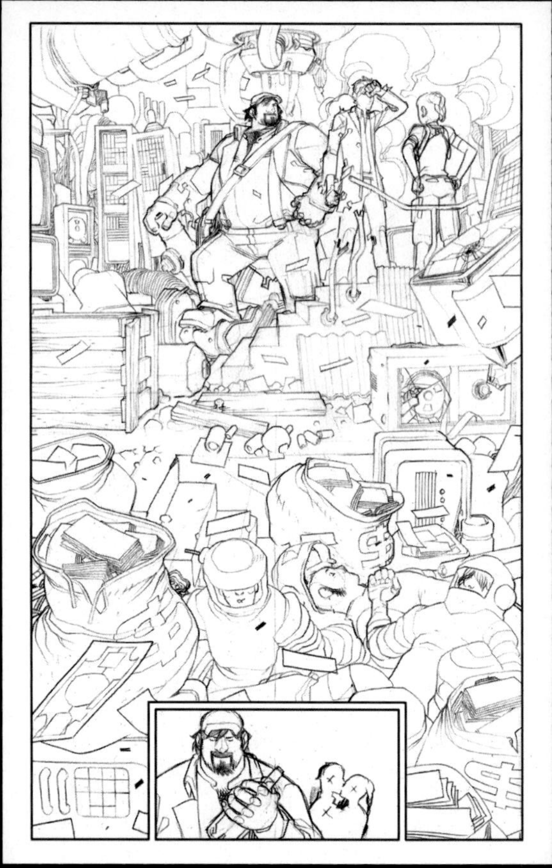

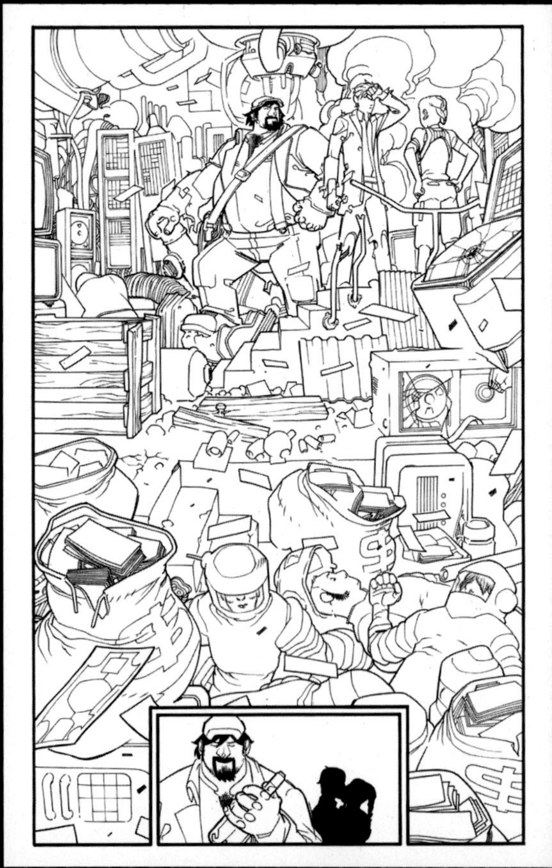

A&A: THE ADVENTURES OF ARCHER & ARMSTRONG #2, p.4
Pencils by DAVID LAFUENTE
Inks by RYAN WINN

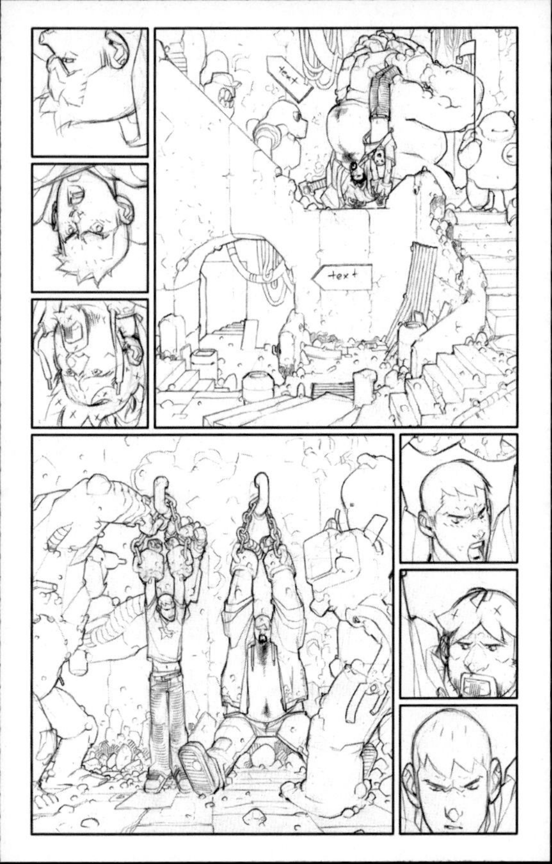
text
text

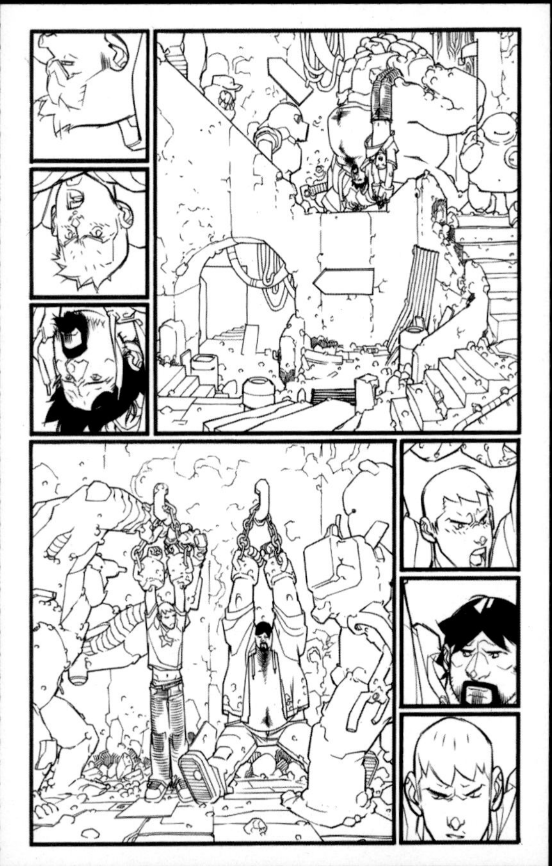

A&A: THE ADVENTURES OF ARCHER & ARMSTRONG #2, p.18
Pencils by DAVID LAFUENTE

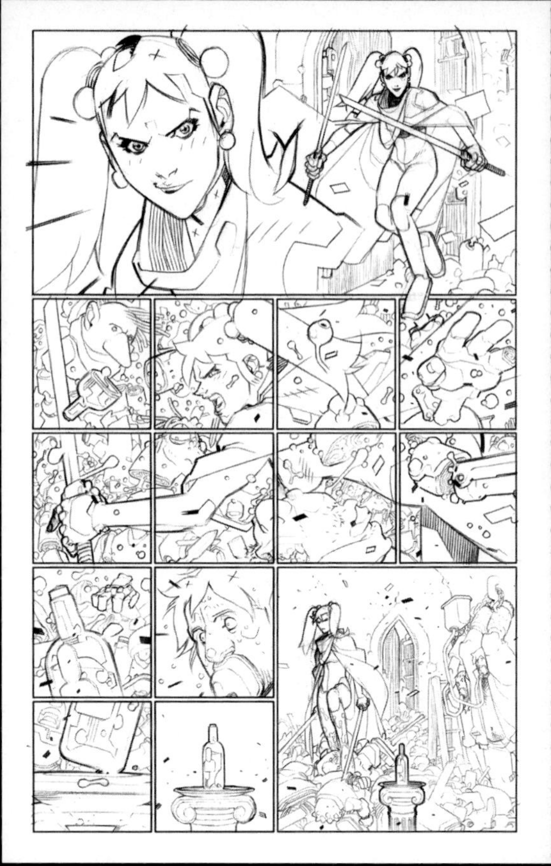

A&A: THE ADVENTURES OF ARCHER & ARMSTRONG #2, p.19
Pencils by DAVID LAFUENTE

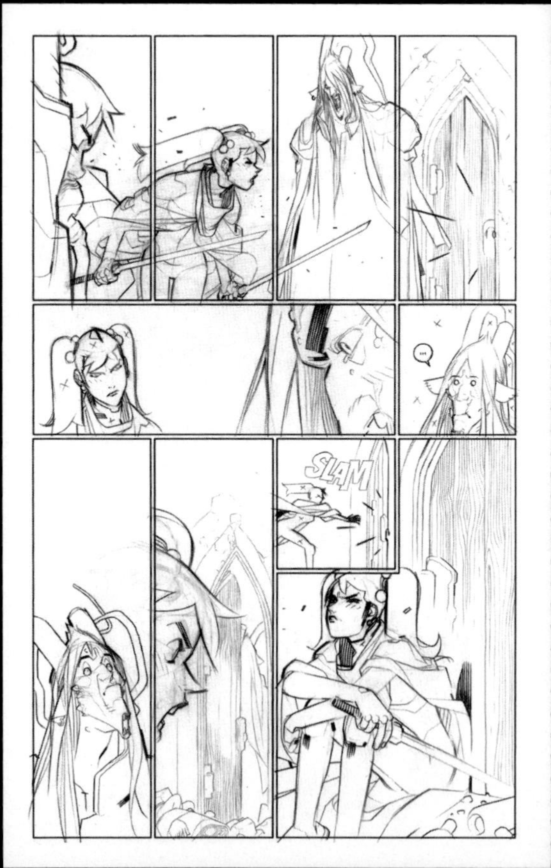
...
SLAM

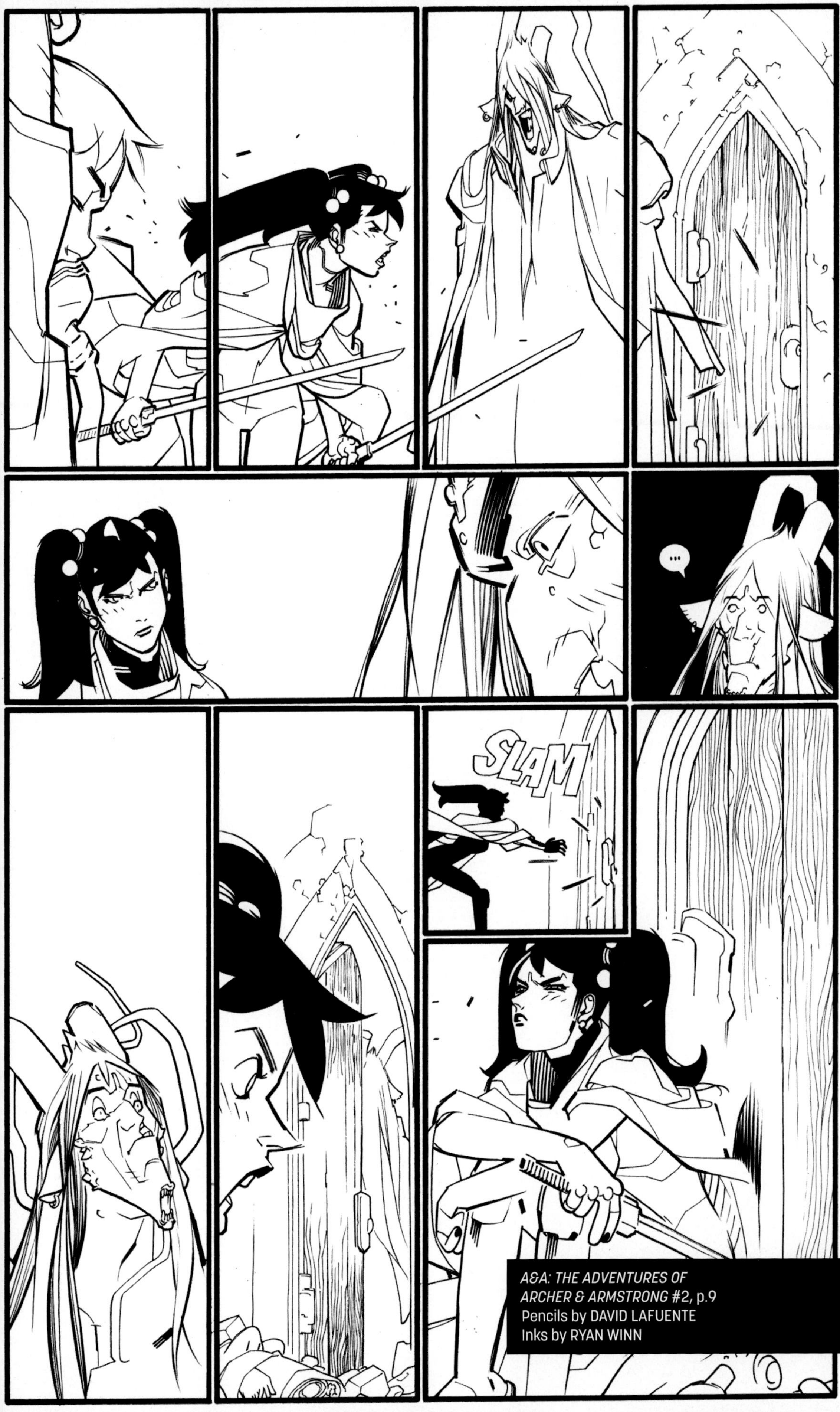
...
SLAM

A&A: THE ADVENTURES OF ARCHER & ARMSTRONG #2, p.9
Pencils by DAVID LAFUENTE
Inks by RYAN WINN

A&A: THE ADVENTURES OF ARCHER & ARMSTRONG #3, p.13
Pencils by DAVID LAFUENTE
Inks by RYAN WINN

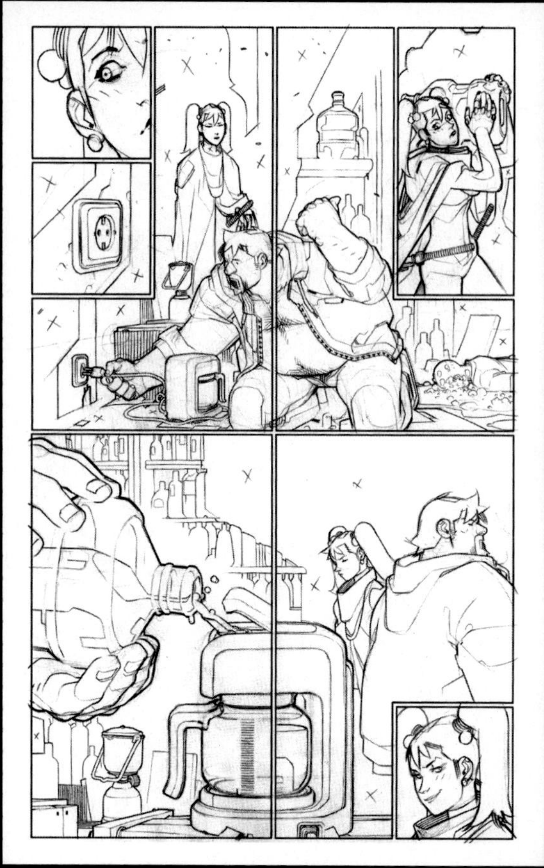

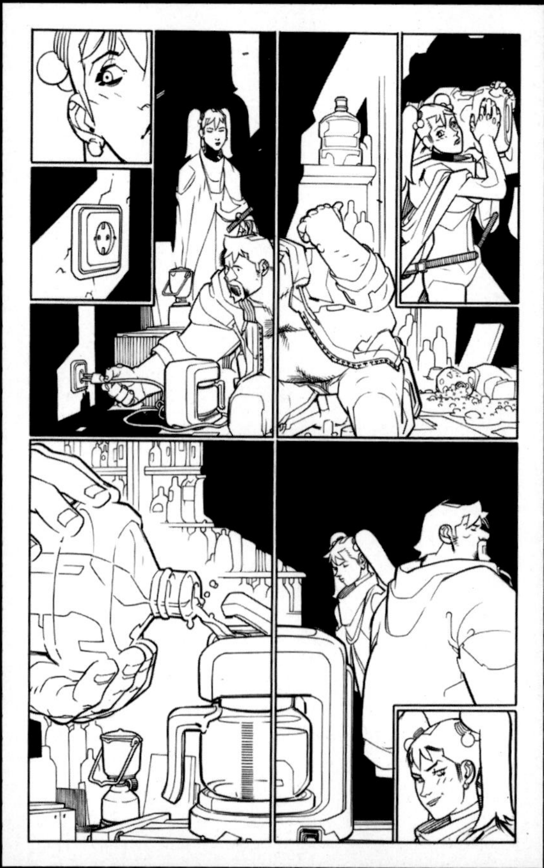

A&A: THE ADVENTURES OF ARCHER & ARMSTRONG #3, p.14
Pencils by DAVID LAFUENTE
Inks by RYAN WINN

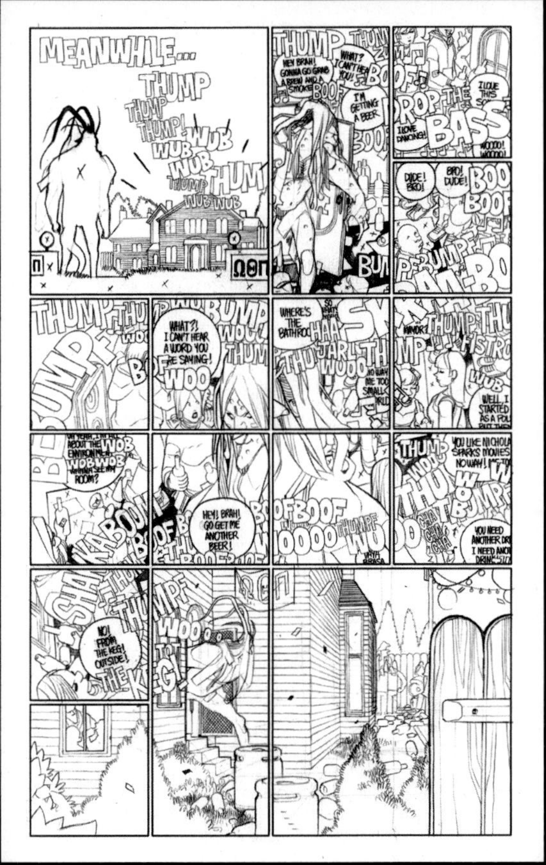
MEANWHILE...
THUMP
THUMP
THUMP! WUB
WUB
WUB THUMP
THUMP
WUB WUB
ΩΘΠ
HEY BRAH! GONNA GO GRAB A BREW AND A SMOKE
WHAT? I CAN'T HEAR YOU!
I'M GETTING A BEER
DROP THE BASS
I LOVE DANCING!
WOOO! WOOO!
DUDE! BRO!
BRO! DUDE!
BOOF
WHAT?! I CAN'T HEAR A WORD YOU'RE SAYING!
WOO
WHERE'S THE BATHROOM?
WELL, I STARTED AS A POL
HEY! BRAH! GO GET ME ANOTHER BEER!
BOOF BOOF
WOOOO
YOU LIKE NICHOLAS SPARKS MOVIES?
NO WAY!
YOU NEED ANOTHER DRINK
I NEED ANOTHER DRINK
NO! FROM THE KEG! OUTSIDE!
THE KEG!
WOOO

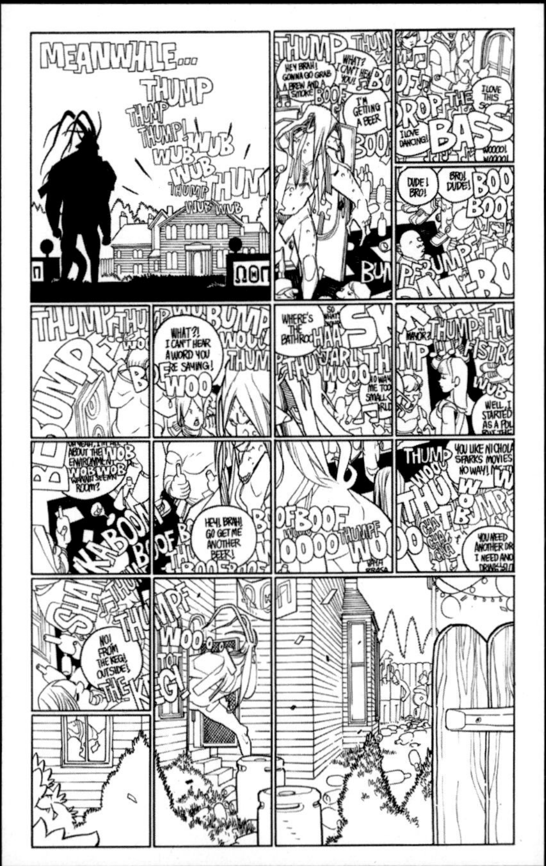
MEANWHILE...
THUMP
THUMP
THUMP! WUB
WUB
WUB THUMP
THUMP
WUB WUB
ΩΘΠ
HEY BRAH! GONNA GO GRAB A BREW AND A SMOKE
WHAT? I CAN'T HEAR YOU!
I'M GETTING A BEER
DROP THE BASS
I LOVE DANCING!
WOOO! WOOO!
DUDE! BRO!
BRO! DUDE!
BOOF
WHAT?! I CAN'T HEAR A WORD YOU'RE SAYING!
WOO
WHERE'S THE BATHROOM?
WELL, I STARTED AS A POL
HEY! BRAH! GO GET ME ANOTHER BEER!
BOOF BOOF
WOOOO
YOU LIKE NICHOLAS SPARKS MOVIES?
NO WAY!
YOU NEED ANOTHER DRINK
I NEED ANOTHER DRINK
NO! FROM THE KEG! OUTSIDE!
THE KEG!
WOOO

A: THE ADVENTURES OF ARCHER &
MSTRONG #3, p.15
cils by DAVID LAFUENTE
s by RYAN WINN

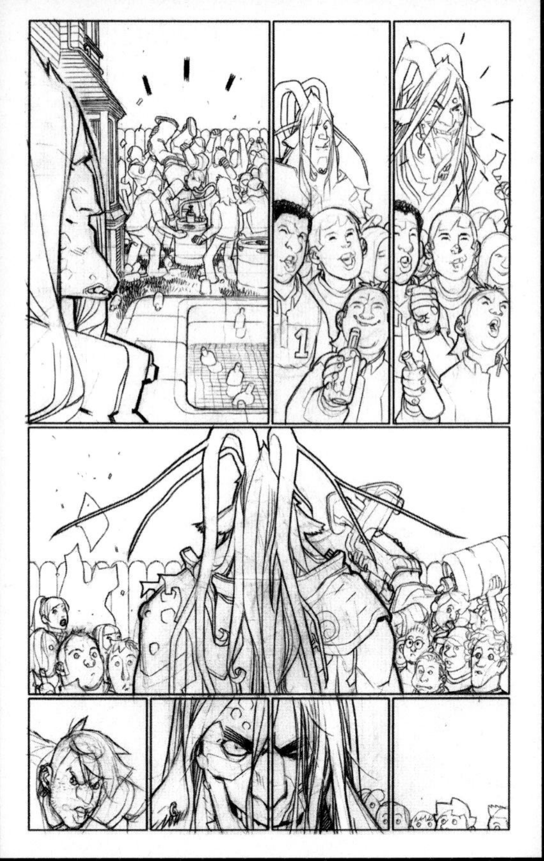

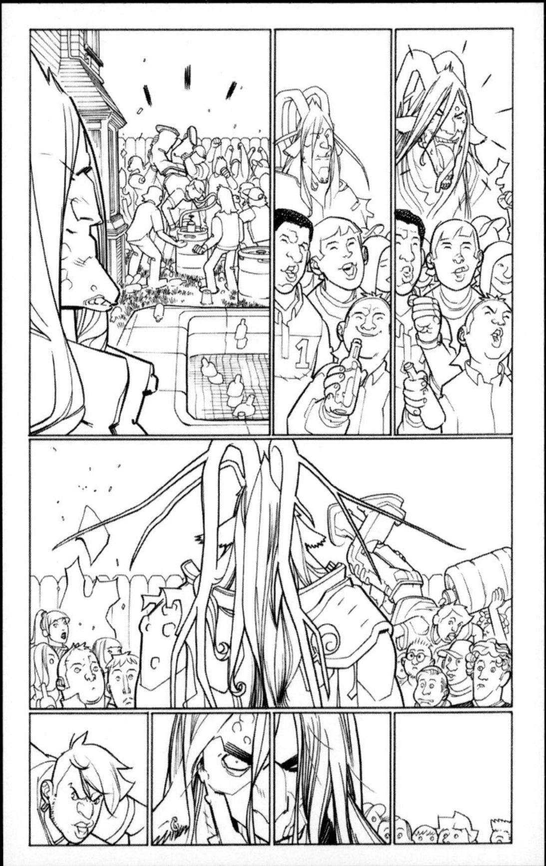

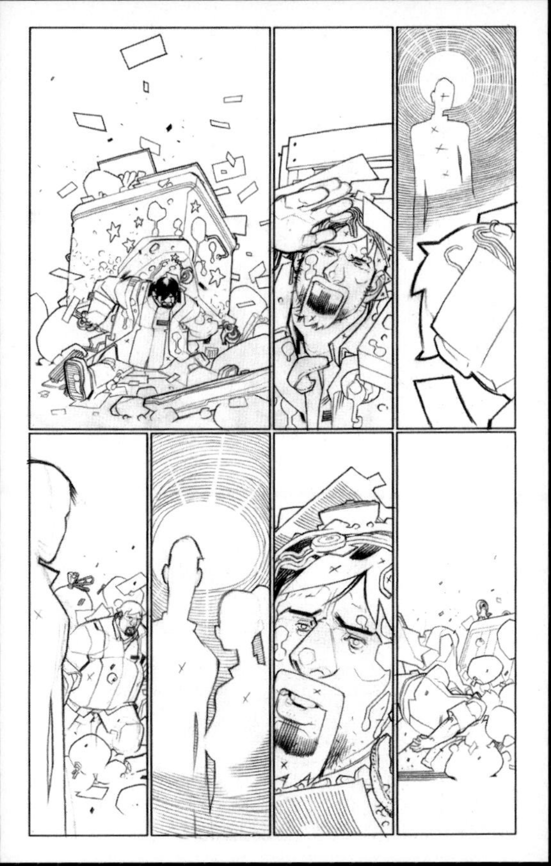

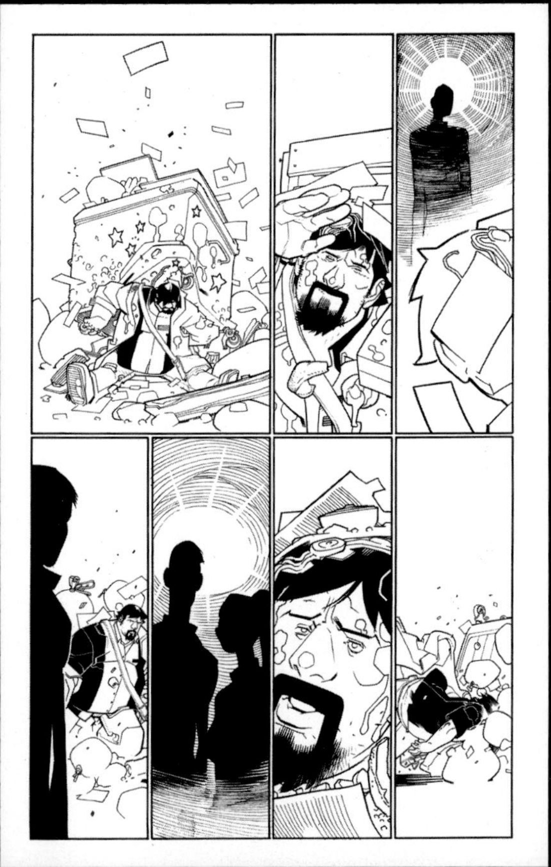

A&A: THE ADVENTURES OF ARCHER & ARMSTRONG #4, p.3
Pencils by DAVID LAFUENTE
Inks by RYAN WINN

A&A: THE ADVENTURES OF ARCHER & ARMSTRONG #4, p.5
Pencils by DAVID LAFUENTE
Inks by RYAN WINN

HEY, BROS!

HEY, BROS!

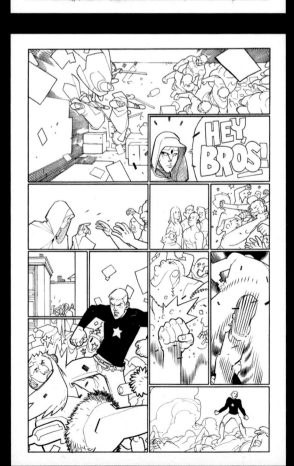

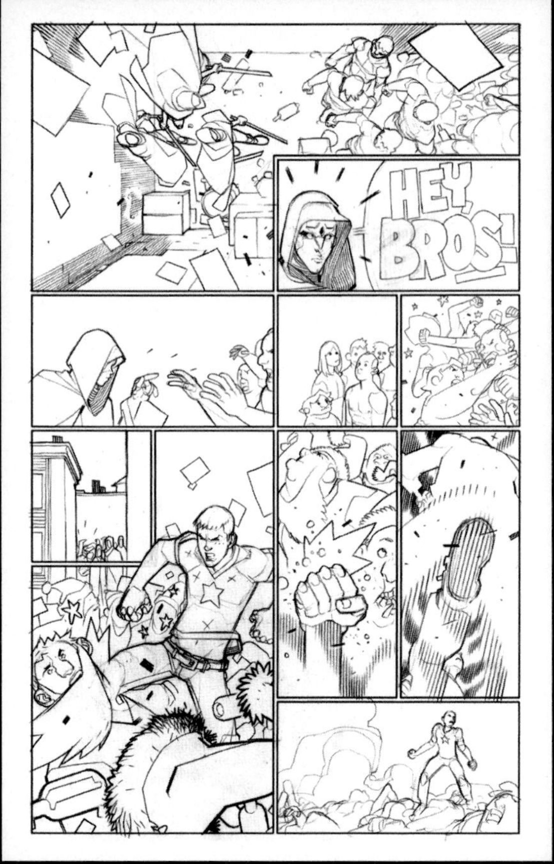

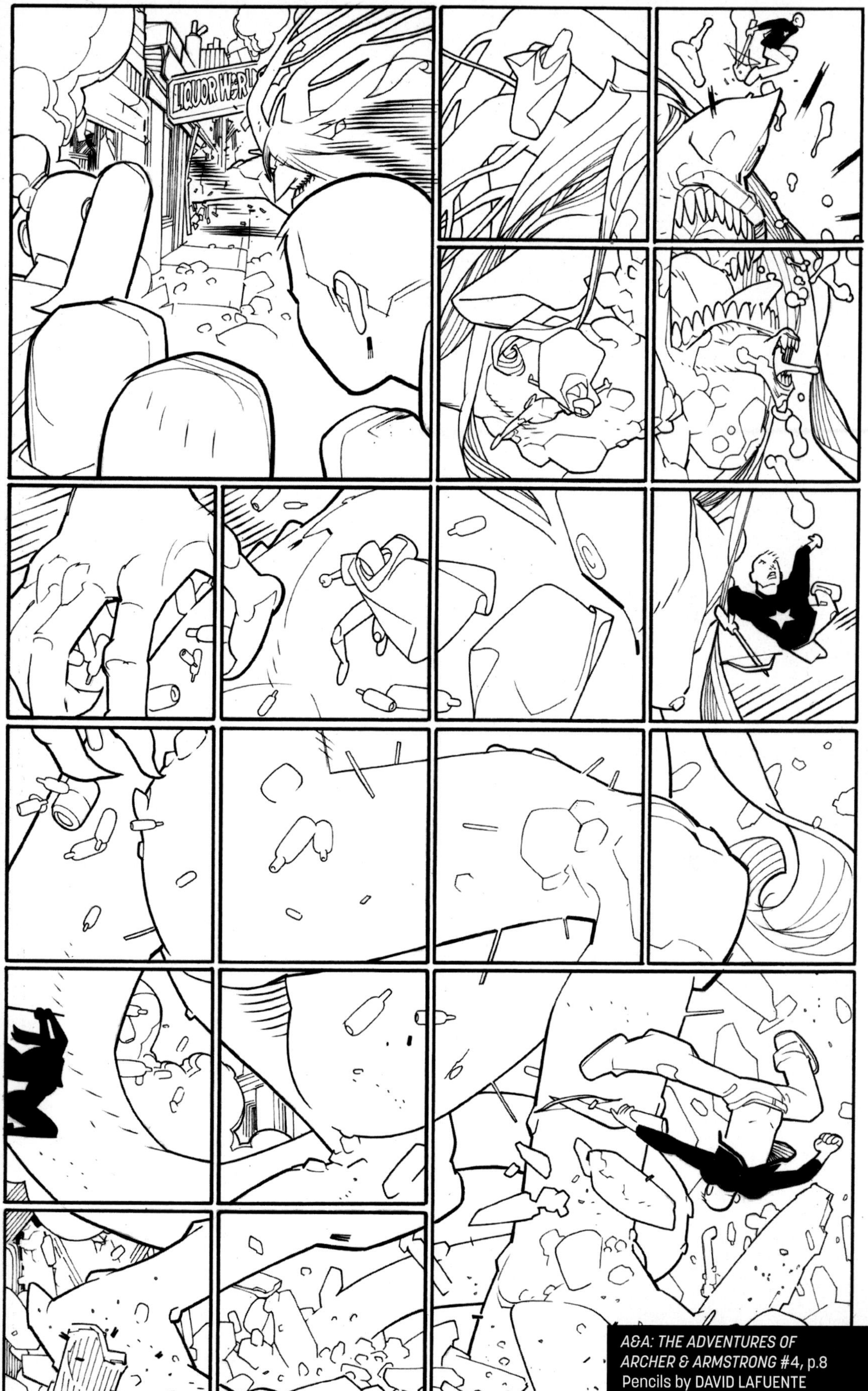
LIQUOR WORLD

A&A: THE ADVENTURES OF ARCHER & ARMSTRONG #4, p.8
Pencils by DAVID LAFUENTE
Inks by RYAN WINN

EXPLORE THE VALIANT UNIVERSE

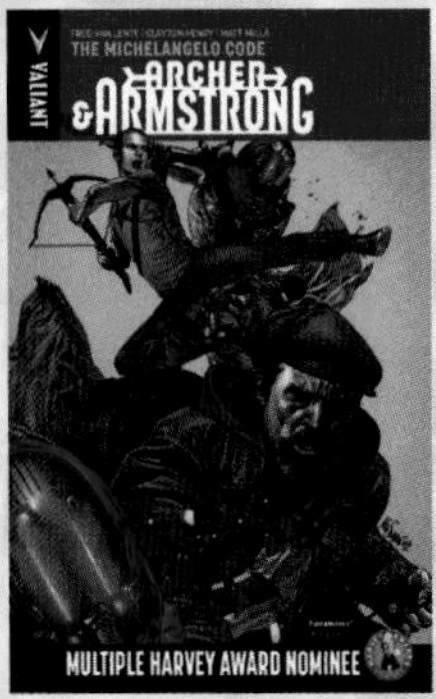
VALIANT
THE MICHELANGELO CODE
ARCHER & ARMSTRONG
MULTIPLE HARVEY AWARD NOMINEE

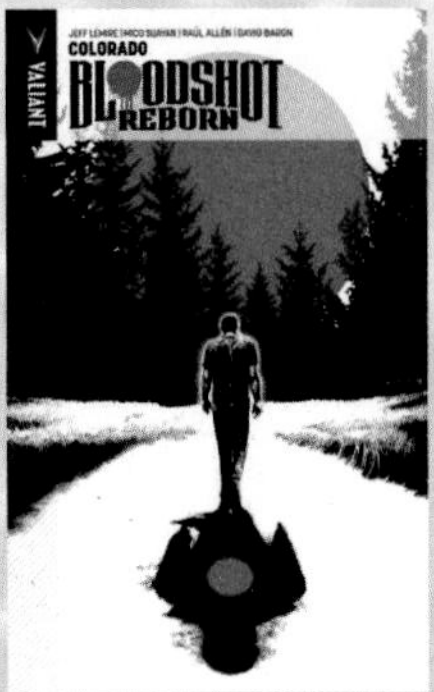
VALIANT
COLORADO
BLOODSHOT REBORN

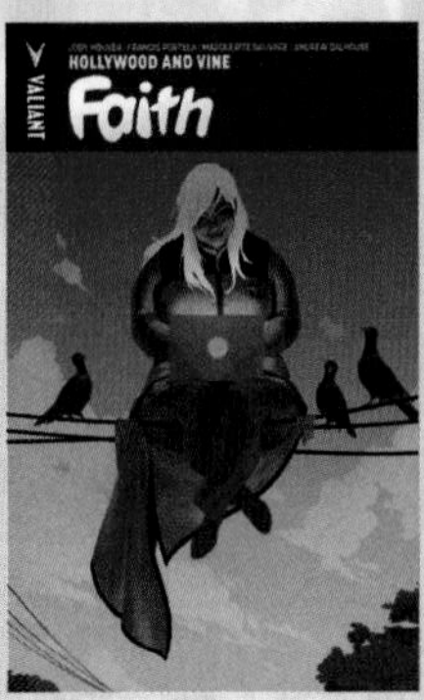
VALIANT
HOLLYWOOD AND VINE
Faith

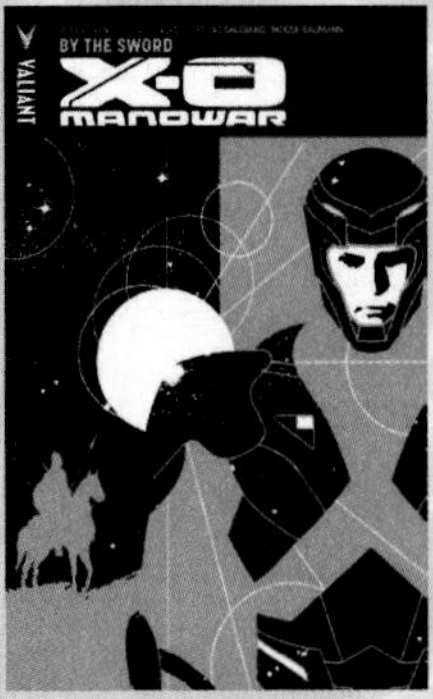
VALIANT
BY THE SWORD
X-O MANOWAR

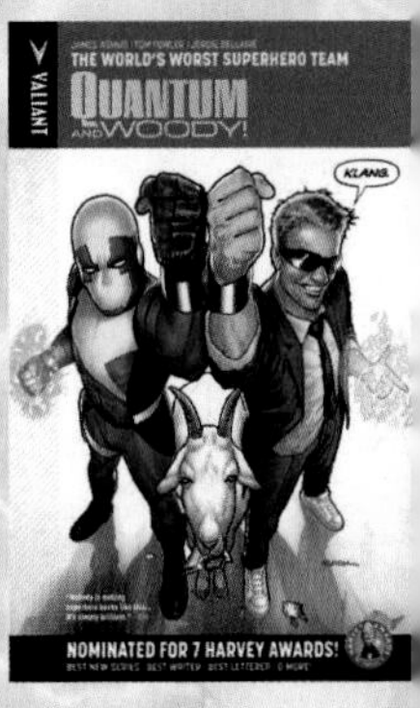
VALIANT
THE WORLD'S WORST SUPERHERO TEAM
QUANTUM AND WOODY!
KLANG
NOMINATED FOR 7 HARVEY AWARDS!

ARCHER & ARMSTRONG

Volume 1: The Michelangelo Code
ISBN: 9780979640988

Volume 2: Wrath of the Eternal Warrior
ISBN: 9781939346049

Volume 3: Far Faraway
ISBN: 9781939346148

Volume 4: Sect Civil War
ISBN: 9781939346254

Volume 5: Mission: Improbable
ISBN: 9781939346353

Volume 6: American Wasteland
ISBN: 9781939346421

Volume 7: The One Percent and Other Tales
ISBN: 9781939346537

ARMOR HUNTERS

Armor Hunters
ISBN: 9781939346452

Armor Hunters: Bloodshot
ISBN: 9781939346469

Armor Hunters: Harbinger
ISBN: 9781939346506

Unity Vol. 3: Armor Hunters
ISBN: 9781939346445

X-O Manowar Vol. 7: Armor Hunters
ISBN: 9781939346476

BLOODSHOT

Volume 1: Setting the World on Fire
ISBN: 9780979640964

Volume 2: The Rise and the Fall
ISBN: 9781939346032

Volume 3: Harbinger Wars
ISBN: 9781939346124

Volume 4: H.A.R.D. Corps
ISBN: 9781939346193

Volume 5: Get Some!
ISBN: 9781939346315

Volume 6: The Glitch and Other Tales
ISBN: 9781939346711

BLOODSHOT REBORN

Volume 1: Colorado
ISBN: 9781939346674

Volume 2: The Hunt
ISBN: 9781939346827

Volume 3: The Analog Man
ISBN: 9781682151334

BOOK OF DEATH

Book of Death
ISBN: 9781939346971

Book of Death: The Fall of the Valiant Universe
ISBN: 9781939346988

DEAD DROP

ISBN: 9781939346858

THE DEATH-DEFYING DOCTOR MIRAGE

Volume 1
ISBN: 9781939346490

Volume 2: Second Lives
ISBN: 9781682151297

THE DELINQUENTS

ISBN: 9781939346513

DIVINITY

ISBN: 9781939346766

ETERNAL WARRIOR

Volume 1: Sword of the Wild
ISBN: 9781939346209

Volume 2: Eternal Emperor
ISBN: 9781939346292

Volume 3: Days of Steel
ISBN: 9781939346742

WRATH OF THE ETERNAL WARRIOR

Volume 1: Risen
ISBN: 9781682151235

FAITH

Volume 1: Hollywood and Vine
ISBN: 9781682151211

HARBINGER

Volume 1: Omega Rising
ISBN: 9780979640957

Volume 2: Renegades
ISBN: 9781939346025

Volume 3: Harbinger Wars
ISBN: 9781939346117

Volume 4: Perfect Day
ISBN: 9781939346155

Volume 5: Death of a Renegade
ISBN: 9781939346339

Volume 6: Omegas
ISBN: 9781939346384

HARBINGER WARS

Harbinger Wars
ISBN: 9781939346094

Bloodshot Vol. 3: Harbinger Wars
ISBN: 9781939346124

Harbinger Vol. 3: Harbinger Wars
ISBN: 9781939346117

EXPLORE THE VALIANT UNIVERSE

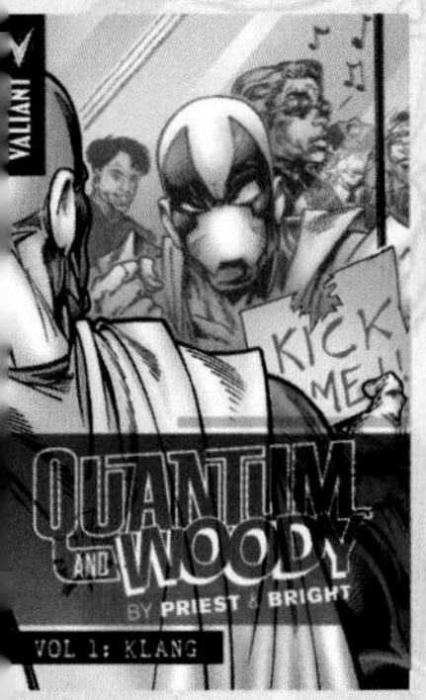
VALIANT
KICK ME
QUANTUM AND WOODY
BY PRIEST & BRIGHT
VOL 1: KLANG

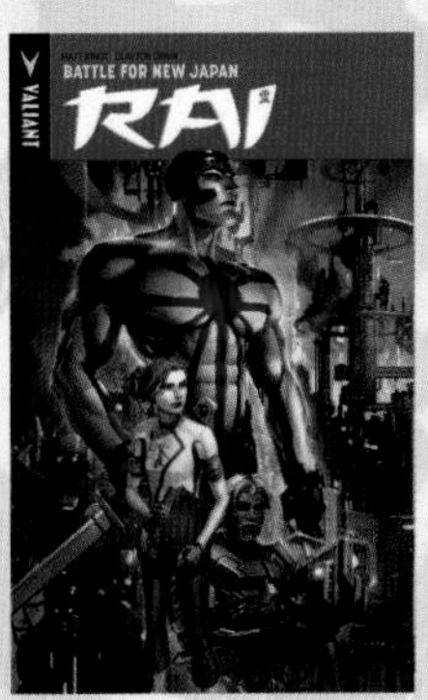
VALIANT
BATTLE FOR NEW JAPAN
RAI

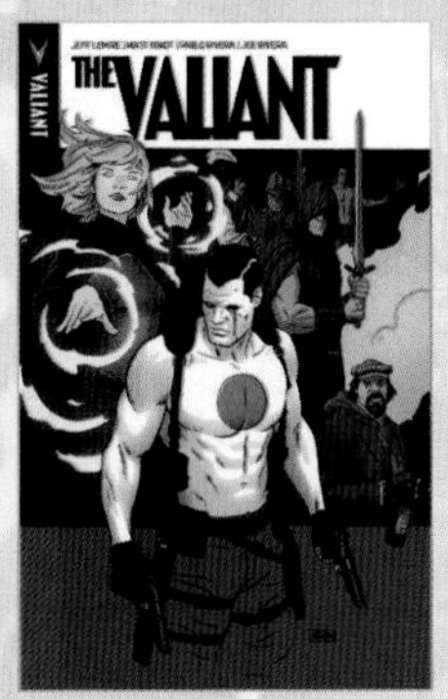
VALIANT
THE VALIANT

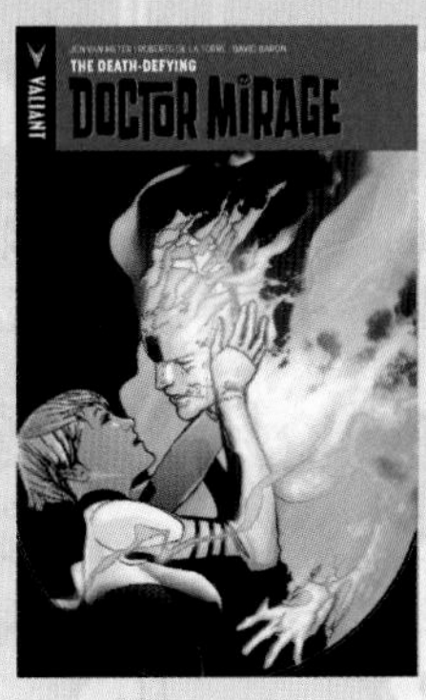
VALIANT
THE DEATH-DEFYING
DOCTOR MIRAGE

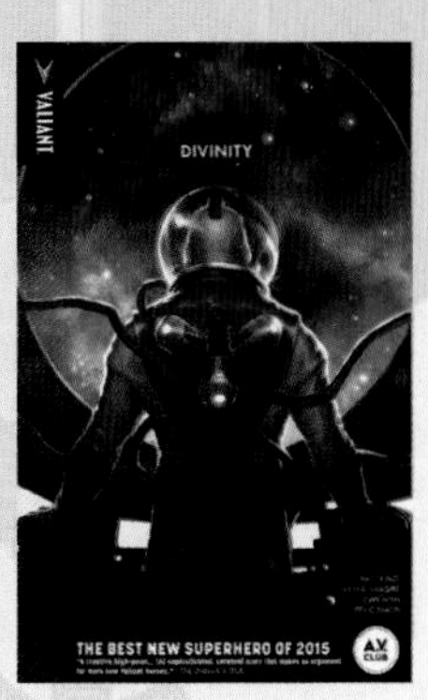
VALIANT
DIVINITY
THE BEST NEW SUPERHERO OF 2015

IMPERIUM

Volume 1: Collecting Monsters
ISBN: 9781939346759

Volume 2: Broken Angels
ISBN: 9781939346896

Volume 3: The Vine Imperative
ISBN: 9781682151112

NINJAK

Volume 1: Weaponeer
ISBN: 9781939346667

Volume 2: The Shadow Wars
ISBN: 9781939346940

Volume 3: Operation: Deadside
ISBN: 9781682151259

QUANTUM AND WOODY

Volume 1: The World's Worst Superhero Team
ISBN: 9781939346186

Volume 2: In Security
ISBN: 9781939346230

Volume 3: Crooked Pasts, Present Tense
ISBN: 9781939346391

Volume 4: Quantum and Woody Must Die!
ISBN: 9781939346629

QUANTUM AND WOODY BY PRIEST & BRIGHT

Volume 1: Klang
ISBN: 9781939346780

Volume 2: Switch
ISBN: 9781939346803

Volume 3: And So...
ISBN: 9781939346865

Volume 4: Q2 - The Return
ISBN: 9781682151099

RAI

Volume 1: Welcome to New Japan
ISBN: 9781939346414

Volume 2: Battle for New Japan
ISBN: 9781939346612

Volume 3: The Orphan
ISBN: 9781939346841

SHADOWMAN

Volume 1: Birth Rites
ISBN: 9781939346001

Volume 2: Darque Reckoning
ISBN: 9781939346056

Volume 3: Deadside Blues
ISBN: 9781939346162

Volume 4: Fear, Blood, And Shadows
ISBN: 9781939346278

Volume 5: End Times
ISBN: 9781939346377

IVAR, TIMEWALKER

Volume 1: Making History
ISBN: 9781939346636

Volume 2: Breaking History
ISBN: 9781939346834

Volume 3: Ending History
ISBN: 9781939346995

UNITY

Volume 1: To Kill a King
ISBN: 9781939346261

Volume 2: Trapped by Webnet
ISBN: 9781939346346

Volume 3: Armor Hunters
ISBN: 9781939346445

Volume 4: The United
ISBN: 9781939346544

Volume 5: Homefront
ISBN: 9781939346797

Volume 6: The War-Monger
ISBN: 9781939346902

Volume 7: Revenge of the Armor Hunters
ISBN: 9781682151136

THE VALIANT

ISBN: 9781939346605

VALIANT ZEROES AND ORIGINS

ISBN: 9781939346582

X-O MANOWAR

Volume 1: By the Sword
ISBN: 9780979640940

Volume 2: Enter Ninjak
ISBN: 9780979640995

Volume 3: Planet Death
ISBN: 9781939346087

Volume 4: Homecoming
ISBN: 9781939346179

Volume 5: At War With Unity
ISBN: 9781939346247

Volume 6: Prelude to Armor Hunters
ISBN: 9781939346407

Volume 7: Armor Hunters
ISBN: 9781939346476

Volume 8: Enter: Armorines
ISBN: 9781939346551

Volume 9: Dead Hand
ISBN: 9781939346650

Volume 10: Exodus
ISBN: 9781939346933

Volume 11: The Kill List
ISBN: 9781682151273

EXPLORE THE VALIANT UNIVERSE

VALIANT
JOSHUA DYSART | BARRY KITSON | CLAYTON HENRY | KHARI EVANS | RAFA SANDOVAL
HARBINGER
DELUXE EDITION 2

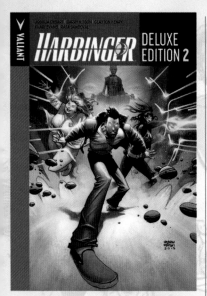

Omnibuses

Archer & Armstrong: The Complete Classic Omnibus
ISBN: 9781939346872
Collecting ARCHER & ARMSTRONG (1992) #0-26, ETERNAL WARRIOR (1992) #25 along with ARCHER & ARMSTRONG: THE FORMATION OF THE SECT.

Quantum and Woody: The Complete Classic Omnibus
ISBN: 9781939346360
Collecting QUANTUM AND WOODY (1997) #0, 1-21 and #32, THE GOAT: H.A.E.D.U.S. #1, and X-O MANOWAR (1996) #16

X-O Manowar Classic Omnibus Vol. 1
ISBN: 9781939346308
Collecting X-O MANOWAR (1992) #0-30, ARMORINES #0, X-O DATABASE #1, as well as material from SECRETS OF THE VALIANT UNIVERSE #1

VALIANT
ROBERT VENDITTI MATT KINDT JOSHUA DYSART JOE HARRIS ROBERT GILL DOUG BRAITHWAITE DIEGO BERNARD TREVOR HAIRSINE STEPHEN SEGOVIA
ARMOR HUNTERS
DELUXE EDITION

Deluxe Editions

Archer & Armstrong Deluxe Edition Book 1
ISBN: 9781939346223
Collecting ARCHER & ARMSTRONG #0-13

Archer & Armstrong Deluxe Edition Book 2
ISBN: 9781939346957
Collecting ARCHER & ARMSTRONG #14-25, ARCHER & ARMSTRONG: ARCHER #0 and BLOODSHOT AND H.A.R.D. CORPS #20-21.

Armor Hunters Deluxe Edition
ISBN: 9781939346728
Collecting Armor Hunters #1-4, Armor Hunters: Aftermath #1, Armor Hunters: Bloodshot #1-3, Armor Hunters: Harbinger #1-3, Unity #8-11, and X-O MANOWAR #23-29

Bloodshot Deluxe Edition Book 1
ISBN: 9781939346216
Collecting BLOODSHOT #1-13

Bloodshot Deluxe Edition Book 2
ISBN: 9781939346810
Collecting BLOODSHOT AND H.A.R.D. CORPS #14-23, BLOODSHOT #24-25, BLOODSHOT #0, BLOODSHOT AND H.A.R.D. CORPS: H.A.R.D. CORPS #0, along with ARCHER & ARMSTRONG #18-19

Divinity Deluxe Edition
ISBN: 97819393460993
Collecting DIVNITY #1-4

Harbinger Deluxe Edition Book 1
ISBN: 9781939346131
Collecting HARBINGER #0-14

Harbinger Deluxe Edition Book 2
SBN: 9781939346773
Collecting HARBINGER #15-25, HARBINGER: OMEGAS #1-3, and HARBINGER: BLEEDING MONK #0

Harbinger Wars Deluxe Edition
ISBN: 9781939346322
Collecting HARBINGER WARS #1-4, HARBINGER #11-14, and BLOODSHOT #10-13

Quantum and Woody Deluxe Edition Book 1
ISBN: 9781939346681
Collecting QUANTUM AND WOODY #1-12 and QUANTUM AND WOODY: THE GOAT #0

Q2: The Return of Quantum and Woody Deluxe Edition
ISBN: 9781939346568
Collecting Q2: THE RETURN OF QUANTUM AND WOODY #1-5

Shadowman Deluxe Edition Book 1
ISBN: 9781939346438
Collecting SHADOWMAN #0-10

Shadowman Deluxe Edition Book 2
ISBN: 9781682151075
Collecting SHADOWMAN #11-16, SHADOWMAN #13X, SHADOWMAN: END TIMES #1-3 and PUNK MAMBO #0

Unity Deluxe Edition Book 1
ISBN: 9781939346575
Collecting UNITY #0-14

The Valiant Deluxe Edition
ISBN: 97819393460986
Collecting THE VALIANT #1-4

X-O Manowar Deluxe Edition Book 1
ISBN: 9781939346100
Collecting X-O MANOWAR #1-14

X-O Manowar Deluxe Edition Book 2
ISBN: 9781939346520
Collecting X-O MANOWAR #15-22, and UNITY #1-4

VALIANT
VALIANT MASTERS
JIM SHOOTER | DAVID LAPHAM
CHILDREN OF THE EIGHTH DAY
HARBINGER

Valiant Masters

Bloodshot Vol. 1 - Blood of the Machine
ISBN: 9780979640933

H.A.R.D. Corps Vol. 1 - Search and Destroy
ISBN: 9781939346285

Harbinger Vol. 1 - Children of the Eighth Day
ISBN: 9781939346483

Ninjak Vol. 1 - Black Water
ISBN: 9780979640971

Rai Vol. 1 - From Honor to Strength
ISBN: 9781939346070

Shadowman Vol. 1 - Spirits Within
ISBN: 9781939346018

VALIANT
VALIANT MASTERS
KEVIN VANHOOK | DON PERLIN
BLOOD OF THE MACHINE
BLOODSHOT

A&A: The Adventures of Archer &
Armstrong Vol. 1: In the Bag

A&A: The Adventures of Archer &
Armstrong Vol. 2: Romance and
Road Trips

Follow all of the critically acclaimed adventures of Valiant's history-smashing duo!

Archer & Armstrong Vol. 1:
The Michelangelo Code

Archer & Armstrong Vol. 2:
Wrath of the
Eternal Warrior

Archer & Armstrong Vol. 3:
Far Faraway

Archer & Armstrong Vol. 4:
Sect Civil War

Archer & Armstrong Vol. 5:
Mission: Improbable

Archer & Armstrong Vol. 6:
American Wasteland

Archer & Armstrong Vol. 7:
The One Percent and
Other Tales

The Delinquents

VALIANT

THE ADVENTURES OF ARCHER AND ARMSTRONG

VOLUME TWO: ROMANCE AND ROAD TRIPS

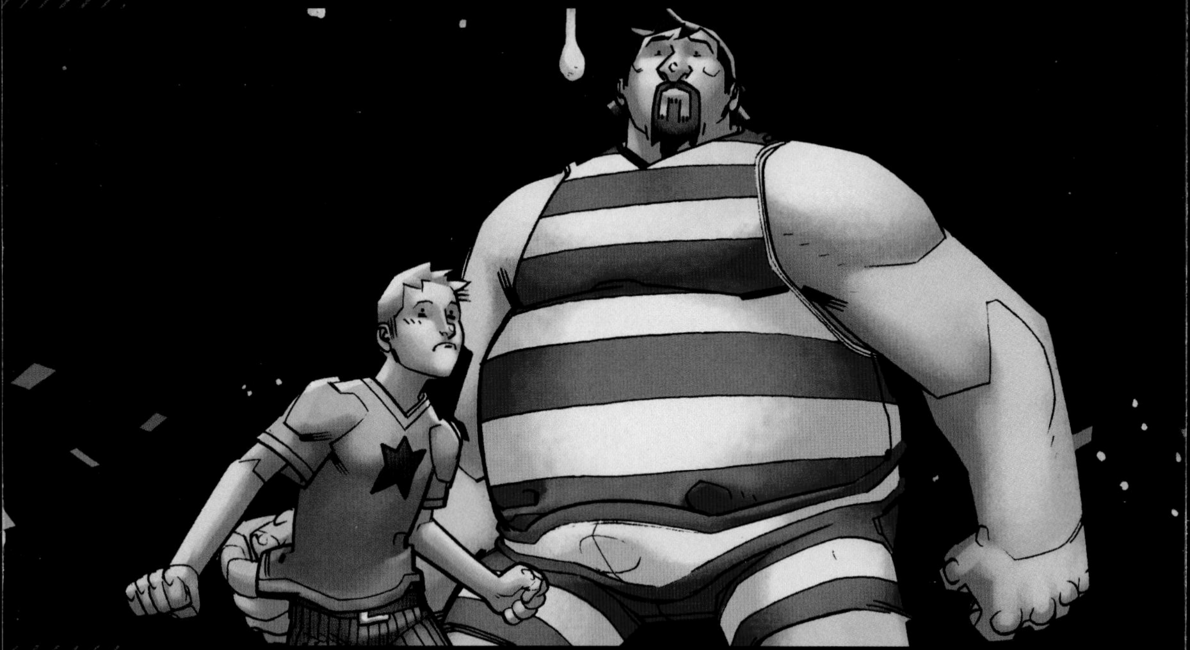

A VALIANT TALE FOR THE AGES! THIS AIN'T NO ORDINARY TEAM-UP... IT'S ARCHER & FAITH'S FIRST DATE!

First, A&A's whirlwind ongoing series is hitting the town with the one and only FAITH! With Armstrong on the road, Archer is taking some much-needed personal time...and bringing his long-distance romance with Los Angeles's number-one superhero off of FaceTime and into the real world! Then, Archer and Armstrong go on the hunt for Armstrong's long-lost wife, and the clues will put them on the trail of America's craziest traveling circus!

Come on board here as red-hot writer Rafer Roberts (*Plastic Farm*) and Eisner Award-winning artist Mike Norton (*Revival*) bring you more crossbows than *Sleepless in Seattle* and more fistfights than *The Notebook*!

Collecting A&A: THE ADVENTURES OF ARCHER & ARMSTRONG #5-8

TRADE PAPERBACK
ISBN: 978-1-68215-171-6

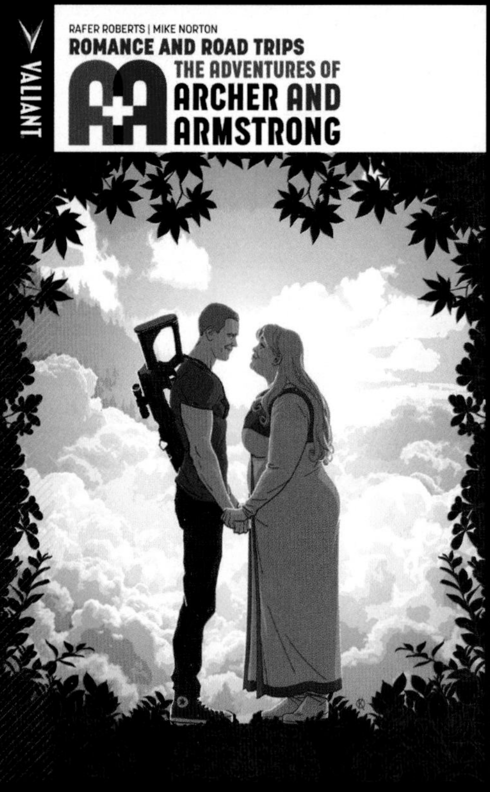
VALIANT
RAFER ROBERTS | MIKE NORTON
ROMANCE AND ROAD TRIPS
THE ADVENTURES OF
ARCHER AND
ARMSTRONG